Henry F. Whish

Clavis Syriaca

Henry F. Whish

Clavis Syriaca

ISBN/EAN: 9783337290610

Printed in Europe, USA, Canada, Australia, Japan

Cover: Foto ©ninafisch / pixelio.de

More available books at **www.hansebooks.com**

CLAVIS SYRIACA:

A KEY TO THE

ANCIENT SYRIAC VERSION, CALLED "PESHITO,"

OF THE FOUR HOLY GOSPELS.

BY THE

REV. HENRY F. WHISH, M.A.,
CORPUS CHRISTI COLLEGE, CAMBRIDGE.

LONDON:
GEORGE BELL AND SONS.
CAMBRIDGE: DEIGHTON, BELL AND CO.
1883

TO

THE RIGHT REVEREND FATHER IN GOD

RICHARD

LORD BISHOP OF CHICHESTER

THIS VOLUME

DESIGNED TO ELUCIDATE THE VENERABLE AND ANCIENT SYRIAC

(PESHITO) VERSION OF THE FOUR HOLY GOSPELS

IS

WITH HIS LORDSHIP'S PERMISSION

MOST RESPECTFULLY AND DUTIFULLY

INSCRIBED

BY THE AUTHOR.

PREFACE.

LITTLE need be said in the way of introduction to the following Work, which in answering to its title sufficiently explains its own object: viz. to furnish a complete analysis of the text of the Four Gospels, as it exists in that ancient and venerable Syriac Version of the New Testament, commonly called Peshito—i.e. the simple, or literal:—a Version which loses nothing of its value from the fact, that whereas for a long time it was regarded as the most ancient, the researches of later years have brought to light a MS. of the Gospels in Syriac, supposed to be at least as ancient as the Old Latin, and which is now in the British Museum.

The plan which I have endeavoured to carry out in the following pages is this:—To give

1. The Syriac word, as it stands in the text.
2. The English rendering, according to the Authorized Version, with a more literal translation where it seems necessary.
3. The corresponding Greek word, or words,—preceded, where not strictly literal, by the abbreviation Gr.
4. The parsing of the word, with all its various forms, as occurring in the Gospels, or in other parts of the New Testament, with references.

As a rule, I have not thought it necessary to give the affixed forms, except where the simple form does not otherwise occur, or where the affix seems to present any peculiarity.

5. The derived forms traced to their respective Roots. Under this head are in some cases added derivatives from verbs and nouns, which, although not occurring in the Gospels, often serve to illustrate the meaning of the original Root.

6. The analogous, or cognate, form, where such exists,
   (a) In Hebrew, with reference (except in a few very common words) to one or more familiar passages in the Old Testament.
   (b) In Chaldee, with similar, but fuller, references to the Books of Daniel and Ezra.

7. A literal translation of such passages as deviate in any remarkable degree from the Original, whether in grammatical construction, or in the actual reading of the text. Where the Syriac Version, thus deviating from the Received Text, agrees with one or more of the most ancient Greek MSS., such agreement is noted: the MSS. referred to being principally the Sinaitic, the Vatican, and the Alexandrine.

I have appended a complete Index to the whole Work, by reference to which the Student will readily find every word—including every conjugation of the Verb—where it first occurs, and where it is fully explained.

In the arrangement of this Clavis, the Gospel of S. John is placed first in order; since, as in Greek, so in Syriac, its language and construction is the simplest, and presents fewer difficulties to the beginner: and by this plan, the Gospel of S. Luke, which is the most difficult, stands last.

The Text which I have followed is that published by Mr Bagster, and bound up with Gutbir's Lexicon.

Although designed, in the first instance, for the use of beginners, this Work does not profess to be, in the strictest sense, *elementary*; it being taken for granted that the student has mastered at least the Elements of Syriac Grammar, and is acquainted with the forms of Nouns and Adjectives, Paradigms of Verbs, &c. The Grammars to which I have occasionally referred are those of Dr Phillips, President of Queens' College, Cambridge (Deighton, Bell and Co.), and B. Harris Cowper, Esq. (Williams and Norgate). There is also a very useful little Grammar prefixed to the "Syriac Reading Lessons," published by Mr Bagster.

PREFACE.

I take this opportunity of expressing my great obligation to the Rev. J. Sandford Bailey, for his kind counsel and invaluable assistance while this work was preparing for the press:—to the Very Rev. the Dean of Canterbury, for his great kindness in allowing me to submit the MS. to his inspection; and to my revered Diocesan, the Lord Bishop of Chichester, for the high honour he has done me in permitting me to dedicate these pages to him. It is my earnest hope that my work may prove not altogether unworthy of such patronage. I shall feel that my object has been fully attained, and the labour of many years well spent, if it should be the means of affording some assistance to those who have begun, and perhaps of encouraging many to begin, the study of the Syriac Language:—a Language which must commend itself to all, not only for its own intrinsic beauty and sweetness (the very Italian of the Semitic family), and the ease with which, especially with a previous acquaintance with Hebrew, it may be acquired;—but chiefly as being, in all probability, the native Tongue of the Son of God Manifest in the Flesh,—the Language in which His "Gracious Words" were uttered, His Sermon on the Mount, His Parables, His Words of love, reproof, and warning;—the Language which gave expression to His last Cry on the Cross,

ܐܒܐ ܒܐܝܕܝܟ ܣܐܡ ܐܢܐ ܪܘܚܝ ܀

HENRY F. WHISH.

BRIGHTON,
June 22, 1883.

ERRATA.

Page 3, line 14, for ܡܢ read ܡܼܢ.

„ 21, „ 16, for ܡܢ ܩܕܡܘܗܝ read ܡܼܢ ܩܕܡܘܗܝ.

„ 88, „ 4 from the bottom, for "quadrilateral," read "quadriliteral."

„ 90, „ 4, for ܚܒܐ read ܚܒܼܐ.

„ 101 (Chap. v. 2), for ܕܪܘܚܐ read ܕܪܘܚܐ.

„ 103, lines 21, 22, for ܐܡܼܬܝ ܟܕܐܡܬܝ, read ܐܡܼܬܝ ܟܕܐܡܼܬܝ.

„ 134, line 13, for ܐܝܕܝܗ read ܐܝܕܗ.

„ 145, „ 13, for ܕܡܫܬܒܗܪܢܘ read ܠܡܫܬܒܗܪܢܘ.

„ 149, „ 5, for ܕܒܣܕܬܗ read ܕܒܣܕܬܗ.

„ 163, „ 4 from the bottom, for ܚܣܡܝܗ read ܚܣܡܼܝܗ.

„ 175, „ 12, for ܕܐܚܕܗ read ܕܐܚܕܗ.

„ 183, „ 5, for ܢܚܘܪ read ܢܚܘܼܪ.

„ 199, „ 1, for ܐܬܚܙܝܬܗ̈ read ܐܣܬܚܙܝܬܗ.

„ 240, „ 14, for "Editors" read "Editions".

„ 262, „ 23, for ܣܝܘܡܘ read ܣܝܘܡܐ.

„ 310, „ 3 from the bottom, for ܚܦܘܟܘܣ read ܚܦܘܟܘܣ.

„ 322, „ 6, for ܒܚܙܬܐ read ܒܚܙܬܐ.

„ 386, 387, top of page, for "Matthew" read "Mark".

„ 391, line 15, for ܕܟܣܦܐ read ܕܟܣܦܐ.

„ 480, „ 4, for ܩܕܘܫܐ read ܩܕܘܫܐ.

CLAVIS.

THE GOSPEL ACCORDING TO
S. JOHN.

ܐܘܢܓܠܝܘܢ ܩܕܝܫܐ ܟܪܘܙܘܬܐ ܕܝܘܚܢܢ ܟܪܘܙܐ ܕܗܘ ܡܠܠ ܘܐܟܪܙ ܝܘܢܐܝܬ ܒܐܦܣܘܣ ܀

The Holy Gospel, the Preaching of John the Preacher, which he spoke and preached in Greek at Ephesus.

CHAPTER I.

(ܩܦܠܐܘܢ, *a chapter*—from the Gr. κεφάλαιον.)

Ver. 1. ܒܪܫܝܬ *in the beginning*—ἐν ἀρχῇ.

— ܒ *inseparable preposition*.

— ܪܫܝܬ *noun fem. denom. from* ܪܫ, *head.*—*A beginning.* ܡܢ ܪܫܝܬ, *from the beginning*, ἀπ' ἀρχῆς, ch. viii. 44: S. Matt. xix. 4, 8; S. Mark x. 6.—Def. ܪܫܝܬܐ, *the beginning*, Hebr. iii. 14; vii. 3. *The first*, Acts xxvi. 23. *First-fruits*, S. James i. 18.—Pl. def. ܪܫܝܬܐ, Hebr. vii. 4 (Gr. ἐκ τῶν ἀκροθινίων). Heb. רֵאשִׁית, Gen. i. 1.

— ܐܝܬܘܗܝ ܗܘܐ *was*—ἦν—ܐܝܬ, *is*; properly a primitive and indeclinable noun signifying "existence, being". With pl. suffixes,

W. C.   1

Ver. 1. it forms the pres. tense of the subst. verb, as ܐܝܬܘܗܝ, *he is*, ܐܝܬܝܗܘܢ, *they are*, &c.: the imperf. tense being expressed by the addition of ܗܘܐ, ܗܘܘ, &c. In the 3rd pers. of both numbers the affix is often omitted; as ܐܝܬ ܗܘܐ *he was*, ܐܝܬ ܗܘܘ, *they were*.

ܐܝܬ followed by the dative expresses the verb "to have"; as ܐܝܬ ܠܝ, *I have*, Lat. *Est mihi*; ܐܝܬ ܠܟ, *thou hast*, ch. iv. 11. Similarly is used ܠܝܬ = ܠܐ ܐܝܬ, *is not*.

— ܡܠܬܐ *the Word* — ὁ Λόγος — Def. of ܡܠܐ (S. Matt. iv. 4, &c.) noun fem. (here masc. in sense, and therefore joined with a masc. verb), *A word, speech*, or *thing, cause, reason* (as Heb. דָּבָר). Pl. ܡܠܐ, def. ܡܠܐ, ch. iii. 34. — Constr. ܡܠܬ ܩܘܫܬܐ, *the words of truth*, Acts xxvi. 25. Root ܡܠܠ Pa. ܡܠܠ, *spoke*.

Heb. מִלָּה, Ps. xix. 5. *Thing* (as דָּבָר), Job xxxii. 11.— Chald. מִלָּה (for מִלָּא) *word*, Dan. ii. 9. Def. מִלְּתָה, and מִלְּתָא, ver. 5, 15. *Thing*, ii. 5, 8, &c.

— ܘܗܘ pers. pron. 3. sing. masc. prefixed with the copulative conj. ܘ, *and*. It expresses here the force of the Gr. art. ὁ. — Pl. masc. ܗܢܘܢ.

— ܠܘܬ *with* — πρός — Preposition. With affixes, ܠܘܬܝ, *with me*, ܠܘܬܢ, *with us*, &c. Also signifying *to, towards, at the hands of* (S. Matt. vi. 1).—ܡܢ ܠܘܬ, *from*; ܡܢ ܠܘܬܗ, *from Him*, ch. vii. 29, below.

— ܐܠܗܐ *GOD* — τὸν Θεόν — Def. of ܐܠܗ, Rev. viii. 2; xxii. 9, according to De Dieu; — Others read the def. form, as here and elsewhere in the N.T.—Fem. def. ܐܠܗܬܐ, *the Goddess*, Acts xix. 27: with aff. ver. 37. — Pl. masc. def. ܐܠܗܐ, ch. x. 34, 35, below.

Heb. אֱלוֹהַּ, Ps. l. 22.—Chald. אֱלָהּ, Dan. ii. 18. Def. אֱלָהָא, ver. 20. Pl. אֱלָהִין, ver. 11.

2. ܗܢܐ *this, the same* — οὗτος — Demonstr. pron. masc. sing. — Pl. masc. ܗܠܝܢ, *these, those*.

Ver. 3. ܟܠ *all, all things*—πάντα—Properly a noun masc. denoting *entirety, universality*, but used adjectively. With affixes, ܟܠܢ, *we all, all of us*; ܟܠܟܘܢ, *all of you*, &c.—When referring to a following noun, the affix agrees with that noun, and is pleonastic; as ܟܠܗ ܥܡܐ, *all (of it) the people*.

Heb. and Chald. בָּל־, בָּל, of frequent use.

— ܒܐܝܕܗ *by His hand*, i.e. *by Him*—Gr. δι' αὐτοῦ—Def. (with prefixed preposition, to which the first vowel is remitted,—and affixed pron. 3. sing. masc.) of ܝܕ, noun fem. *The hand*, seldom occurring as a noun. Def. ܐܝܕܐ (S. Mar. vii. 32) *the hand*, also *power, dominion*.—Pl. (of masc. form) ܐܝܕܝܢ, S. Mar. ix. 43; Col. ii. 11.—Def. ܐܝܕܝܐ, S. John vii. 30, 44.

ܝܕ with pref. ܒ, ܒܝܕ is used as a preposition. ܥܡ, *by, by means of*. ܝܕ ܥܠ, *at, near, by the side, shore, of*.

Heb. יָד. Chald. יַד def. יְדָא, Dan. v. 5, 24.

— ܗܘܐ *was, was made, came into existence*—ἐγένετο—The Substantive verb, pret. 3. sing.—Fut. ܢܗܘܐ, S. Matt. xxvi. 35.—Imperat. ܗܘܝ, S. Matt. ii. 13; pl. ܗܘܘ, v. 48: S. Luke xii. 36, 40.— Inf. with pref. ܠ, ܠܡܗܘܐ, S. John iii. 9; ix. 27; S. Matt. xix. 21.—Part. ܗܘܐ, S. Mark iv. 28. Fem. ܗܘܝܐ, S. Matt. xii. 45; xiii. 22; S. Mark iv. 19, 32.—Pl. masc. ܗܘܝܢ, S. Matt. xiv. 21; xv. 38; S. Luke ix. 14.—Fem. ܗܘܝܢ, S. Mar. xii. 25; S. Luke xx. 34, 35.

For the complete paradigm of this verb, see Phillips's Gram. § 33.

Added to the participle or preterite of verbs, it forms their imperfect and pluperfect tense respectively, and the two words coalesce, ܗ taking the *linea occultans*. Thus:

Imperf. ܗܘܐ ܩܛܠ (Kotelvo) *he was killing*.

Pluperf. ܗܘܐ ܩܛܠ (K'talvo) *he had killed*.

Similarly, it forms its own tenses; as,

Imperf. ܗܘܐ ܗܘܐ (hovĕvo) *he was*.

S. JOHN I. 3, 4.

Ver. 3.   Pluperf. ܗܘܳܐ ܗܘܳܐ (h'vōvo) *he had been.*
   Yet in some cases we find the imperf. with the force of a pluperf. and vice versâ.
   Heb. הָיָה. Chald. הֲוָה.

— ܒܶܠܥܳܕܰܘܗ̄ܝ *without Him*—χωρὶς αὐτοῦ—ܒܶܠܥܳܕ (Rom. vii. 8; Philem. ver. 14) prep. *Without, besides.* Followed by ܡܶܢ, S. Matt. x. 29; S. Luke xxii. 6.—Takes affixes as a pl. noun, as here 3. masc. So ܒܶܠܥܳܕܶܝܗ̇, *without it* (sc. ܩܰܕܺܝܫܘܽܬܐ, fem. *holiness*), Hebr. xii. 14; ܒܶܠܥܳܕܰܝܢ, *without us,* Hebr. xi. 40.

   Heb. בִּלְעֲדֵי, with aff. בִּלְעָדֶיךָ, בִּלְעָדַי, Gen. xli. 16, 44. Comp. of בַּל, *not,* and עֲדֵי, *until.* Compare בִּלְעֲדֵי, always with pref. מִן, מִבַּלְעֲדֵי, Ps. xviii. 32.

— ܐܳܦܠܳܐ *not, not even*—οὐδέ—Comp. of ܐܳܦ, *also,* and ܠܳܐ *not.*

— ܚܰܕ *one*—ἕν—Fem. of ܚܰܕ (ver. 40) where see note. *One, a certain one* (τις).

— ܗܘܳܬ *was*—ἐγένετο—Pret. 3. sing. fem. of ܗܘܳܐ. See note above. The point over ܙ marks the feminine gender.

— ܡܶܕܶܡ *something, anything*—Indeclinable. Followed, as here, by ܕ *that which, whatsoever.* It forms phrases: as ܡܶܕܶܡ ܡܶܕܶܡ *various,* Acts xxi. 34;—ܡܶܕܶܡ ܠܳܐ and ܠܳܐ ܡܶܕܶܡ, *nothing,* S. John xvi. 23; S. Matt. v. 13:—ܟܠ ܡܶܕܶܡ, *all, whatsoever,* S. John xvi. 23:— ܡܶܕܶܡ ܟܠ, *in every way,* Gr. κατὰ πάντα τρόπον, Rom. iii. 2.

— ܗܘܳܐܕ *that which was, existed*—ὃ γέγονεν—ܕ, relative pronoun, with ܘ before a vowelless consonant.

4. ܒܶܗ *in Him*—ἐν αὐτῷ—Preposition with affix 3. sing. masc.

— ܚܰܝ̈ܶܐ *life*—ζωή—Def. of ܚܰܝ̈ܶܐ, pl. noun masc. *life, health.* The two dots (Ribui) mark the plural. Agrees, as an abstract noun, with the verb ܗܘܳܐ in the singular. But in the next clause it is joined with the pl. form ܐܺܝܬܰܝܗܘܢ.

   Heb. חַיִּים, Gen. ii. 7.—Chald. חַיִּין, as an abstract noun, Dan. vii. 12. Constr. חַיֵּי, Ezr. vi. 10.

— ܢܘܽܗܪܳܐ *the light*—τὸ φῶς—Noun masc. def.—Root ܢܗܰܪ, *shone.*

S. JOHN I. 4—6.

Ver. 4. ܕܲܒ̈ܢܰܝܢܳܫܳܐ *of men*—lit. *of the sons of men*—τῶν ἀνθρώπων—Plur. of ܒܰܪܢܳܫܳܐ (ch. ii. 25) def. ܒܰܪܢܳܫܳܐ, ver. 6, below. Noun masc. compounded of ܒܰܪ, *son*, and ܐܢܳܫ, def. ܐܢܳܫܳܐ, *man*, by aphæresis of ܐ. The sing. def. in a separate form, ܒܰܪ ܐܢܳܫܳܐ, occurs, S. Matt. xii. 12: also the pl. ܒܢܰܝ ܐܢܳܫܳܐ, S. Matt. vi. 5, &c.

5. ܒܚܶܫܽܘܟܳܐ *in the darkness*—ἐν τῇ σκοτίᾳ—Def. (with pref. prep. ܒ) of ܚܶܫܽܘܟܳܐ (ch. xx. 1) noun masc. *Dark, darkness*—R. ܚܣܟ, *was dark*.
    Heb. חֹשֶׁךְ, Gen. i. 2.—Chald. חֲשׁוֹךְ, Dan. ii. 22.

— ܡܰܢܗܰܪ *shining, shineth*—φαίνει.—Aphel part. of ܢܗܰܪ, *shone*. Aph. ܐܰܢܗܰܪ (Acts xvi. 29), *lightened, illuminated*;— Pret. 3. fem. ܐܰܢܗܪܰܬ̤, S. Luke ii. 9.—Fut. ܢܰܢܗܰܪ, Eph. v. 14.—Infin. with ܠ, ܠܡܰܢܗܳܪܽܘ, S. Luke i. 79.—Part. fem. ܡܰܢܗܪܳܐ, S. Luke xv. 8.— Pl. masc. ܡܰܢܗܪܺܝܢ, S. Matt. v. 15.—Part. pass. pl. masc. (of the same form), S. Luke xii. 35.

— ܠܳܐ *not*—οὐ.

— ܐܰܕܪܟܶܗ *comprehended it*—αὐτὸ...κατέλαβεν.—Aphel pret. 3. sing. (with aff. 3. sing. masc.) of ܕܪܰܟ or ܕܪܶܟ, *trod with the feet, proceeded*. Aph. ܐܰܕܪܶܟ (Rom. ix. 31) *trod out* corn: *attained to, reached, seized, overtook, perceived, experienced, followed to perfection*. Pret. 1. sing. ܐܰܕܪܟܶܬ, Acts x. 34; xxv. 25; Phil. iii. 13.—3. pl. ܐܰܕܪܶܟܘ Rom. ix. 30.—Fut. ܢܶܕܪܽܘܟ, with aff. ܢܶܕܪܟܟܽܘܢ, 1 Thess. v. 4.— 1. sing. ܐܶܕܪܽܘܟ, Phil. iii. 12;—3. pl. ܢܶܕܪܟܽܘܢ, 1 Tim. vi. 19:—1. pl. ܢܶܕܪܽܘܟ, 1 Thess. iv. 15.—Imperat. ܐܰܕܪܶܟ, 1 Tim. vi. 12.—Inf. ܠܡܶܕܪܟܽܘܬܳܐ, Eph. iii. 18.—Part. ܡܰܕܪܶܟ, 1 Cor. ix. 9; Fem. ܡܰܕܪܟܳܐ, S. Mark ix. 18.
    Heb. Hiph. הִדְרִיךְ, *caused to walk*, Ps. xxv. 5, 9; cvii. 7; cxix. 35; *overtook*, with acc. Judg. xx. 43.

Derivatives, ܕܪܳܟܬܳܐ, noun fem. def. *a treading out* corn, 1 Tim. v. 18.

ܕܽܘܪܟܬܳܐ, noun fem. def. *a footstep*, Acts vii. 5.

6. ܕܐܶܫܬܰܕܰܪ *who was sent*—Gr. ἀπεσταλμένος—Ethpaal pret. 3. sing. (with

Ver. 6. pref. relat. ܕ, to which the first vowel is remitted) of ܫܰܕܰܪ (not used in Peal); Pael ܫܰܕܰܪ, *sent*—Ethpa. ܐܶܫܬܰܕܰܪ, S. Luke iv. 26 (where however the Vienna and some other Edits. read ܐܶܫܬܰܕܰܪ, Ethpeel) *was sent*. Pret. 3. sing. fem. ܐܶܫܬܰܕܪܰܬ, Acts xiii. 26:— 2. sing. ܐܶܫܬܰܕܰܪܬ, S. John iii. 2:—1. sing. ܐܶܫܬܰܕܪܶܬ, S. Matt. xv. 24; S. Luke iv. 43:—3. pl. ܐܶܫܬܰܕܰܪܘ, ver. 24, below; S. Luke vii. 10; xix. 32; Acts v. 22 (Vienna and some others ܐܶܫܬܰܕܰܪܘ); x. 17; xi. 11.—3. pl. fem. ܐܶܫܬܰܕܰܪ, Rev. v. 6.—Part. ܡܶܫܬܰܕܰܪ, pl. masc. ܡܶܫܬܰܕܪܺܝܢ, 1 S. Pet. ii. 14.

Chald. Ithpa. part. מִשְׁתַּדַּר, *exerted himself, endeavoured,* followed by לְ, Dan. vi. 15.

— ܡܶܢ *from*—παρά—Preposition.
— ܫܡܶܗ *his name*—ὄνομα αὐτῷ—ܫܡܳܐ (Eph. i. 21) noun masc. *A name*.
Wit haff. pron. of the 3rd pers.—Def. ܫܡܳܐ, S. Mark iii. 16, 17. —Constr. ܫܶܡ, S. John v. 43; S. Matt. xxviii. 19. With affixes, ܫܡܳܟ, *Thy name*, S. Matt. vi. 9, &c. ܫܶܡܝ, *My name*, S. John xiv. 13, 26, &c. For an explanation of this latter form, see Phillips's Gr. § 29 (4); Cowper's Gr. § 154 (3).—Pl. ܫܡܳܗܶܐ (irreg.) Phil. ii. 9.—Def. ܫܡܳܗܶܐ, S. Matt. x. 2.—With aff. ܫܡܳܗܰܝܗܘܢ, S. John x. 3; ܫܡܳܗܳܬܗܶܝܢ, S. Luke x. 20.

Heb. שֵׁם (of very frequent occurrence)—Chald. שֵׁם, Dan. iv. 5; Ezr. v. 1. Takes affixes as from שֵׁם, see Dan. ii. 20; iv. 5, &c.—Pl. שְׁמָהָן, Ezr. v. 4, 10.

7. ܐܶܬܳܐ *came*—ἦλθεν—Verb pret. 3. sing. *Came, arrived*. Joined with ܩܕܳܡ, it signifies *made progress*, as in 1 Cor. xi. 17:—with ܒܳܬܰܪ, *followed*, as in ver. 27, 38, below. Pret. 3. sing. fem. ܐܶܬܳܬ, ch. ii. 4.—2. sing. ܐܶܬܰܝܬ, ch. vi. 25, &c.—1. sing. ܐܶܬܺܝܬ, ver. 31, below.—3. pl. ܐܶܬܰܘ, ver. 39, below.—2. pl. ܐܶܬܰܝܬܘܢ, S. Matt. xxv. 36.—1. pl. ܐܶܬܰܝܢ, S. Matt. ii. 2.—Fut. ܢܺܐܬܶܐ, ch. iv. 4, &c.—Fem.

Ver. 7. ܢܸܗܘܸܐ, S. Luke i. 43.—2. sing. ܢܸܗܘܸܐ, 2 Tim. iv. 21.—1. sing. ܐܸܗܘܸܐ, S. John xiv. 3.—3. pl. ܢܸܗܘܘܿܢ, S. Matt. viii. 11:—Fem. ܢܸܗܘܝܵܢ̈, S. Matt. xxiii. 36, &c.—2. pl. ܬܸܗܘܘܿܢ, ch. v. 40, below.—1. pl. ܢܸܗܘܸܐ, Hebr. vi. 1. Imperat. ܗܘܝܼ, ver. 43, 46, below.—Fem. ܗܘܵܝ, S. John iv. 16.—Pl. ܗܘܘܿ, ver. 39, below; Fem. ܗܘܝܼ̈ܝܢ, S. Matt. xxviii. 6.—Inf. (with ܠ) ܠܡܸܗܘܵܐ, S. John vii. 34, 36.—Part. ܗܘܸܐ, ver. 9, below;—Fem. ܗܘܝܵܐ, ch. iv. 15.—Pl. masc. ܗܘܹܝܢ, ver. 38, below:—combined with ܐܸܢܵܐ, ܗܘܝܼܬ, ch. xiv. 23; xxi. 3: —Fem. ܗܘܝܵܐ, 1 S. Pet. ii. 19.—Part. Peil ܗܘܝܼ, S. John vi. 17;— pl. ܗܘܹܝܢ, ch. xi. 19.

Heb. אָתָה (used in poetry only) Deut. xxxiii. 2.—Chald. אֲתָה, Dan. vii. 22.—Inf. לְמֵתֵא, ch. iii. 2.

— ܠܣܵܗܕܘܼܬܐ for a witness—εἰς μαρτυρίαν—ܠ, to, for—Inseparable preposition —used also to mark the accusative case.

ܣܵܗܕܘܼܬܐ, def. of ܣܵܗܕܘܼ (Acts xiv. 16) noun fem. Testimony, witness.—Constr. form. ܣܵܗܕܘܼܬ ܕܩܘܼܫܬܐ, witness of untruth, i.e. false witness, S. Matt. xv. 19.—Pl. ܣܵܗܕܘܵܢ̈, def. ܣܵܗܕܘܵܬܐ̈, with aff. ܣܵܗܕܘܵܬܗܘܿܢ, S. Mark xiv. 56. Compare Gen. xxxi. 47, where this word is used by Laban the Syrian. Root ܣܗܕ, witnessed.

The Heb. word שָׂהֵד, with aff. שָׂהֲדִי, my witness, record, is found once, Job xvi. 19.

— ܕܢܣܗܕ to bear witness, that he might bear witness—ἵνα μαρτυρήσῃ— Aphel fut. 3. sing. (pref. ܕ here a causal conjunction) of ܣܗܕ, witnessed.—Aph. ܐܣܗܕ (ver. 32, below), bore witness:—Pret. 2. sing. ܐܣܗܕܬ, Acts xxiii. 11:—1. sing. ܐܣܗܕܬ, ver. 34, below: —3. pl. ܐܣܗܕܘ, Acts x. 43:—1. pl. ܐܣܗܕܢ, 1 Cor. xv. 15.— Fut. 1. sing. ܐܣܗܕ, S. John xviii. 37.—Imperat. ܐܣܗܕ, ver. 23. —Infin. ܠܡܣܗܕܘ, Rev. xxii. 16.—Part. ܡܣܗܕ, S. John iii. 32; vii. 7; viii. 13, 14:—Fem. ܡܣܗܕܐ, Rom. ii. 15.—Pl.

S. JOHN I. 7.

Ver. 7. masc. ܡܿܚܟܣܘܕ݂ܐ, S. Matt. xxiii. 31, &c.   Combined with ܡܿܚܟܣܘܕ݂ܢܝ̈, ܣܢܝ̈, S. John iii. 11.

— ܥܲܠ concerning—περί—Preposition.

— ܕܟ݂ܠܢܳܫ that every man, all men—Gr. ἵνα πάντες—Compounded of ܐܢܳܫ + ܟܠ, by aphæresis of ܐ, but often used as separate words. Pref. ܕ, causal conjunction.

— ܢܗܰܝܡܢܘܢ might believe—Gr. πιστεύσωσι—Aphel fut. 3. sing. (with ܕ prefixed to the foregoing word, having the force of the subjunctive) of ܐܡܢ, persevered, was constant, faithful; used only in part. Peil ܐܡܝܢ, def. ܐܡܝܢܐ, faithful, constant, Phil. i. 3:—Fem. (same form) 1 Tim. v. 5:—def. ܐܡܝܢܬܐ, Acts xii. 5.—Pl. ܐܡܝܢܝܢ, Acts i. 14, &c.:—def. ܐܡܝܢܬܐ, 1 Tim. v. 23.—Ethpeel ܐܬܐܡܢ, remained firm, constant, once in Imperat. pl. ܐܬܐܡܢܘ, Col. iv. 2.

Aph. ܗܰܝܡܢ (S. John iii. 18) believed. In this form the characteristic ה of the Heb. Hiph. הֶאֱמִין is retained, and the 1st radical changed to Yud. Usually followed by ܒ or ܠ; but sometimes immediately by the noun, as in S. Mark xvi. 11: S. Luke xxiv. 11. Pret. 3. sing. fem. ܗܰܝܡܢܰܬ, S. Luke i. 45—2. sing. ܗܰܝܡܢܬ, S. John xx. 29, &c.—1. sing. ܗܰܝܡܢܬ, Acts xvi. 15.—3. pl. ܗܰܝܡܢܘ, S. John ii. 11, &c.—2. pl. ܗܰܝܡܢܬܘܢ, S. John v. 46, &c.—1. pl. ܗܰܝܡܢܢ, S. John vi. 69.—Fut. 2. sing. ܬܗܰܝܡܢ, S. Mark ix. 23.—1. sing. ܐܗܰܝܡܢ, S. John ix. 36.—3. pl. ܢܗܰܝܡܢܘܢ, S. John xi. 42, &c.—2. pl. ܬܗܰܝܡܢܘܢ, S. John iv. 48; v. 47, &c.—1. pl. ܢܗܰܝܡܢ, S. John vi. 30, &c.—Imperat. ܗܰܝܡܢ, S. Mark v. 36:—Fem. ܗܰܝܡܢܝ, with aff. ܗܰܝܡܢܝܢܝ, S. John iv. 21:—Pl. ܗܰܝܡܢܘ, ch. x. 38, &c.—Inf. ܠܡܗܰܝܡܢܘ, ch. v. 44.—Part. ܡܗܰܝܡܢ, ver. 50, below, and frequently. Def. ܡܗܰܝܡܢܐ, ch. xx. 27:—Fem. (same form) ch. xi. 26, 27:—Def. ܡܗܰܝܡܢܬܐ, Acts xvi. 1.—Pl.

Ver. 7. masc. ܡܗܝܡܢܝܢ, ver. 12, below;—combined with ܚܢܢ, ܡܗܝܡܢܝܢܢ, ch. iv. 42:—Def. ܡܗܝܡܢܐ, Acts viii. 2, &c. —Part. pass. ܡܗܝܡܢ, *one who is faithful, in whom trust is reposed*, S. Matt. xxv. 23; S. Luke xvi. 10.—Def. ܡܗܝܡܢܐ, S. Matt. xxiv. 45; xxv. 21, 23; S. Luke xii. 42. Used also in def. state as a substantive, *an Eunuch*, Acts viii. 27, &c.—Fem. (same form) 1 Tim. i. 15:—Def. ܡܗܝܡܢܬܐ, Acts xiii. 34. Pl. masc. def. ܡܗܝܡܢܐ, S. Luke xvi. 11, 12. As a substantive, S. Matt. xix. 12.—Pl. fem. ܡܗܝܡܢܢ, 1 Tim. iii. 11;—Def. ܡܗܝܡܢܬܐ, Rev. xxi. 5.

Heb. Hiph. (as above) Gen. xv. 6.—Chald. Aph. הֵימִן, Dan. vi. 24. Part. pass. ch. ii. 45; vi. 5.

8. ܐܠܐ, *but*—ἀλλά—Conjunction, commonly regarded as identical with the Gr. word which it here represents. But its etymology as compounded of ܐܢ + ܠܐ is evident from its meaning in ch. x. 10, *except, unless*—Gr. εἰ μή.—ܐܠܐ ܐܢ, ἐὰν μή, ch. iii. 27.

9. ܓܝܪ, *for*, is the Gr. γάρ; and, like it, never begins a sentence.

— ܕܫܪܪܐ, *of the truth*, i.e. *the true* Light—Gr. (τὸ φῶς) τὸ ἀληθινόν—Noun masc. def. *firmness, sincerity, integrity, verity.* With pref. ܕ of the genitive, which takes ̇ before a vowelless consonant.—Pref. ܒ, ܒܫܪܪܐ, *in truth, of a truth, verily*, Acts x. 34.—Root ܫܪ ܫܪܪ, *was firm.*

— ܕܡܢܗܪ ܠܟܠܢܫ, *which lighteth every man*—ὃ φωτίζει πάντα ἄνθρωπον. Here ܕ is the rel. pronoun; ܠ marks the object.

— ܕܐܬܐ, *that cometh*—Gr. ἐρχόμενον. Participle of ܐܬܐ, *came* (see note, ver. 7). The first vowel remitted to ܕ.

— ܠܥܠܡܐ, *into the world*—εἰς τὸν κόσμον. Def. (with pref. prep. ܠ) of ܥܠܡ (ch. iii. 15), noun masc. primarily signifying *a long or indefinite space of time—eternity* (αἰών, Lat. *ævum*); then *the world*, Lat. *mundus*. Pl. ܥܠܡܝܢ, S. Matt. vi. 13. Def. ܥܠܡܐ, Rom. xvi. 25. ܡܠܟܐ ܕܥܠܡܐ, Gr. ὁ βασιλεὺς τῶν ἁγίων (al. ἐθνῶν), Rev. xv. 3.

S. JOHN I. 9—11.

Ver. 9. Heb. עוֹלָם, Ps. xxv. 6.—Chald. עָלַם, *perpetuity*, Dan. iii. 33.

10. ܝܰܕܥܶܗ, *knew Him*—αὐτὸν...ἔγνω—Pret. 3. sing. (with aff. 3. sing. masc.) of ܝܺܕܰܥ (ch. iv. 1) *knew, understood*. For the rule of the vowels, see Phillips's Gr. § 48; Cowper § 102.

Pret. 3. sing. fem. ܝܶܕܥܰܬ݂, S. Mark v. 33; S. Luke vii. 37.—2. sing. ܝܺܕܰܥܬ݁, with aff. S. John xiv. 9:—Fem. ܝܺܕܰܥܬ݁ܝ, S. Luke xix. 44.—1. sing. ܝܶܕܥܶܬ݂, S. John xvii. 7; S. Luke xvi. 4.—3. pl. ܝܺܕܰܥܘ, S. John vii. 26, &c.—2. pl. ܝܺܕܰܥܬ݁ܽܘܢ, Gal. iv. 9: with aff. S. John viii. 55.—1. pl. ܝܺܕܰܥܢ, S. John iv. 42, &c.—Fut. ܢܶܕܰܥ, S. John vii. 51, &c.:—Fem. ܬܶܕܰܥ, S. Matt. vi. 3.—2. sing. ܬܶܕܰܥ, S. John xiii. 7; S. Luke i. 4.—1. sing. ܐܶܕܰܥ, S. Luke i. 18.—3. pl. ܢܶܕܥܽܘܢ, Rom. i. 28:—with aff. S. John xvii. 3; S. Luke ix. 45:—Fem. ܢܶܕܥܳܢ, Rev. ii. 23.—2. pl. ܬܶܕܥܽܘܢ, S. John viii. 28, 32, &c.—1. pl. ܢܶܕܰܥ, 1 Cor. ii. 12; 1 S. John v. 20.—Imperat. ܕܰܥ, Hebr. viii. 11:—Pl. ܕܰܥܘ, S. Matt. xxiv. 33, 43.—Inf. with ܠ, ܠܡܶܕܰܥ, S. John xiv. 5.—Part. ܝܳܕܰܥ, ch. i. 31:—Fem. ܝܳܕܥܳܐ, ch. iv. 10; coalescing with ܐܰܢ̱ܬ݁, ܝܳܕܥܰܬ݁, S. Luke xix. 42.—Pl. masc. ܝܳܕܥܺܝܢ, ver. 26, below: coalescing with ܐ̱ܢܶܢ, ܝܳܕܥܺܝܢܰܢ, ch. iii. 2;—with ܐܰܢ̱ܬ݁ܽܘܢ, ܝܳܕܥܺܝܬܽܘܢ, 2 Cor. iii. 3.—Constr. ܝܳܕܥܰܝ̈, Rom. vii. 1.—For the part. Peil, see note, S. Matt. xxvii. 16.

Heb. יָדַע (very frequent)—Chald. יְדַע, Dan. ii. 8, &c.

11. ܕܺܝܠܶܗ, *to his own*—εἰς τὰ ἴδια—Prep. ܠ, prefixed to ܕ, a particle compounded of ܕ (or ܕ݁), Chald. דִּי) and ܠ of the dative. With affixes (here 3. masc. sing.) it serves for personal pronouns of all persons and genders. See Phillips, Gr. § 28: Cowper § 67, 68.

Compare Heb. שֶׁלִּי, אֲשֶׁר־לִי.

— ܩܰܒ݁ܠܽܘܗ̱ܝ, *received Him*—αὐτὸν...παρέλαβον—Pael pret. 3. pl. (with aff. 3. sing. masc.) of ܩܒܰܠ, *demanded of a person*, with aff. ܡܩܰܒ݁ܠܳܢܺܝܬܳܐ, Acts xxv. 24. *Exclaimed*, part. ܡܩܰܒ݁ܠܳܐ, Rom. xi. 2.

S. JOHN I. 11, 12.   11

Ver. 11. *Opposed himself*, fut. ܢܶܩܰܒܶܠ, Rom. viii. 33.—Pa. ܩܰܒܶܠ (ch. iii. 33; S. Luke ix. 11), *took, received, accepted.*—Pret. 3. fem. ܩܰܒܠܰܬ, 1 Tim. v. 10.—2. sing. ܩܰܒܶܠܬ, S. Luke xvi. 25.—1. sing. ܩܰܒܠܶܬ, S. John x. 18.—3. pl. ܩܰܒܶܠܘ, ch. xvii. 8.—2. pl. ܩܰܒܶܠܬܘܢ, S. Luke vi. 24.—1. pl. ܩܰܒܶܠܢ, Acts xxviii. 21.—Fut. ܢܩܰܒܶܠ, S. Matt. xviii. 5; xix. 29, &c.—Fem. ܬܩܰܒܶܠ, Hebr. xi. 11.—2. sing. ܬܩܰܒܶܠ, 1 Tim. v. 19;—Fem. ܬܩܰܒܠܝܢ, S. Luke i. 31.—1. sing. ܐܶܩܰܒܶܠ with aff. 2 Cor. vi. 17.—3. pl. ܢܩܰܒܠܘܢ, S. Mark xii. 40; S. Luke xx. 47; with aff. S. John vi. 21.—2. pl. ܬܩܰܒܠܘܢ, ch. v. 43.—1. pl. ܢܩܰܒܶܠ, Gal. iv. 5.— Imperat. ܩܰܒܶܠ, S. Luke xvi. 7.—Pl. ܩܰܒܶܠܘ, S. John xx. 22; S. Matt. xi. 14.—Inf. ܠܰܡܩܰܒܳܠܘ, S. John vii. 39; with aff. (pleonastic) ch. xiv. 17.—Part. ܡܩܰܒܶܠ, ch. iii. 32, &c. Fem. ܡܩܰܒܠܐ, Hebr. vi. 7.—Pl. masc. ܡܩܰܒܠܝܢ, S. John iii. 11, &c.—Coalescing with ܠܢܝ, ܡܩܰܒܠܝܢܝ, Acts xxiv. 3:—with ܐܢܬܘܢ, ܡܩܰܒܠܝܬܘܢ, Col. iii. 24.—Part. pass. ܡܩܰܒܠܐ, used as a noun; see note, S. Luke iv. 19.

Heb. Piel קִבֵּל, Prov. xix. 20.—Chald. Pa. קַבֵּל, Dan. ii. 6; vi. 1; vii. 18.

12. ܐܝܠܝܢ, *they, as many (as)*—ὅσοι—Demonstr. pron. pl., usually followed (as here) by ܕ.

— ܕܝܢ, the same as the Gr. δέ, used in the same way and signification.

— ܝܰܗܒ, *He gave*—ἔδωκεν—For the peculiarities of this verb, see Phillips's Gr. § 40 (9); Cowper's Gr. § 113 (6).—A verb defective in the Fut. tense and Inf. Mood, which are supplied by the verb ܢܬܠ, found in these two forms only. See note, ver. 22, below. Pret. 3. fem. ܝܶܗܒܰܬ, S. Mark vi. 28.—2. sing. ܝܰܗܒܬ, S. John xvii. 2, &c.—1. sing. ܝܶܗܒܶܬ, ch. xiii. 15; xvii. 8, 14, 22.—3. pl. ܝܰܗܒܘ, S. Matt. xv. 36.—2. pl. ܝܰܗܒܬܘܢ, S. Matt. xxv. 35, 42.—1. pl. ܝܰܗܒܢ, Acts xxi. 7, 19.—Imperat. ܗܒ,

Ver. 12. S. John iv. 15, &c. Fem. ܝܶܗܒ݂ܰܬ݂, ch. iv. 7, 10.—Pl. ܝܰܗ̱ܒ݂ܘ, S. Matt. x. 8:—Fem. ܝܰܗ̱ܒ݂ܶܝܢ, S. Matt. xxv. 8.—Part. ܝܳܗܶܒ݂, S. John iv. 10, &c.—Fem. ܝܳܗ̱ܒ݂ܳܐ, ch. xv. 2.—Pl. masc. ܝܳܗ̱ܒ݂ܺܝܢ, S. Matt. xxi. 41, &c.—Coalescing with ܢܰܢ, ܝܳܗ̱ܒ݂ܺܝܢܰܢ, 2 Cor. i. 20, &c.—Pl. fem. ܝܳܗ̈ܒ݂ܳܢ, 1 Cor. xiv. 7.—Part. Peil, ܝܗܺܝܒ݂, S. John vi. 65:—Fem. ܝܗܺܝܒ݂ܳܐ, Acts xix. 39.—Pl. masc. ܝܗܺܝܒ݂ܺܝܢ, Acts ii. 47.

Heb. יָהַב, only in imperat. Prov. xxx. 15; Gen. xxix. 21, and a few other places only.—Chald. יְהַב, Dan. ii. 37, &c.

— ܠܗܽܘܢ, *to them*—*αὐτοῖς*—ܠ of the dative with affixed pronoun 3. masc. pl.

— ܫܽܘܠܛܳܢܳܐ, *the power*—*ἐξουσίαν*—Def. of ܫܽܘܠܛܳܢ (S. Matt. xxviii. 18) noun masc. *rule, dominion, one who has power* (Arab. *Sultan*). Pl. def. ܫܽܘܠܛܳܢ̈ܶܐ, Rom. viii. 38. Gr. *ἀρχαί*. R. ܫܠܶܛ, *had power*.

Chald. שָׁלְטָן, Dan. iii. 33, &c. Pl. def. שָׁלְטָנַיָּא, ch. vii. 27. —שִׁלְטוֹן, *ruler*, ch. iii. 2.

— ܢܶܗܘܽܘܢ . . . . ܕ, *that they might become*—*to become*—Gr. *γενέσθαι*—Fut. 3. pl. of ܗܘܳܐ, *was, became*. The ܕ, with ܼ before a vowelless consonant, prefixed to ܒ݁ܢܰ̈ܝܳܐ.

— ܒ݁ܢܰ̈ܝܳܐ, *the sons*—*τέκνα*—Pl. def. of ܒ݁ܪ (ver. 45, below), noun masc. *a son*. Def. ܒ݁ܪܳܐ, ch. iii. 35. Pl. (irreg.) ܒ݁ܢܺܝܢ, Acts vii. 29; Gal. iv. 22.—Constr. ܒ݁ܢ̈ܰܝ, S. Matt. xx. 20; S. Mark iii. 17; S. Luke i. 16.—ܒ݁ܪ with aff. 1. sing. and 2, 3 pl. takes the vowel ܶ; as ܒ݁ܶܪܝ, *my son*, S. Matt. ii. 15; iii. 17, &c.—ܒ݁ܶܪܟ݂ܽܘܢ, *your son*, S. John ix. 19.

ܒ݁ܪ, ܒ݁ܢ̈ܰܝ, enter into certain idiomatic expressions; as ܒ݁ܪ ܐ݈ܢܳܫܳܐ or ܒ݁ܪܢܳܫܳܐ, *son of man*, i.e. *man*, pl. ܒ݁ܢ̈ܰܝ ܐ݈ܢܳܫܳܐ or ܒ݁ܢ̈ܰܝܢܳܫܳܐ, see ver. 4, above.

Ver. 12. ܒܢܝ ܐܘܪܫܠܡ, *people of Jerusalem,* S. Mark i. 5.

ܒ݁ܪ ܚܡܫܝܢ ܫܢܝܢ, *fifty years old,* S. John viii. 57.

ܒ݁ܪ ܬܪܬܥܣܪܐ ܫܢܝܢ, *twelve years old,* S. Luke ii. 42.

ܒܢܝ ܒܝܬܐ, *those of the household,* viz. all but the heads of the family, father and mother, S. Matt. x. 25, 36; xxiv. 45; S. Luke ix. 61.

ܒܢܝ ܚܐܪܐ, *sons of the free,* i.e. *the free,* S. John viii. 33, 36; S. Matt. xvii. 26.

ܒܢܝ ܛܘܗܡܐ, *sons of relationship,* i.e. *kindred,* S. Luke i. 58.

ܒܢܝ ܟܘܡܐ, *acquaintance,* S. Luke ii. 44.

ܒܢܝ ܡܕܝܢܬܐ, *sons of the city, citizens,* S. Luke vii. 12; xv. 15; xix. 14.

ܒܢܝ ܥܡܐ, *sons of the people—nation,* S. John xviii. 35.

ܒܪ ܫܠܡܐ, *the son of peace,* i.e. *one worthy of your favour or regard,* S. Luke x. 6.

ܒܪ ܫܥܬܗ, *the son of his time,* i.e. *in that very hour, immediately,* S. John v. 9; xiii. 30; S. Matt. xiii. 5, 20; xxi. 20.

Similar phrases occur in other parts of the N. T.; as,

ܒܪ ܐܘܡܢܘܬܗܘܢ, and ܒܢܝ ܐܘܡܢܘܬܗܘܢ, *a son of their craft,* or *occupation, fellow-craftsman; fellow-craftsmen,* Gr. ὁμότεχνος, ὁμότεχνοι. Acts xviii. 3, and xix. 24, 25, 38.

ܒܢܝ ܐܬܪܐ, *sons of the place,* i.e. *they of that place,* Gr. οἱ ἐντόπιοι, Acts xxi. 12.

ܒܢܝ ܒܢܝܐ, *grandchildren,* Gr. ἔκγονα, 1 Tim. v. 4.

ܒܢܝ ܒܣܪܝ, *sons of my flesh,* i.e. *my own people,* Rom. xi. 14.

ܒܪ ܐܢܝܪܝ *son of my yoke, yokefellow,* Phil. iv. 3; and ܒܢܝ ܐܢܝܪܐ, 2 Cor. vi. 14.

ܒܢܝ ܝܪܬܘܬܐ, *joint-heirs,* Rom. viii. 17; Eph. iii. 6.

ܒܢܝ ܡܠܟܘܗܝ, *his councillors,* Acts xxv. 12.

ܒܪ ܡܬܪܒܝܢܘܗܝ, *son of the educators (of Herod),* i.e. *one who was brought up with him* (aff. pleon.), Acts xiii. 1.

ܒܢܝ ܦܬܟܪܐ, *sons of idols, idolaters,* Rev. ii. 14, 20.

Ver. 12. ܒܢܝ̈ ܫܢܝ̈, *sons of my years, my equals in age*, Gr. συνηλικιώτας, Gal. i. 14.

ܒܢܝ̈ ܫܪܒܬܟܘܢ, *children of your own tribe, your own countrymen*, 1 Thess. ii. 14.

Heb. בֵּן, very frequently; בַּר, Ps. ii. 12; Prov. xxxi. 2.—Chald. בַּר, Dan. iii. 25; Ezr. v. 1.—Pl. בְּנִין, constr. בְּנֵי, Dan. ii. 25; Ezr. vi. 9.

13. ܠܘ, *not*—compounded of ܠܐ ܗܘ, *is not*—Interrogatively, ch. vii. 25, below.

— ܡܢ ܕܡܐ, *from the blood, of blood*—Gr. ἐξ αἱμάτων—Def. of ܕܡ (Acts xvii. 26.) noun masc. *Blood*—Takes with aff. 1. sing. and 2, 3. pl. the vowel of its abs. state, as ܕܡܝ, ch. vi. 54, seqq.; S. Matt. xxvi. 28, &c.; ܕܡܗܘܢ, S. Luke xiii. 1.

Heb. דָּם, Ps. xciv. 21.

— ܡܢ ܨܒܝܢܐ, *of the will*—ἐκ θελήματος—Def. of ܨܒܝܢ, noun masc. *Will, good pleasure.* With pref. ܒ, adv. *willingly, suâ sponte*, Gr. ἑκοῦσα, Rom. viii. 20.—Constr. ܒܨܒܝܢ ܢܦܫܗܘܢ, *by the will of their soul, willingly*, 2 Cor. viii. 3.—Pl. with aff. ܨܒܝܢܝ̈, *my desires, will*, Acts xiii. 22.—R. ܨܒܐ, *willed.*

— ܕܒܣܪܐ, *of the flesh*—σαρκός—Def. (with ܕ of the gen.) of ܒܣܪ (ch. xvii. 2) noun masc. *Flesh.*—Pl. def. ܒܣܖ̈ܐ, S. Jude ver. 7.

Heb. בָּשָׂר, Gen. vi. 13; Ps. lxv. 3.—Chald. בְּשַׂר, Dan. vii. 5. Def. בִּשְׂרָא, ch. ii. 11; iv. 9.

— ܕܓܒܪܐ, *of man*—ἀνδρός—Def. (with ܕ of the gen.) of ܓܒܪ, noun masc. *A man*, and *man*, i.e. the male sex in general.—Pl. ܓܒܖ̈ܝܢ, def. ܓܒܖ̈ܐ, Acts i. 16, &c.

Heb. גֶּבֶר (chiefly in poetry) Ps. xxxiv. 9.—Chald. גְּבַר, Dan. ii. 25; v. 11.—Pl. גֻּבְרִין, def. גֻּבְרַיָּא, ch. iii. 8, 12. Root Heb. גָּבַר, *was strong, prevailed*—Syr. Ethpe. or (Ethpa.) ܐܬܓܒܪ, *showed himself strong*, Imperat. pl. ܐܬܓܒܪܘ, *quit you like men*, 1 Cor. xvi. 13.

— ܐܬܝܠܕܘ, *were born*—ἐγεννήθησαν—Ethpeel pret. 3. pl. of ܝܠܕ, *gave*

S. JOHN I. 13, 14.

Ver. 13. *birth to.*—Ethpe. ܐܶܬ݂ܺܝܠܶܕ݂ (ix. 19), *was born.* Followed by ܡܶܢ ܕ݁ܪܺܝܫ? *was born again*, see ch. iii. 3, 7.—Pret. 2. sing. ܐܶܬ݂ܺܝܠܶܕ݁ܬ݁, ch. ix. 34:—1. sing. ܐܶܬ݂ܺܝܠܶܕ݂ܬ݁, Acts xxii. 8:—2. pl. ܕ݁ܶܐܬ݂ܺܝܠܶܕ݁ܬ݁ܽܘܢ 1 S. Pet. i. 23.—Fut. ܢܶܬ݂ܺܝܠܶܕ݂, S. John iii. 4.—Part. ܡܶܬ݂ܺܝܠܶܕ݂, ver. 3, 5.—Inf. ܠܡܶܬ݂ܺܝܠܳܕ݂ܽܘ, ver. 7.

14. ܘܰܐܓܶܢ, *and dwelt, tabernacled*—καὶ ἐσκήνωσεν—Aph. pret. 3. sing. (pref. ܘ, to which the vowel is remitted) of ܓܢܐ, used only in Aph. ܐܰܓܶܢ, *overshadowed, protected, fell* or *rested upon.* Followed by ܒ, as here; or, as elsewhere, by ܥܰܠ.—Pret. 3. fem. ܐܰܓܢܰܬ݂, Acts x. 44; xi. 15.—Fut. ܢܰܓܶܢ (or ܢܰܓܶܢ) S. Luke i. 35. Gr. ἐπισκιάσει—Acts ii. 26; 2 Cor. xii. 9.—3. fem. ܬܰܓܶܢ, Acts v. 15. Heb. גָּנַן, with עַל, 2 Kings xx. 6.—Hiph. יָגֵן, with עַל, Isa. xxxi. 5.

— ܒܰܢ, *in us*—ἐν ἡμῖν—Prepos. ܒ with aff. 1. pl.

— ܘܰܚܙܰܝܢ, *and we beheld*—καὶ ἐθεασάμεθα—Pret. 1. pl. (pref. ܘ with ' before a vowelless consonant) of ܚܙܐ (ver. 18) *saw, beheld.*—Pret. 3. fem. ܚܙܳܬ݂, ch. xx. 1, 12, 14, 18, &c.—2. sing. ܚܙܰܝܬ݁, Acts xxii. 15: with aff. S. John ix. 37; xx. 29.—1. sing. ܚܙܺܝܬ݂, ch. viii. 38. —3. pl. ܚܙܰܘ, ver. 39, below, &c.; Fem. ܚܙܰܝ, S. Mark xv. 47, &c.—2. pl. ܚܙܰܝܬ݁ܽܘܢ, S. John v. 37, &c.—Fut. ܢܶܚܙܶܐ, ch. iii. 3.— 2. sing. ܬܶܚܙܶܐ, ver. 46, 50, below.—1. sing. ܐܶܚܙܶܐ, S. Mark x. 51: —3. pl. ܢܶܚܙܽܘܢ, S. John vii. 3:—2. pl. ܬܶܚܙܽܘܢ, ver. 39, 51, below;—1. pl. ܢܶܚܙܶܐ, ch. vi. 30.—Imperat. ܚܙܺܝ, ch. vii. 52, &c.;—pl. ܚܙܰܘ, ch. iv. 29:—Fem. ܚܙܰܝܶܝܢ, S. Matt. xxviii. 6.— Inf. ܠܡܶܚܙܳܐ, S. Matt. xiii. 14; pref. ܠ, S. Matt. xi. 7, 8, 9, &c.— Part. ܚܳܙܶܐ, ver. 33, below; fem. ܚܳܙܝܳܐ, ch. iv. 19.—Pl. masc. ܚܳܙܶܝܢ, ch. vi. 2, &c.:—coalescing with ܠܢ, ܚܳܙܶܝܢܰܢ, ch. ix. 41;—with ܐܰܢܬ݁ܽܘܢ, ܚܳܙܶܝܬ݁ܽܘܢ, Phil. iii. 17.—Pl. fem. ܚܳܙܝܳܢ, S. Matt. xiii. 16.

Ver. 14. Heb. חָזָה, chiefly in poetry, Ps. xlvi. 9, &c. Chald. חֲזָא, Dan. ii. 31, 34, &c.

— ܫܘܒܚܗ, *his glory*—τὴν δόξαν αὐτοῦ—Def. (with aff. 3. sing. masc.) of ܫܘܒܚ, def. ܫܘܒܚܐ (in the next clause) noun masc. *Praise, glory, Majesty.*—R. ܫܒܚ, Pa. ܫܒܚ, *glorified.*

— ܐܝܟ, *as*—ὡς—Conjunction—answering to the Heb. כְּ.

— ܕܝܚܝܕܝܐ, *of the Only-begotten*—μονογενοῦς—Def. (pref. ܕ of the gen., to which the first vowel is remitted) of ܝܚܝܕܝ, noun masc., *an only one, only child.* Fem. def. ܝܚܝܕܝܬܐ, S. Luke viii. 42.
Heb. יָחִיד, Gen. xxii. 2.—R. יָחַד, *was united.*

— ܕܡܢ ܐܒܐ, *which* (*is*) *from the Father*—Gr. παρὰ Πατρός—Def. of ܐܒ, noun masc. This noun (like ܐܚܐ, *brother*, and ܚܡܐ, *father-in-law*) takes in the sing. ܘ before all affixes, excepting that of 1. sing. in which ̄ is changed to ̇, thus:—ܐܒܝ, *my father*, ch. ii. 16;—ܐܒܘܟ, *thy father*, ch. viii. 19; ܐܒܘܗܝ, *his father*, ver. 18, below;—ܐܒܘܗ, *her father*, ch. viii. 44;—ܐܒܘܢ, *our father*, ch. iv. 12;—ܐܒܘܟܘܢ, *your father*, ch. viii. 38;—ܐܒܘܗܘܢ, *their father*, S. Matt. iv. 21.—The pl. has two forms; masc. ܐܒܗܝܢ, Hebr. xii. 9. def. ܐܒܗܐ, S. Luke i. 17, *patres naturales*;—and fem. def. ܐܒܗܬܐ, S. John vii. 22, *patres spirituales.* According to Amira, this distinction extends to the singular, the first being distinguished by Ruchoch (ܐܒܐ), and the second by Kuschoi (ܐܒܐ).
Heb. אָב Ps. ciii. 13; Constr. lxviii. 6.—Chald. אַב, with aff. אֲבוּהִי, Dan. v. 2.—Pl. אֲבָהָן, with aff. Dan. ii. 23; Ezr. iv. 15; v. 12.

— ܕܡܠܐ, *which* (*is*) *full* (sc. ܡܠܝܬܐ, but masc. see note above, ver. 1)—πλήρης—Part. Peil (pref. rel. ܕ with ̄ before a vowelless consonant) of ܡܠܐ, *filled.* Here, as throughout the N. T., in immediate construction with the following word. Fem. ܡܠܝܐ, ch. xxi. 11; Acts xvii. 16; S. James iii. 17.—Constr. ܡܠܝܬ, S. Luke i. 28;

S. JOHN I. 14, 15.

Ver. 14. Eph. iii. 10.—Pl. masc. ܡܠܝܢ, S. Matt. xiv. 20, &c.—Constr. ܡܠܝܬ, 2 S. Pet. ii. 13.—Pl. fem. ܡܠܝܢ, 1 S. Pet. i. 22.
For the verb itself, see note, S. John ii. 7.

— ܛܝܒܘܬܐ, grace—Gr. χάριτος—Def. of ܛܝܒܘ (Rom. iv. 4) noun fem. *Favour, beneficence.* R. ܛܐܒ, Pa. ܛܝܒ, *did good.*

— ܘܩܘܫܬܐ, *and truth*—Gr. καὶ ἀληθείας—Def. (pref. ܘ) of ܩܘܫܬܐ, noun masc. *Truth.*—Pl. ܩܘܫܬ̈ܐ, not occurring in the N. T.
Heb. קֹשֶׁט, קשְׁטְ, Ps. lx. 6; Prov. xxii. 21.—Chald. קְשׁוֹט, Dan. iv. 34, מִן־קְשׁוֹט, *of a truth, truly,* ch. ii. 47.

15. ܣܗܕ, *bare witness*—μαρτυρεῖ—Verb Peal pret. *Was a witness, testified.* Pret. 2. sing. ܣܗܕܬ, ch. iii. 26.—3. pl. ܣܗܕܘ, Acts vii. 58.—Fut. ܢܣܗܕ, S. John ii. 25;—2. sing. ܬܣܗܕ, S. Matt. xix. 18, &c.—Part. ܣܗܕ, S. John v. 37, &c.—Def. ܣܗܕܐ, used as a noun, *A witness, martyr,* Acts i. 22, &c.—Fem. ܣܗܕܬܐ, Hebr. x. 15.—Pl. masc. ܣܗ̈ܕܐ, S. John iii. 28; coalescing with ܒܢܝ, ܒܢ̈ܝ ܣܗ̈ܕܝ, 1 S. John i. 2. Pl. def. ܣܗ̈ܕܐ, S. Matt. xxvi. 59, &c.

— ܥܠܘܗܝ, *of (concerning) Him*—περὶ αὐτοῦ—ܥܠ, prepos. with aff. 3. sing. masc.

— ܘܩܥܐ, *and cried*—καὶ κέκραγε—Verb Peal pret. (pref. ܘ with ' before a vowelless consonant) *cried out, exclaimed, proclaimed.*—Pret. 3. fem. ܩܥܬ, S. Luke i. 42.—1. sing. ܩܥܝܬ, Acts xxiv. 21.—3. pl. ܩܥܘ, S. John xviii. 40, &c.—Fut. ܢܩܥܐ, S. Matt. xii. 19;—3. pl. fem. ܢܩ̈ܥܢ, S. Luke xix. 40.—Inf. ܠܡܩܥܐ, S. Mark x. 47.—Part. ܩܥܐ, S. John vii. 37, &c.—Fem. ܩܥܝܐ, S. Matt. xv. 22, 23.—Pl. masc. ܩܥܝܢ, S. John xii. 13, &c.
Compare Heb. גָּעָה, *cried, lowed (of cows),* 1 Sam. vi. 12.

— ܘܐܡܪ, *and said*—Gr. λέγων—Verb Peal pret. (the first vowel remitted to ܘ prefixed). *Said, spoke.* Pret. 3. fem. ܐܡܪܬ, S. Mark v. 33; S. Luke ii. 48.—2. sing. masc. ܐܡܪܬ, S. John xviii. 34, &c.—

W. C.

Ver. 15. Fem. ܐܶܡܪܰܬ݂, ch. iv. 18.—1. sing. ܐܶܡܪܶܬ݂, in this ver. and ver. 30, 50.—3. pl. masc. ܐܶܡܰܪܘ, ver. 22, below, &c.; Fem. ܐܶܡܰܪ̈ܝ̱, S. Luke xxiv. 10, 24; and ܐܶܡܰܪ̈ܶܢ, S. Matt. xxv. 8; S. Mark xvi. 8; S. Luke xxiv. 9.—2. pl. ܐܶܡܰܪ̈ܬܽܘܢ, S. Luke xii. 3.—1. pl. ܐܶܡܰܪܢ, Acts xxi. 14.—Fut. ܢܺܐܡܰܪ, S. Matt. xii. 32:—Fem. ܬܺܐܡܰܪ (for ܬܶܐܡܰܪ) S. Mark xiv. 69.—2. sing. ܬܺܐܡܰܪ, S. Matt. xxvi. 63.—1. sing. ܐܺܡܰܪ, S. Luke vii. 40, &c.—3. pl. masc. ܢܺܐܡܪܽܘܢ, S. Matt. vii. 22, &c.—Fem. ܢܺܐܡܪ̈ܳܢ, S. Matt. xxviii. 8.—2. pl. ܬܺܐܡܪܽܘܢ, S. Matt. iii. 9.—1. pl. ܢܺܐܡܰܪ, S. Matt. xxi. 25.—Imperat. ܐܶܡܰܪ, Acts xxii. 27;—Fem. ܐܶܡܰܪ̱ܝ, S. John xx. 17.—Pl. ܐܶܡܰܪܘ, S. Matt. x. 7;—fem. ܐܶܡܰܪ̈ܶܝܢ, ch. xxviii. 7; S. Mark xvi. 7.—Inf. ܠܡܺܐܡܰܪ, S. John viii. 26.—Part. ܐܳܡܰܪ, ver. 23, below.—Fem. ܐܳܡܪܳܐ, ch. ii. 3.—Pl. masc. ܐܳܡܪܺܝܢ, ver. 38, below;—coalescing with ܠܺܝ, ܐܳܡܪܺܝܢ, ch. viii. 48.—Pl. fem. ܐܳܡܪ̈ܳܢ, S. Matt. xxv. 9, 11.—Part. Peil ܐܰܡܺܝܪ, S. Matt. iii. 3:—fem. ܐܰܡܺܝܪܳܐ, Acts ii. 16.

Heb. אָמַר, of very frequent occurrence—Chald. אֲמַר, Dan. ii. 25, &c.

— ܗܳܢܰܘ, *this is*—Gr. οὗτος ἦν—For ܗܽܘ ܗܳܢܐ, the latter word representing the Copula.

— ܗܽܘ, *He*, Demonstr. pronoun. Pl. ܗܶܢܽܘܢ.—Fem. ܗܺܝ, pl. ܗܶܢܶܝܢ.

— ܕܶܐܡܪܶܬ݂, *that I said—of whom I spake*—ὃν εἶπον—Pret. 1. sing. of ܐܶܡܰܪ (see above), with pref. ܕ to which the vowel is remitted.

— ܒܳܬܰܪ̱ܝ, *after me*—ὀπίσω μου—ܒܳܬܰܪ, prep. (ch. ii. 12) *after*; with aff. 1. sing. The particle ܕ is employed to introduce a speech or quotation. This word, besides its simple and affixed forms, occurs in the following compound forms:

1. ܒܳܬܰܪ ܒܳܬܰܪ, *one thing after another, in order*, Acts xi. 4.
2. ܡܶܢܒܳܬܰܪ, S. John xi. 7, 11. ܡܶܢ ܒܳܬܰܪܟܶܢ, S. Luke xii. 4. ܡܶܢ ܒܳܬܰܪܟܶܢ, Hebr. iv. 8. *Afterwards*.
3. ܡܶܢ ܒܳܬܰܪ, *after*, followed by a noun, ch. v. 4; S. Matt. i. 12.—

Ver. 15. ܡܢ ܒܳܬܰܪ ܕ, *after that, postquam*, followed by a verb, S. Matt. xxvi. 32; S. Luke xxii. 20; Acts i. 3, 13.

4. As a noun in the def. state, with pref. ܠ, ܠܒܶܣܬܪܳܐ, *to the back, back again*, 2 S. Pet. ii. 21.

Transl. *That after me He cometh, and was before me.*—ܠܶܗ, *to Him* is here pleonastic. See Cowper's Gr. § 198.

— ܩܕܳܡܰܝ, *before me*—ἔμπροσθέν μου—ܩܕܳܡ (S. Matt. v. 16), prep. *Before;* taking pl. affixes; here with aff. 1. pl.—ܩܕܳܡܰܝܢ, *before*, S. John xvii. 24.—ܩܕܳܡܰܝ ܡܢ, *before me*, ch. v. 7.—ܩܕܳܡ ܕ, *before that, priusquam*, S. Mark xiv. 30.—ܡܢ ܩܕܳܡ ܕ, *the same*, S. John xiii. 19; xvii. 5.

Chald. קְדָם, קֳדָם, Dan. ii. 9, and very frequently.

— ܕ ܡܶܛܽܠ, *because*—ὅτι—ܡܶܛܽܠ, prep. *On account of*, Gr. διά, ch. iii. 29; S. Mark iv. 7; Rom. iv. 25. *For the sake of*, Gr. ἕνεκεν, S. Matt. v. 10.—Followed, as here, by ܕ, *Because, since; in order that*, Gr. ἵνα, S. John vii. 23; S. Mark iii. 10.—Followed by ܗܳܢܳܐ, or ܗܳܕܶܐ, to which it is sometimes joined as one word, it means *Because of this, therefore*, ver. 31, below; S. Matt. xii. 27, 31; xxiii. 34.—Followed by, or joined with, ܡܳܢܳܐ, *Wherefore, why?*— With pron. affixes it takes the form ܡܶܛܽܠܳܬ; as, ܡܶܛܽܠܳܬܝ, *for my sake*, S. Matt. v. 11; ܡܶܛܽܠܳܬܗ (*she heard*) *of Him*, S. Mark vii. 25.

— ܩܕܳܡܰܝ ܗܘܳܐ ܠܶܗ, *He is before, anterior to, me*—Gr. πρῶτός μου ἦν —ܗܘܳܐ here represents the logical copula, and the two words are pronounced as one, *Kadmoyu*—ܩܰܕܡܳܝ, noun masc. *The first, preceding, ancient, elder.*—Def. ܩܰܕܡܳܝܳܐ, ch. v. 4.—Fem. def. ܩܰܕܡܳܝܬܳܐ, ch. ii. 11.—Constr. ܩܰܕܡܳܝܰܬ, used as an adverb, *first, for the first time*, Acts xi. 26; xiii. 46.—Pl. masc. def. ܩܰܕܡܳܝܶܐ, *those of old time, the ancients*, S. Matt. v. 21, &c.—Pl fem. def. ܩܰܕܡܳܝܳܬܳܐ, Hebr. v. 12.

Chald. קַדְמָי, pl. def. קַדְמָיֵא, Dan. vii. 24.—Fem. def. קַדְמָיְתָא, ver. 4;—Pl. def. קַדְמָיָתָא, ver. 8.

16. ܡܢ ܡܰܠܝܽܘܬܶܗ, *of His fulness*—ἐκ τοῦ πληρώματος αὐτοῦ—ܡܰܠܝܽܘܬܳܐ, noun fem. *Fulness*—Def. ܡܰܠܝܽܘܬܳܐ. Occurs in the N. T. only

S. JOHN I. 16, 17.

Ver. 16. once elsewhere, with aff. fem. ܡܽܠܳܝܶܗ, *its filling up*, i.e. *that which is put in to fill it up*, S. Matt. ix. 16. R. ܡܠܐ, Pa. ܡܰܠܺܝ, *filled*.

— ܟܽܠܰܢ, *we, all of us; all we*—ἡμεῖς πάντες—ܢܰܢ, pron. 1. pl.— For ܟܽܠ, see note, ver. 3.

— ܢܣܰܒ݂ܢ, *we have received*—ἐλάβομεν—Pret. 1. pl. of ܢܣܰܒ݂ (ch. xiii. 30), *took, obtained, bore away; cut off*, S. Luke xxii. 50.— ܢܣܰܒ݂ ܐܰܢ݈ܬ݁ܬ݂ܳܐ, *duxit uxorem, married*, S. Matt. xxii. 25.—With ܐܰܦ̈ܶܐ (pref. ܕ pleonastic) ܢܣܰܒ݂ ܒ݁ܰܐܦ̈ܶܐ, *assumed an appearance, played the hypocrite;* whence part. pl. ܢܳܣܒ݁ܰܝ̈ ܒ݁ܰܐܦ̈ܶܐ, *hypocrites*, S. Matt. vi. 2, &c.—Pret. 3. fem. ܢܶܣܒ݁ܰܬ݂, S. Luke vii. 37; xiii. 21.—2. sing. ܢܣܰܒ݂ܬ݁, 1 Cor. iv. 7.—1. sing. ܢܶܣܒ݁ܶܬ݂, S. Matt. xxvii. 9; S. Luke xiv. 20.—3. pl. masc. ܢܣܰܒ݂ܘ, S. Matt. xvi. 7, &c. Fem. ܢܣܰܒ݂̈ܝ, ch. xxv. 1, 3.—2. pl. ܢܣܰܒ݂ܬ݁ܽܘܢ, ch. x. 8.— Fut. ܢܶܣܰܒ݂, S. John vi. 7.—2. sing. ܬ݁ܶܣܰܒ݂, S. Mark vi. 18.— 1. sing. ܐܶܣܰܒ݂, Phil. iii. 14.—Pl. ܢܶܣܒ݂ܽܘܢ, S. Matt. xvi. 5.—2. pl. ܬ݁ܶܣܒ݂ܽܘܢ, S. John xvi. 24.—1. pl. ܢܶܣܰܒ݂, S. Mark vii. 27.—Imperat. ܣܰܒ݂, S. Matt. xvii. 27, &c.—Pl. ܣܰܒ݂ܘ, ch. xxv. 28, &c. —Inf. ܠܡܶܣܰܒ݂, S. John iii. 27, &c.—Part. ܢܳܣܶܒ݂, S. John iv. 36, &c. Fem. ܢܣܳܒ݂ܳܐ, S. Mark ii. 21.—Pl. masc. ܢܳܣܒ݁ܺܝܢ, S. Matt. xvii. 24, &c.—Coalescing with ܢܰܢ, ܢܳܣܒ݁ܺܝܢܰܢ, 1 S. John iii. 22.—Constr. ܢܳܣܒ݁ܰܝ̈, in the above-mentioned phrase.

— ܚܠܳܦ, *for, answerable to*—ἀντί—Preposition, *in the room of*, S. Matt. ii. 22.—Takes affixes of nouns masc. pl. as ܚܠܳܦܰܝ, ܚܠܳܦܰܝܟ݁, *for Me...for thee*, S. Matt. xvii. 27.— ܚܠܳܦܰܘܗ݈ܝ, *for him*, S. Luke ii. 27.—ܚܠܳܦܰܝܟ݁ܽܘܢ, *for you*, S. Mark ix. 40.— ܕ݁ܰܚܠܳܦ, *because*, S. Luke xix. 44.—R. ܚܠܦ, Pa ܚܰܠܶܦ, *changed, exchanged*.

Heb. חֵלֶף, noun, used as a prep. Numb. xviii. 21, 31.

17. ܢܳܡܽܘܣܳܐ, *the Law*—ὁ νόμος—Def. of ܢܳܡܽܘܣ (1 Cor. ix. 21) noun masc. *Law*.—Pl. def. ܢܳܡܽܘ̈ܣܶܐ, Acts xxii. 3.

S. JOHN 1. 17, 18. 21

Ver. 17. ܒܝܕ, *by, through*, lit. *at the hand of*—διά—See note, ver. 3.

— ܐܬܝܗܒ, *was given*—ἐδόθη—Ethpeel pret. 3. sing. of ܝܗܒ, *gave*.—
Pret. 3. fem. ܐܬܝܗܒܬ, ch. vii. 39; S. Mark vi. 2.—In Hebr. viii. 6 the Vien. and some other Editions read ܐܬܝܗܒܬ.—3. pl. masc. ܐܬܝܗܒܘ, Hebr. ii. 4:—Fem. ܐܬܝܗܒ, 1 Cor. ii. 12.—
Fut. ܢܬܝܗܒ, S. Matt. vii. 7, &c. Fem. ܬܬܝܗܒ, S. Matt. xii. 39; without final ܢ, S. Matt. xxi. 43; S. Mark viii. 12; S. Luke xi. 29; Eph. iv. 19.—Inf. ܠܡܬܝܗܒܘ, S. Mark xiv. 5.
—Part. ܡܬܝܗܒ, S. Matt. x. 19.—Fem. ܡܬܝܗܒܐ, ch. xvi. 4.
—Pl. masc. ܡܬܝܗܒܝܢ, 1 S. John v. 16.

— ܡܫܝܚܐ, *the Anointed, Christ*—Χριστός—noun masc. def. *The Messiah*. Of form part. Peil of ܡܫܚ, *anointed*.—ܡܫܝܚܐ ܕܓܠܐ, *a false Christ, Antichrist*, 1 S. John ii. 18, &c.—Pl. def. ܡܫܝܚܐ ܕܓܠܐ, S. Matt. xxiv. 24.
Heb. מָשִׁיחַ, Dan. ix.:—with aff. Ps. ii. 2, &c.

18. ܠܐ...ܐܢܫ ܡܢ ܡܬܘܡ, *no man ever, at any time*—οὐδεὶς πώποτε—ܡܬܘܡ, ܡܢ ܡܬܘܡ, ܡܬܘܡܐܝܬ, *ever, sometimes*. Preceded or followed by ܠܐ, *never*, in various forms; as:

1. ܠܐ ܡܬܘܡ, S. Luke xv. 29; 2 S. Pet. i. 10.
2. ܠܐ ܡܢ ܡܬܘܡ, S. Matt. xxi. 42; S. John v. 37; Gal. v. 16.
3. ܡܢ ܡܬܘܡ ܠܐ, S. Luke xv. 29; xix. 30; S. John viii. 33.
4. ܡܬܘܡܐܝܬ ܠܐ, S. Matt. xxi. 16; S. Mark ii. 12, 25; S. Luke xxi. 34; S. John vii. 46; Eph. v. 29; 2 S. Pet. i. 21.
5. ܠܐ ܡܬܘܡܐܝܬ, S. Matt. vii. 23; ix. 33; xxvi. 33; Acts x. 14; xiv. 7.

— ܝܚܝܕܝܐ ܐܠܗܐ, *the Only-begotten God*—Gr. ὁ μονογενὴς υἱός.

— ܒܥܘܒܐ, *in the bosom*—εἰς τὸν κόλπον—Def. (with pref. prep. ܒ) of ܥܘܒܐ, noun masc. *Bosom*. Pl. def. ܥܘܒܐ, with aff. ܥܘܒܗ, S. Luke vi. 38.

S. JOHN I. 18, 19.

Ver. 18. ܐܶܫܬܰܥܺܝ, *He hath declared—ἐξηγήσατο*—Ethpael pret. 3. sing. of ܫܥܺܝ, *smeared over, smoothed*—Ethpe. ܐܶܫܬܰܥܺܝ, *delighted himself, was delighted.* Inf. ܠܡܶܫܬܰܥܳܝܽܘ, *to play*, Gr. παίζειν, 1 Cor. x. 7. Ethpa. *delighted (others) by discourse, narrated, brought back news.*—Pret. 3. pl. ܐܶܫܬܰܥܺܝܘ, S. Mark v. 16, &c.—Fut. ܢܶܫܬܰܥܶܐ, Acts viii. 33.—1. sing. ܐܶܫܬܰܥܶܐ, ch. xxviii. 20.—Imperat. ܐܶܫܬܰܥܳܐ, S. Mark v. 19. — Pl. ܐܶܫܬܰܥܰܘ, S. Matt. xi. 4. — Part. ܡܶܫܬܰܥܶܐ, Acts xiii. 41.—Pl. ܡܶܫܬܰܥܶܝܢ, ch. xv. 3, 12.

Heb. שָׁעַע *was smeared over;* of the eyes, *was closed, dim,* Isai. xxxii. 3.

19. ܘܗܳܕܶܐ, *and this is—καὶ αὕτη ἐστίν—*ܗܳܕܶܐ (always thus pointed when alone, as below, ch. ii. 12), Demonstr. pron. fem.

ܗܺܝ, person. pron. fem. here supplying the place of the subst. verb, and therefore losing its own vowel and taking the *linea occultans*. Pronounced with the preceding word as one, *Hodoi*.

— ܣܳܗܕܽܘܬܶܗ, *the record*, lit. *his record*—ἡ μαρτυρία—See note, ver. 7.—The affixed pronoun is pleonastic, referring to the following noun.

— ܟܰܕ, *when—ὅτε*—Conjunction.

— ܫܰܕܰܪܘ, *they sent—ἀπέστειλαν—*Pael pret. 3. pl. of ܫܕܰܪ (Peal not used) Pa. ܫܰܕܰܪ (iii. 17.) *Sent, sent forth, sent away*—Fut. ܢܫܰܕܰܪ, S. Matt. xiii. 41.—1. sing. ܐܫܰܕܰܪ, S. Luke xx. 13; with aff. S. John xvi. 7. —3. pl. ܢܫܰܕܪܽܘܢ, S. Matt. xxi. 34.—Imperat. ܫܰܕܰܪ, S. Mark v. 12. —Infin. ܠܡܫܰܕܳܪܽܘ, S. Luke iv. 18.—Part. ܡܫܰܕܰܪ, ch. xiii. 20, below.—Pl. ܡܫܰܕܪܺܝܢ, coalescing with ܒܢܰܝ, ܡܫܰܕܪܰܝ, Acts xxv. 27.

— ܟܳܗܢܶܐ, *priests—ἱερεῖς—*Pl. def. of ܟܳܗܶܢ, def. ܟܳܗܢܳܐ (S. Luke i. 5) noun masc. *A priest*.

Heb. כֹּהֵן, Ps. cx. 4, and very frequently.—Chald. כָּהֵן, def. כָּהֲנָא, Ezr. vii. 12, 21. Pl. def. כָּהֲנַיָּא, ch. vi. 18, &c.

— ܕܰܢܫܰܐܠܽܘܢܳܝܗܝ, *that they might ask him—to ask him—*ἵνα ἐρωτήσωσιν αὐτόν—Pael fut. 3. pl. with aff. 3. sing. (used as a subjunctive with pref. ܕ) of ܫܐܶܠ, *asked, sought for*, intransitive.—Pa. ܫܰܐܶܠ (ch. iv. 52) *questioned, demanded.*—Pret. 3. pl. ܫܰܐܶܠܘ, ch. ix. 19.

S. JOHN I. 19, 20.

Ver. 19. —Fut. ܢܫܐܠ, with aff. ch. xiii. 24; xvi. 30.—1. sing. ܐܫܐܠ,
with aff. S. Matt. xxi. 24, &c.—Imperat. ܫܐܠ, S. John xviii. 21.
—Pl. ܫܐܠܘ, ch. ix. 21, 23.—Inf. ܠܡܫܐܠܬܗ, with aff. S. Matt.
xxii. 46. Part. ܫܐܠ, S. John xvi. 5, &c.—Pl. ܫܐܠܝܢ,
S. Matt. xii. 10.
 Heb. Pi. שָׁאַל, *begged*, Ps. cix. 10.

— ܐܢܬ ܡܢ ܐܢܬ, *who art thou?*—σὺ τίς εἶ;—

 ܐܢܬ, pers. pronoun; standing, in the second instance, for the subst.
verb.
 ܡܢ, pron. interrog. of the person. Of the thing, S. Luke viii. 30.
Followed by ܕ it becomes a relative, S. John iii. 2.
 Chald. מָן, מַן־, Dan. iii. 15; Ezr. v. 3, 4, 9.

20. ܘܐܘܕܝ, *and he confessed*—καὶ ὡμολόγησε—Aphel pret. 3. sing. of ܝܕܐ
(not used in Peal). Pref. ܘ, to which the first vowel is remitted.
Aph. ܐܘܕܝ, *confessed, professed*, with ܒ of the object, S. Matt.
iii. 6; x. 32. *Gave thanks to*, with ܠ, S. John xi. 41.—Pret. 3.
fem. ܐܘܕܝܬ, S. Luke ii. 38.—Fut. ܢܘܕܐ, S. Matt. x. 32; S. Luke
xii. 8.—2. sing. ܬܘܕܐ, Rom. x. 9.—1. sing. ܐܘܕܐ, S. Matt. vii. 23;
x. 32.—Inf. ܠܡܘܕܝܘ, Eph. i. 16.—Part. ܡܘܕܐ, S. John xi. 41;
S. Matt. xi. 25, &c.—Pl. masc. ܡܘܕܝܢ, S. John xii. 42, &c.—
Coalescing with ܠܢ, ܡܘܕܝܢܢ, 1 S. John i. 9.
 Heb. Hiph. הוֹדָה, *confessed*, Ps. xxxii. 5. Chald. Aph.
הוֹדָא, *praised.* Part. מְהוֹדָא, contr. מוֹדָא, Dan. ii. 23; vi. 11.
N.B. For verbs doubly imperfect, see Cowper's Gr. § 129.

— ܟܦܪ, *denied*—ἠρνήσατο—Verb Peal pret. *Denied; refused*, Hebr. xi.
24.—Pret. 2. sing. ܟܦܪܬ, Rev. ii 13; iii. 8.—3. pl. ܟܦܪܘ, Acts
vii. 35.—2. pl. ܟܦܪܬܘܢ, ch. iii. 13, 14.—Fut. ܢܟܦܘܪ, S. Matt.
x. 33, &c.—2. sing. ܬܟܦܘܪ, S. John xiii. 38, &c.—1. sing.
ܐܟܦܘܪ, S. Matt. x. 33, &c.—1. pl. ܢܟܦܘܪ, Acts iv. 16.—Part.
ܟܦܪ, S. Luke xii. 9.—Pl. masc. ܟܦܪܝܢ, ch. viii. 45.—Constr.
ܟܦܪܝ, *refusers of (thanks), unthankful*, Gr. ἀχάριστοι, 2 Tim.
iii. 2.

S. JOHN I. 20, 21.

Ver. 20. ܐܢܐ ܐܢ ܐܢܐ ܕܠܐ?, *that I am not*—ὅτι οὐκ εἰμὶ ἐγώ—ܐܢܐ, personal pron.; in the second instance supplying the place of the subst. verb, and forming the pres. tense of ܐܝܬܘܗܝ. See Phillips' Gr. § 33.

21. ܘܫܐܠܘܗܝ, *and they asked him*—καὶ ἠρώτησαν αὐτόν—Peal (or Pael, see below) pret. 3. pl. (pref. ܘ and aff. 3. sing. masc.) of ܫܐܠ (S. Matt. xxvii. 58) *asked, requested.*—Pret. 3. fem. ܫܐܠܬ݁, S. Luke i. 40.—2. sing. ܫܐܠܬ, Hebr. x. 6.—3. pl. ܫܐܠܘ, S. Mark ix. 15.—2. pl. ܫܐܠܬܘܢ, S. John xvi. 24.—1. pl. ܫܐܠܢ, 1 S. John v. 15.—Fut. ܢܫܐܠ, S. James i. 6:—fem. ܬܫܐܠ, S. Matt. xiv. 7.—2. sing. ܬܫܐܠ, S. John xi. 22.—3. pl. ܢܫܐܠܘܢ, S. Matt. xviii. 19.—2. pl. ܬܫܐܠܘܢ, S. John xiv. 13, &c.—1. pl. ܢܫܐܠ, S. Mark x. 35.—Imperat. ܫܐܠ (in phrase) Tit. iii. 15; 3 S. John ver. 15. Fem. ܫܐܠܝ, S. Mark vi. 22.—Pl. ܫܐܠܘ, S. John ix. 21, 23 (Vienna,—others read ܫܐܠܘ, Pa.) xvi. 24; S. Matt. vii. 7, &c.—Inf. ܠܡܫܐܠܘ, S. John xv. 7.—Part. ܫܐܠ, ch. iv. 9, &c.—Coalescing with ܐܢܐ, ܫܐܠܢܐ, *I ask, desire*, Eph. iii. 13.—Fem. ܫܐܠܐ, S. Matt. xx. 20.—Pl. masc. ܫܐܠܝܢ, S. Matt. vii. 11, &c. Coalescing with ܠܢ, ܫܐܠܝܢܢ, Eph. iii. 20:—with ܐܝܠܝܢ ܕܫܐܠܝܢ, S. Matt. v. 47.—Pl. fem. ܫܐܠܢ, Rom. xvi. 16; 1 Cor. xvi. 19.

The phrase frequently occurs ܫܐܠ ܫܠܡܗ (or ܫܠܡܟܘܢ) *enquired after the peace of*, i.e. *saluted*, in various forms and persons; see S. Matt. v. 47; x. 12; S. Luke i. 40.

N.B. The affixed pret. forms ܫܐܠܗ (ch. xviii. 19), ܫܐܠܘܗܝ (as above), ܫܐܠܬܗ (Acts xxviii. 18) are commonly regarded as Peal. But ܫܐܠ is intransitive, or transitive only as regards the thing asked, e. g. ܫܐܠ ܦܓܪܗ ܕܝܫܘܥ, *he asked*—i.e. *asked for —the body of Jesus*. So in the Future forms with affixes, the meaning is, *asked a person for a thing*, i.e. *asked a thing of a person*, the object being the thing asked for:—e. g. ܢܫܐܠܝܘܗܝ, *petet ab eo*, S. Matt. vii. 9, 10; S. Luke xi. 11, 12:—so also

Ver. 21. ܫܐܠܘܗܝ, S. Mark vi. 23:—ܐܫܐܠܝܗ̇, ver. 24; ܬܫܐܠܘܢܝܗܝ, S. Matt. vi. 8;—ܬܫܐܠܘܢܢܝ, S. John xiv. 4.—Such pret. forms therefore, as, with affixes, have the same vowels in Pael as in Peal, and signify *questioned*, or *demanded of*—the direct object being *the person asked or questioned*, should be regarded as Pael. Compare S. John iv. 52; ix. 19, where this is the meaning, and the verb clearly Pael.

Heb. שָׁאַל, Ps. ii. 8.—Chald. שְׁאֵל, Dan. ii. 10, 11, &c.

— ܬܘܒ, *again*—(this is not in the Gr.) Adverb: *again, besides; yet*, ch. xvi. 12.

— ܡܢܐ, *what?*—τί;—Interrog. pron. usually of *things*. Its simplest form is ܡܢ, which occurs once, S. Luke i. 29, in the form of ܡܢ ܗܘ = ܡܢܘ. Such is the reading of the Vienna and many Editions: others read ܡܢܐ ܗܘ = ܡܢܘ.—It is joined both with masculines and feminines, as may be seen, S. Mark i. 27.—When joined with prepositions it becomes an adverb; as, ܒܡܢܐ, *with what, how?* S. Matt. v. 13.—ܠܡܢܐ, *for what, why?* S. John xii. 5.

— ܗܟܝܠ, *therefore, then*—οὖν—Conjunction.

— ܢܒܝܐ, *the Prophet, that Prophet*—ὁ προφήτης—For ܢܒܝܐܐ, def. of ܢܒܝܐ or ܢܒܝ, noun masc. *A prophet*.—Pl. def. ܢܒܝ̈ܐ, ch. viii. 52, 53.

Heb. נָבִיא, Deut. xiii. 2.—Chald. נְבִיא, def. נְבִיאָה, pl. def. נְבִיאַיָּא, Ezr. v. 1; vi. 14.

22. ܘܡܢܘ ܐܢܬ, *and who art thou?*—Gr. τίς εἶ;—ܡܢ, interrog. pron. of the person, coalescing with ܗܘ, which represents the subst. verb, in pres. 3. sing.—Lit. *Who is it (that) thou (art)?*

— ܕܢܬܠ, *that we may give*—ἵνα δῶμεν—Fut. 1. pl. (as subjunct. with ܕ) of ܢܬܠ, *gave*. A verb used only in the Future and Infinitive, the rest being supplied by ܝܗܒ, see note, ver. 12.—Fut. ܢܬܠ, ch. iii. 16, &c.—Fem. ܬܬܠܝܢ, Eph. iv. 29; and without final ܢ, S. John xv. 4.—2. sing. ܬܬܠ, S. Matt. v. 26, &c.—1. sing. ܐܬܠ,

Ver. 22. S. John iv. 14, &c.—3. pl. ܢܬܠܘܢ, S. Matt. xii. 36, &c. Fem. ܢܬܠܢ, S. Luke i. 48; 1 Tim. v. 14.—2. pl. ܕܬܠܘܢ, S. Matt. vii. 6.—Inf. ܠܡܬܠ, S. Matt. vii. 11, &c.

Heb. נָתַן, Ps. i. 3; and very frequently. Chald. נְתַן, like the Syr. only in fut. יִנְתֵּן, Dan. ii. 16; iv. 14; Ezr. iv. 13; vii. 20:—and inf. לְמִנְתַּן, Ezr. vii. 20.

— ܦܬܓܡܐ, *an answer*—ἀπόκρισιν—Def. of ܦܬܓܡ, noun masc. *A word, matter, cause, reply*.—Constr. ܦܬܓܡ ܕܙܒܢܐ, S. Luke iv. 4.—Pl. def. ܦܬܓܡܐ, with aff. ܦܬܓܡܘܗܝ, S. Luke ii. 47.

In later Heb. פִּתְגָם, Esth. i. 20.—Chald. the same, def. פִּתְגָמָא, Dan. iii. 16. *Edict*, ch. iv. 14. *Letter*, Ezr. v. 7.

— ܢܦܫܟ ܕܝܠܟ, *of, concerning, thyself*, lit. *thy soul*—περὶ σεαυτοῦ—ܢܦܫ (Acts i. 14) noun fem. *The soul, life*.—Def. ܢܦܫܐ, S. Matt. vi. 25, &c.—Pl. ܢܦܫ, Acts ii. 41.—Def. ܢܦܫܬܐ, S. Luke ix. 56; xxi. 26.—With affixes, as above, often used as a reflexive pronoun, *ipse, ipsa*.

Heb. נֶפֶשׁ, Gen. i. 20, 30; and very frequently.

23. ܩܠܐ, *the voice*—φωνή—Def. of ܩܠ, noun masc. *Voice, sound*. Constr. ܩܠ ܙܡܪܐ, *the voice of music*, S. Luke xv. 25.—Pl. def. ܩܠܐ, in phrase ܒܢܬ ܩܠܐ, lit. *daughters of voices*, Acts xii. 22; 1 Tim. vi. 20.

Heb. קוֹל, Ps. xxix. 3.—Chald. קָל, Dan. iii. 5.—Root Arab. قَالَ, *said*.

— ܩܪܐ?, *of one crying*—βοῶντος—Part. (with aff. ܕ of the genitive) of ܩܪܐ (ch. ii. 9) *called, exclaimed*; read (ch. xix. 20).—Pret. 3. fem. ܩܪܬ, S. Matt. i. 25; S. John xi. 28.—1. sing. ܩܪܝܬ, S. Matt. ii. 15; with aff. S. John xv. 15.—3. pl. ܩܪܘ, S. John ix. 18, &c.—2. pl. ܩܪܝܬܘܢ, S. Matt. xii. 3, 5.—Fut. ܢܩܪܐ, S. John xiii. 38; with aff. ver. 48, below:—fem. ܬܩܪܐ, 1 Cor. xiv. 8; xv. 52.—2. sing. ܬܩܪܐ, S. Matt. i. 21; S. Luke i. 13; S. Matt. vi. 2 (Gr. σαλπίσῃς):—fem. ܬܩܪܝܢ, S. Luke i. 31.—1. sing. ܐܩܪܐ, S. Matt. ix. 13, &c.—3. pl. ܢܩܪܘܢ, S. Matt. i. 23, &c.—2. pl. ܬܩܪܘܢ, S. Matt. xxiii.

Ver. 23. 9—Imperat. ܩܪܝ, S. Matt. xx. 8; S. Luke xiv. 13.—Pl. ܩܪܘ, S. Matt. xxii. 9.—Inf. ܠܡܩܪܐ, S. Luke iv. 16.—Part. fem. ܩܪܝܐ, S. Luke xv. 9.—Pl. masc. ܩܪܝܢ, S. John xiii. 13, &c. coalescing with ܠܝ, ܩܪܝܢܠܝ, Rom. viii. 15.—Part. Peil ܩܪܐ, Rev. xix. 13.—Def. ܩܪܝܐ, Rom. i. 1; 1 Cor. i. 1.—Pl. masc. ܩܪܝܢ, S. Luke xiv. 17, 24. Def. ܩܪܝܐ, S. Matt. xx. 16; xxii. 14.

Heb. קָרָא, Ps. xiv. 4; and very frequently. Chald. קְרָא, *proclaimed*, Dan. iii. 4, &c. *Read*, ch. v. 8, &c. Part. Peil קְרִי, Ezr. iv. 18.

— ܒܚܘܪܒܐ, *in the wilderness*—ἐν τῇ ἐρήμῳ—Noun masc. def. (pref. prep. ܒ) *a desert place*, i.e. uninhabited, but adapted for pasturing flocks, *driven* thither for that purpose. R. ܕܒܪ, *drove*; the noun being formed from Aph. ܐܕܒܪ, part. ܡܕܒܪ.

— ܐܫܘܘ, *make straight*—εὐθύνατε—Quotation introduced by pref. ܕ, to which the first vowel is remitted.

Aphel imperat. pl. of ܫܘܐ, *was equal to, worthy of.*—Aph. ܐܫܘܝ, *made equal* or *straight*, *agreed together, judged rightly.* With aff. ܐܫܘܝܢ, *hath made us able*, Gr. ἱκάνωσεν ἡμᾶς, 2 Cor. iii. 6.— Pret. 2. sing. ܐܫܘܝܬ, S. Matt. xx. 12.—2. pl. ܐܫܘܝܬܘܢ, Acts v. 9.—Fut. ܢܫܘܐ, 1 Cor. vi. 5.—Imperat. ܐܫܘܝ, pl. ܐܫܘܘ, as above.—Part. ܡܫܘܐ, S. John v. 18.

Heb. Hiph. הִשְׁוָה, *likened, compared*, Isa. xlvi. 5; Lam. ii. 13.

— ܐܘܪܚܗ, *the way*—lit. *His way*, affix pleonastic, referring to the following word—Gr. τὴν ὁδόν. ܐܘܪܚܐ, noun fem. *a way, path, journey*. Def. ܐܘܪܚܐ, ch. iv. 6, &c.—Pl. def. ܐܘܪܚܬܐ, S. Matt. xxii. 9, &c.

Heb. אֹרַח, Ps. xix. 6.—Chald. אֹרַח, pl. אָרְחָן, with aff. Dan. iv. 34; v. 23.

— ܕܡܪܝܐ, *of the Lord*—Κυρίου—Def. (pref. ܕ of the gen.) of ܡܪܐ (S. Matt. ix. 38). The def. form sing. is used exclusively for *The LORD*,— יְהוָה— and is by the Syrians styled the *Tetragrammaton;* in which (they say) the ܡ represents ܡܪܘܬܐ, *Dominion;*—the ܪ, ܪܒܘܬܐ, *Majesty;*—and the ܝ, ܐ, ܐܝܬܘܬܐ, *Essence* or *Substance*.

Ver. 23. —Pl. def. ܡܳܪܶܐ, Eph. vi. 9.—There is also a pl. of fem. form, ܡܳܪ̈ܳܬܐ, S. Matt. vi. 24; S. Luke xvi. 13.—Def. ܡܳܪܽܘܬܐ, 1 Cor. viii. 5 (with adject. masc.); 1 Tim. vi. 15.

Chald. ܡܳܪܶܐ, *lord,* Dan. ii. 47; iv. 16, 21; v. 23.

— ? ܐܰܝܟܢܐ, *as*—καθώς—Adverb, in its simplest form ܐܰܝܟ (S. Matt. xvi. 11). *How?*—Gr. πῶς. ܐܰܝܟܢܐ, either interrogative, *How?* πῶς; S. John iii. 9; Acts ii. 8; Rom. vi. 2; 1 S. John iii. 17;—or, *As,* Gr. καθώς, Hebr. iv. 3;—*How,* Gr. πῶς, Rev. iii. 3;—ὡς, Phil. i. 8 (the pref. ? is here pleonastic).

? ܐܰܝܟܢܐ, *as,* καθώς, S. John xx. 21;—ὡς, S. Matt. i. 24; vi. 12;—ὥσπερ, S. Matt. xiii. 40;—*That,* ὥστε, S. John iii. 16;—*That, how,* ὅπως, S. Mark iii. 6.

24. ܗܳܢܘܢ, *they, these.* Pl. of ܗܘ, demonstr. pron. masc.

— ܡܢ ܦܪ̈ܝܫܐ, *of, from among, the Pharisees*—ἐκ τῶν Φαρισαίων—Pl. def. of ܦܪܝܫܐ (Acts xxiii. 6); noun masc. def. *a Pharisee;* of form Part. Peil of ܦܪܫ, *separated.*—Another form is ܦܪܝܫܐ, Phil. iii. 15.

— ܗܘܘ, *were*—ἦσαν—Pret. 3. pl. of ܗܘܐ, with the *linea occultans,* as representing the logical copula.

25. ܡܥܡܕ ܐܢܬ, *baptizest thou*—βαπτίζεις—Aphel part. (representing, with ܐܢܬ, the present tense 2. sing.) of ܥܡܕ, *washed himself; was immersed, baptized.*—Aph. ܐܥܡܕ (Acts i. 5), *immersed, baptized.*—Pret. 1. sing. ܐܥܡܕܬ, 1 Cor. i. 14, 15, 16.—Fut. ܢܥܡܕ, with aff., S. Mark i. 8; S. Luke iii. 16;—1. sing. ܐܥܡܕ, ver. 31, 33, below.—Imperat. ܐܥܡܕ, pl. ܐܥܡܕܘ, S. Matt. xxviii. 19.—Inf. ܡܥܡܕܘ, 1 Cor. i. 17.

— ܐܢ, *if*—εἰ—Conjunction.

— ܠܐ ܐܢܬ, *thou be not*—σὺ οὐκ εἶ—ܐܢܬ with affix, for verb subst. pres. 2. sing. See note, ver. 1.

26. ܥܢܐ, *answered*—ἀπεκρίθη—Verb Peal pret. 3. sing. *Replied, began to speak.* Followed by ܒ, *was anxious, careful about,* S. Luke x. 40.—Pret. 1. sing. ܥܢܝܬ, Acts xxii. 8.—3. pl. ܥܢܘ, S. Matt. xxi 27.—Fut. ܢܥܢܐ, S. Matt. xxv. 45, &c.—3. pl. ܢܥܢܘܢ,

S. JOHN I. 26.   29

Ver. 26. S. Matt. xxv. 44.—Part. ܟܳܢܶܐ, fem. ܟܳܢܝܳܐ, S. Luke x. 40.—Part. Peil ܟܢܶܐ, pl. ܟܢܶܝܢ, 1 Thess. iv. 11; 2 Tim. ii. 16.

Heb. עָנָה, Gen. xxiii. 14; Ps. iii. 5.—Chald. עֲנָה or עֲנָא, Dan. ii. 7, &c. &c.

— ܠܗܽܘܢ, *to them*—αὐτοῖς—Prepos. with aff. 3. pl. masc.

— ܒܡܰܝܳܐ, *with water*—ἐν ὕδατι—Noun masc. used in the pl. only. So also

Heb. מַיִם, Ps. xviii. 17;—and frequently.

— ܒܰܝܢܳܬܟܽܘܢ, *among you*—Gr. μέσος ὑμῶν—Preposition ܒܰܝܢܰܝ (S. Matt. xix. 10) and ܒܰܝܢܳܬ (S. John iv. 31) *Between.* Both take plural affixes; as ܒܰܝܢܰܘܗ̄ܝ ܘܠܗܽܘܢ, *between Him and them*, i.e. *in secret*, S. Matt. xx. 17.—ܒܰܝܢܰܝܟ, *between thee*, ch. xviii. 15.—ܒܰܝܢܳܬܗܽܘܢ, *among them*, ver. 2, 20.

— ܩܳܐܶܡ, *standing* i.e. *there standeth*—ἕστηκεν—Part. of ܩܳܡ ܩܳܐܶܡ (ch. ii. 22) *arose, stood up.* With ܠܽܘܩܒܰܠ, *was opposed to, resisted*, S. Matt. v. 39; Acts xxvii. 15; S. James iv. 7; v. 6.—Pret. 3. fem. ܩܳܡܰܬ, S. John xi. 29, &c.—1. sing. ܩܳܡܶܬ, Acts xxiv. 20.—3. pl. ܩܳܡܘ, S. Matt. xxvii. 52, &c. Fem. ܩܳܡܶܝܢ, Acts ix. 39.—2. pl. ܩܳܡܬܽܘܢ, 1 Cor. xv. 1.—Fut. ܢܩܽܘܡ, S. Matt. xvi. 21, &c. Fem. (without final ܢ) ܬܩܽܘܡ, S. Matt. xviii. 16; ܬܩܽܘܡܘܢ, Acts xxvii. 15.—2. pl. ܬܩܽܘܡܘܢ, S. Matt. v. 39.—3. pl. ܢܩܽܘܡܘܢ, S. Matt. x. 21.—Imperat. ܩܽܘܡ, S. Matt. ii. 13, 20, &c. Fem. ܩܽܘܡܝ, S. Mark v. 41.—Pl. ܩܽܘܡܘ, S. Matt. xvii. 7.—Inf. ܠܰܡܩܳܡ, S. Matt. vi. 5, &c.—Part. ܩܳܐܶܡ (pron. *Kho-yem*) as above; Fem. ܩܳܝܡܳܐ, S. Matt. xxiv. 15.—Pl. masc. ܩܳܝܡܺܝܢ, S. Matt. xi. 5; coalescing with ܐܢܳܐ, ܩܳܝܡܺܝܢܰܢ, Acts xix. 40.—Pl. fem. ܩܳܝܡܳܢ, S. Luke v. 2.

Heb. קוּם, Ps. iii. 8; and very frequently. Chald. קוּם, Dan. ii. 39, &c. &c.

— ܕܠܳܐ......?, *whom*—Comp. Heb. אֲשֶׁר...אֹתוֹ.

— ܝܳܕܥܺܝܢ ܐܢ̄ܬܽܘܢ, *ye know*—οἴδατε—Part. pl. of ܝܕܰܥ, forming with ܐܢ̄ܬܽܘܢ the present tense, 2. pl., and pronounced with it as one word,

Ver. 26. *yodĭtun.* The words are often joined, as ܢܳܕܥܝܼܢ. See Phillips' Gr. § 38: Cowper § 91.

27. ܐܢܳܐ ܫܳܘܶܐ (pron. *Shovéno*), *I am worthy*—εἰμὶ ἄξιος—Part. (with pron. expressing the Pres. 1. sing.) of ܫܳܘܶܐ, *was equal to, worthy, fitted for, sufficient for.*—Pret. 1. sing. ܫܳܘܺܬ, S. Luke vii. 7.—3. pl. ܫܳܘܘ, ch. xx. 35.—The object (if any) when a noun, is preceded by ܠ (except, in the Gospels, S. Matt. x. 10; S. Luke x. 7);—when a verb, by ܕ, as in this place.—Fut. ܢܫܘܶܐ, 2 Cor. ii. 16.—3. pl. ܢܫܘܘܢ, 1 Tim. v. 17.—2. pl. ܬܫܘܘܢ, S. Luke xxi. 36.—Part. fem. ܫܳܘܝܳܐ, S. Luke xxiii. 22.—Pl. masc. ܫܳܘܶܝܢ, S. Matt. iii. 8, &c.—Part. Peil ܫܶܘܶܐ, 1 Cor. xv. 39:—Fem. ܫܘܝܳܐ, S. Mark xiv. 59.—Constr. ܫܘܝܰܬ ܐܝܩܳܪܳܐ, *equal in honour*, 2 S. Pet. i. 1. —Pl. masc. ܫܘܶܝܢ, def. ܫܘܰܝܳܐ, Rev. xxi. 16.—Pl. fem. ܫܘܝܳܢ̈, S. Mark xiv. 56.—From this verb are derived:

ܫܘܝܘܼܬܐ, noun fem. def. *Parity, equality, justice*, Rom. xv. 5; 2 Cor. viii. 13, 14; Col. iv. 1.

ܫܘܝܳܐܝܬ, adv. *Equally*, Acts xi. 17; 1 Cor. xii. 25.

Heb. שָׁוָה, followed by בְּ, Prov. iii. 15; viii. 11. Also Esth. v. 13; vii. 4. By לְ, Esth. iii. 8.—Chald. see note, S. John xi. 2.

— ܕܐܫܪܶܐ, *that I should unloose, to unloose*—ἵνα λύσω—Fut. 1. sing. (pref. ܕ, to which the vowel is remitted) of ܫܪܳܐ (S. Matt. xiv. 23), *loosened, dissolved, broke* a law, *dispersed, destroyed; sent away, absolved; freed from bonds* or *burdens;* whence, *took up abode,* and, generally, *dwelt.* From the original idea of *loosing,* are derived other secondary meanings; as, Pa. *opened* an undertaking, i. e. *began.* Ethpa. *was loosed* from hunger, i. e. *dined;* whence

ܫܳܪܘܬܐ, *a meal, feast.*

Pret. 3. fem. ܫܪܳܬ, *dwelt,* 2 Tim. i. 5.—1. sing. ܫܪܺܝܬ, *I sent (them) away*, 2 Cor. ii. 13.—3. pl. ܫܪܰܘ, Acts iv. 21, &c.—1. pl. ܫܪܰܝܢ, *we abode*, Acts xxi. 7.—Fut. ܢܫܪܶܐ, S. Matt. v. 19; with aff. S. John xix. 12;—Fem. ܬܫܪܶܐ (without final ܐ), S. Mark x. 12.—2. sing. ܬܫܪܶܐ, S. Matt. xvi. 19.—3. pl. ܢܫܪܘܢ, *(that) they may lodge*, S. Luke ix. 12.—2. pl. ܬܫܪܘܢ, S. Matt. xviii. 18; xix. 8.—1. pl. ܢܫܪܶܐ, S. Mark x. 4.—Imperat. ܫܪܺܝ, S. Matt. xiv. 15,

Ver. 27. &c.—Pl. ܫܪܘ, ch. xxi. 2, &c.—Infin. ܠܡܫܪܐ, S. Mark xv. 6.—
Part. ܫܪܐ, S. John v. 18; xix. 12, &c.—Pl. masc. ܫܪܝܢ, S. Mark
xi. 4, 5, &c.—Part. Peil ܫܪܐ, S. Matt. xvi. 19; xviii. 18:—Fem.
ܫܪܝܐ, *remaining, abiding,* 1 S. John ii. 14: coalescing with
ܐܢܬ, ܫܪܝܐܢܬ, S. Luke xiii. 12.—Pl. masc. ܫܪܝܢ, S. Matt. ix.
36; *lodging,* S. Luke ii. 7; *abiding,* ver. 8:—coalescing with
ܚܢܢ, ܫܪܝܢܢ, *we abide, are at home,* 2 Cor. v. 6. From this verb
are derived:

ܫܪܝ, noun masc. *A loosening.* Def. ܫܪܝܐ, *Divorce,* 1 Cor. vii. 27.
—*Interpretation,* 2 S. Pet. i. 20.

ܫܪܝܬܐ, noun fem. def. *A joint.* Pl. ܫܪ̈ܝܢ, Eph. iv. 16.—Def. ܫܪ̈ܝܬܐ,
Heb. iv. 12. Form of Peal part. act.

Heb. שָׁרָה, *let loose, set at liberty,* once, Job xxxvii. 3.—
Chald. שְׁרָא or שְׁרֵא (Dan. ii. 22) *loosed knots, hard questions;*
set free; remained, dwelt, Dan. iii. 25; v. 16.

— ܥܪ̈ܩܐ, *the latchets*—Gr. τὸν ἱμάντα—Pl. def. (of masc. form) of ܥܪܩܐ,
noun fem. *A cincture, girdle, fastening.* Def. ܥܪܩܬܐ, S. Mark i.
6; Acts xxi. 11.—Also, in pl. *Thongs,* Acts xxii. 25.

— ܕܡܣܐܢܘܗܝ, *of His shoes*—αὐτοῦ...τοῦ ὑποδήματος—Pl. (with aff.
pron. and pref. ܕ of the gen. with ʼ before a vowelless letter) of
ܡܣܢ or ܡܣܐܢ, noun masc. *A sandal.*—Def. ܡܣܢܐ or ܡܣܐܢܐ.
Pl. def. ܡܣ̈ܢܐ (or ܡܣ̈ܐܢܐ), S. Matt. x. 10, &c.—R. ܣܐܢ, *put on
shoes.*

28. ܗܘ̈ܝ, *were done, took place*—Gr. ἐγένετο—Pret. 3. pl. fem. of ܗܘܐ,
agreeing with ܗܠܝܢ, demonstr. pron. pl. com. gender. See
Cowper's Gr. § 179 (4).

— ܒܥܒܪܐ ܕ, *on the other side of, beyond*—πέραν—ܥܒܪ, def. ܥܒܪܐ, noun
masc. *The act of passing over; the region beyond.*—ܒܥܒܪܐ,
on the other side, S. Luke viii. 26.—ܠܥܒܪܐ, *to the other side,*
S. Matt. xiv. 22; xvi. 5, &c. Also, as a preposition, ܥܒܪܐ, *over,*
S. Mark vi. 53.—ܒܥܒܪܐ ܕ, *beyond,* as in this place;—ܡܢ ܥܒܪܐ ܕ,
from beyond, S. Matt. iv. 25, &c.—ܠܥܒܪܐ ܕ, *to the other side of,*

S. JOHN I. 28, 29.

Ver. 28. S. John vi. 1; x. 40; xviii. 1, &c.—Pl. def. ܚܨܒܐ, with aff. ܚܨܒܘ̈ܗܝ, ܚܨܒܘܗܝ, both pleonastic, S. Matt. iv. 15; xii. 42.—Heb. עֵבֶר, Gen. 1. 10.—Chald. עֲבַר, Ezr. iv. 10, &c.

— ܐܝܟܐ ?, *where*—ὅπου—Adverb of place, compounded of ܐܝ + ܟܐ. The particle of interrogation ܐܝ (= Heb. אִי, אֵי) enters into the composition of several words; as ܐܝܡܪ, ܐܝܢܐ, ܐܝܢܘ, &c. So also ܟܐ (Heb. כֹּה, *thus*, also *here*, Gen. xxxi. 37) with prepositions becomes ܠܟܐ, *hither*, S. Matt. viii. 29;—ܡܟܐ, *hence*, S. John ii. 16; xviii. 36.

ܐܝܟܐ (without ?) *where*, S. John xx. 2.—Interrogatively, *where?* ch. xi. 34.—With pref. ܠ, ܠܐܝܟܐ, *whither*, ch. iii. 8.—Followed by ܗܘ, it becomes ܐܝܟܘ, *where is?* ch. vii. 11.—ܡܢ ܐܝܟܐ, *where, from whence*, S. Matt. xxv. 26.

Heb. אֵיכָה, Song of Sol. i. 7.—אֵיכֹה, 2 Kings vi. 13.

— ܡܥܡܕ ܗܘܐ, *was baptizing*—ἦν...βαπτίζων—See note, ver. 25, above. Part. and subst. verb, forming the imperf. tense. See Phillips's Gr. § 38; Cowper § 82.

29. ܘܠܝܘܡܐ ܕܒܬܪܗ, *and on the day which (was) after it*, i. e. *the next day*—Gr. τῇ ἐπαύριον—Pref. ܘ with ܠ before a vowelless consonant; and prep. ܠ, marking the time at which an action is performed; as Lat. *ad diem insequentem*.

ܝܘܡܐ, def. of ܝܘܡ, noun masc. *A day*, occurring in the expressions ܝܘܡ ܡܢ ܝܘܡ, *day by day*, 2 Cor. iv. 16; 2 S. Pet. ii. 8.—ܟܠ ܝܘܡ or ܟܠܝܘܡ, *every day, daily*, S. Matt. xxvi. 55, &c.—The pl. has a masc. form ܝܘ̈ܡܝܢ, S. John ii. 19, 20, &c.—Def. ܝܘ̈ܡܐ, Gal. iv. 10.—Constr. ܝܘ̈ܡܝ, S. Matt. ii. 1, &c.;—and a fem. def. ܝܘ̈ܡܬܐ (S. John ii. 12), which is joined with masc. verbs, &c. see S. John vii. 14; S. Matt. iii. 1.

Heb. and Chald. יוֹם, frequently.

— ܗܐ, *behold!*—ἴδε—Interjection.

— ܐܡܪܗ, *the Lamb* (affix pleon.)—ὁ Ἀμνός—ܐܡܪ (Rev. xvii. 14) noun masc. *A lamb, sheep*. Def. ܐܡܪܐ, Acts viii. 32.—Pl. def. ܐܡ̈ܪܐ, S. Matt. vii. 15, &c.

S. JOHN I. 29—31.

Ver. 29. Chald. אָמַר, pl. אָמְרִין, Ezr. vi. 9, 17; vii. 17.

— ܕܫܳܩܶܠ ܗܽܘ, *who, which* (lit. *He who*) *taketh away*—ὁ αἴρων—Part. of ܫܩܰܠ (ch. v. 9). *Carried, bore up, took, removed; took to wife, married* (S. Matt. v. 32), corresponding with the Heb. נָשָׂא; also *departed*, S. Matt. xix. 1. Pret. 3. fem. ܫܶܩܠܰܬ, S. Matt. xiii. 33.—3. pl. ܫܩܰܠܘ, ch. xiv. 12, &c.—2. pl. ܫܩܰܠܬܽܘܢ, ch. xvi. 8.— Fut. ܢܶܫܩܽܘܠ, S. Matt. v. 40.—1. sing. ܐܶܫܩܽܘܠ, with aff. S. John xx. 15.—3. pl. ܢܶܫܩܠܽܘܢ, S. Mark vi. 8.—Imperat. ܫܩܽܘܠ, S. Matt. ix. 6; with aff. S. John xix. 15.—Pl. ܫܩܽܘܠܘ, S. Matt. xi. 29.—Part. pl. masc. ܫܳܩܠܺܝܢ;—Constr. ܫܳܩܠܰܬ, *those bearing the fasces*, i.e. *the lictors*—Gr. τοὺς ῥαβδούχους, Acts xvi. 35, 38. Part. Peil ܫܩܺܝܠ, S. Mark ii. 3, and actively, S. John xix. 17, &c.—Fem. constr. ܫܩܺܝܠܰܬ, Rev. xii. 15.— Pl. masc. ܫܩܺܝܠܺܝܢ, S. Mark vi. 55, &c.:—coalescing with ܣܢܰܝ, ܡܣܰܝܒܠܺܝܢ, 2 Cor. iv. 10.—Constr. ܡܫܰܩܠܰܝ ܩܽܘܒܠܺܝܢ, *bearing burdens*, i.e. *heavy laden*, S. Matt. xi. 28.

Heb. שָׁקַל, *suspended, weighed out* money, Gen. xxiii. 16.

— ܚܛܺܝܬܶܗ, *the sin* (affix pleonastic)—τὴν ἁμαρτίαν—ܚܛܺܝܬܳܐ, def. ܚܛܺܝܬܳܐ (ch. viii. 34, 46), noun fem. *A sin, crime.*—R. ܚܛܳܐ, *sinned.*

Chald. חֲטָא, with aff. Dan. iv. 24.

31. ܠܳܐ ܝܳܕܰܥ ܗܘܺܝܬ ܠܶܗ, *I knew him not*—οὐκ ᾔδειν αὐτόν—Part. and subst. verb forming the imperf. tense, 1. sing.

— ܕܢܶܬܺܝܕܰܥ, *that He should be known, made manifest*—ἵνα φανερωθῇ— Ethpeel fut. 3. sing. (pref. ܕ, giving force of subj. mood) of ܝܺܕܰܥ, *Knew.*—Ethpe. ܐܶܬܺܝܕܰܥ (S. Mark vi. 14) *Was known, made known.*— Pret. 3. fem. ܐܶܬܺܝܕܥܰܬ, Acts i. 19, &c.—1. sing. ܐܶܬܺܝܕܥܶܬ, 1 Cor. xiii. 12.—2. pl. ܐܶܬܺܝܕܰܥܬܽܘܢ, Gal. iv. 9.—Fut. 3. sing. fem. (without final ܢ) ܬܶܬܺܝܕܰܥ, Acts ii. 14, &c.—3. pl. ܢܶܬܺܝܕܥܽܘܢ, S. John iii. 21:

S. JOHN I. 31, 32.

Ver. 31. Fem. ܢܵܣܒܹܐ, Phil. iv. 6.—Part. ܡܲܣܸܩ, S. Matt. xii. 33; S. Luke vi. 44: forming pres. tense, S. John x. 14.—Fem. ܡܲܣܩܵܐ, 2 Tim. iii. 9; 1 S. John iv. 2.

— ܗܵܢܵܐ ܡܛܠ, *because of this, therefore*—διὰ τοῦτο—See note, ver. 15, above.

— ܕܐܲܥܡܸܕ ܒܡܲܝܵܐ, *that I might baptize with water*—Gr. ἐν τῷ ὕδατι βαπτίζων—See note, ver. 25, above.

32. ܐܸܡܲܪ ܣܗܸܕ, *bare record and said*—Gr. ἐμαρτύρησεν, λέγων—A past tense followed by a part. in Gr. is usually rendered in Syr. by two preterites connected by ܘ.

— ܠܪܘܚܐ, *the Spirit*—τὸ Πνεῦμα—Pref. ܠ marking the object or accusative.

ܪܘܚ, (S. Matt. v. 3) noun com. but generally used as a feminine, *Spirit, wind, breath.* Def. ܪܘܚܐ.—Pl. (masc. form) ܪܘܚܝܢ, S. Luke xi. 26; 1 S. John iv. 1.—Def. ܪܘܚܐ, S. Matt. vii. 25, &c.—Pl. fem. def. ܪܘܚܬܐ, Hebr. xii. 9, 23.—

Heb. רוּחַ, Gen. i. 2.—Chald. רוּחַ, *spirit, wind, Divine Spirit*, Dan. ii. 35; v. 12, 20, &c. Pl. constr. רוּחֵי, ch. vii. 2.

— ܕܢܚܬܐ, *descending*—καταβαῖνον—Pref. ܕ marking the participle used as such; see Cowper's Gram. § 211. (5).—

Part. fem. of ܢܚܬ (ch. ii. 12) *Went down*. Pret. 3. fem. ܢܚܬܬ, S. Mark i. 10; S. Luke iii. 22.—1. sing. ܢܚܬܬ, S. John vi. 38, &c.—3. pl. ܢܚܬܘ, ver. 16; S. Mark iii. 22.—2. pl. ܢܚܬܬܘܢ, 1 Cor. xi. 17.—1. pl. ܢܚܬܢ, Acts xx. 13; xxvii. 2.—Fut. ܢܚܘܬ, S. Matt. xxiv. 17, &c.—Imperat. ܚܘܬ, S. John iv. 49, &c.—Inf. ܠܡܚܬ, Rev. xiii. 13.

Heb. נָחַת, Ps. xxxviii. 3.—Chald. נְחַת, part. נָחֵת (= נָחֵת) Dan. iv. 10, 20.—

— ܡܢ ܫܡܝܐ, *from Heaven*—ἐξ οὐρανοῦ—A pl. noun def. with or without Ribui: in the former case always constructed as a plural: in the latter sometimes with a pl. (as ver. 51, below),—sometimes with a sing. verb, as in S. Matt. iii. 16.

Heb. שָׁמַיִם, Gen. i. 1.—Chald. Pl. def. שְׁמַיָּא, Dan. ii. 18, &c.—

Ver. 32. ܝܰܘܢܳܐ, *a dove*—περιστεράν—Noun fem. Pl. def. (of masc. form) ܝܰܘܢܶܐ, ch. ii. 14, 16, &c.

Heb. יוֹנָה, Gen. viii. 8. Pl. יוֹנִים, Song of Sol. i. 15.

— ܘܰܩܰܘܺܝ, *and it abode, remained*—καὶ ἔμεινεν—Pael pret. 3. sing. fem. of ܩܘܐ (Peal not used) Pa. ܩܰܘܺܝ (S. Luke i. 22) *Remained, persevered, expected, waited.*—Pret. 1. sing. ܩܰܘܺܝܬ, Gal. i. 18.—3. pl. ܩܰܘܺܝܘ, S. Matt. xv. 32.—1. pl. ܩܰܘܺܝܢ, Acts xx. 15; xxviii. 12.— Fut. ܢܩܰܘܶܐ, S. John iii. 36, &c.; Fem. ܬܩܰܘܶܐ, Rom. ix. 11.— 2. sing. ܬܩܰܘܶܐ, Rom. xi. 22.—1. sing. ܐܩܰܘܶܐ, 1 Cor. xvi. 6; Phil. i. 24.—3. pl. ܢܩܰܘܽܘܢ, S. John xv. 16; Fem. ܢܩܰܘܝܳܢ, ver. 7. 2. pl. ܬܩܰܘܽܘܢ, same verse.—1. pl. ܢܩܰܘܶܐ, Rom. vi. 1.—Imperat. ܩܰܘܳܐ, 2 Tim. iii. 14.—Pl. ܩܰܘܰܘ, S. John xv. 4, 9, &c.—Part. ܡܩܰܘܶܐ, S. John vi. 56, &c.—Fem. ܡܩܰܘܝܳܐ, ver. 33, below.—Pl. masc. ܡܩܰܘܶܝܢ, Acts xxiii. 21; coalescing with ܒܢܝ, ܡܩܰܘܝܳܢܝ, Rom. viii. 25; Gal. v. 5.

Heb. קָוָה, *waited for, hoped in*, only in part. קֹוֵה, Ps. xxv. 3; xxxvii. 9; lxix. 7.—Piel קִוָּה, *trusted in*, Ps. xxv. 5, &c.

33. ܡܰܢ ܕܫܰܕܪܰܢܝ, *He that sent me*—ὁ πέμψας με—Interrog. pron. with ܕ, used as a relative; see Phillips's Gr. § 26, Cowper § 74.

Verb Pael pret. with aff. 1. sing.—See note, ver. 19, above.

— ܚܟܝܡ ܕ ....ܣܘܗܝ, ܕܐܰܝܢܳܐ, *that he, on whom*—Gr. ἐφ' ὅν—ܐܰܝܕܳܐ, fem. ܐܰܝܢܳܐ, interrog. pronoun, used like the preceding, with ܕ as a relative. Pref. ܕ, introducing the speech, and taking the first vowel.

— ܒܪܘܚܳܐ ܕܩܽܘܕܫܳܐ, *with the Spirit of holiness* i.e. *with the Holy Ghost*—ἐν Πνεύματι ἁγίῳ—ܪܘܚܳܐ with pref. prep.—see last verse. ܕ of the gen. prefixed to ܩܘܕܫܳܐ, def. of ܩܘܕܫ (Rom. i. 4) noun fem. *Holiness.* Pl. def. ܩܘܕܫܶܐ, the Holy of Holies, Hebr. ix. 3.—

R. ܩܕܫ, Pa. ܩܰܕܶܫ, *sanctified.*

Heb. קָדַשׁ, Ps. ii. 6 and frequently.

35. ܘܠܝܰܘܡܳܐ ܐܚܪܺܢܳܐ, *the next day*—τῇ ἐπαύριον—Equivalent to ܠܝܰܘܡܳܐ ܕܒܳܬܪܶܗ, ver. 29.

Ver. 35. Def. of ܐܚܪܝܢ (ch. v. 7, 42, 43, &c.). *Another*—.... ܐܚܪܝܢ ܘܐܚܪܝܢ, *one...and another*, ch. iv. 37.—Also *yet;* as ܩܠܝܠ ܐܚܪܝܢ, *yet a little while*, ch. xii. 35; xiii. 33; xiv. 18.—Fem. def. ܐܚܪܬܐ, ch. vi. 22, &c.—Pl. masc. ܐܚܪ̈ܢܝܢ, ch. xix. 18, &c.—Def. ܐܚܪ̈ܢܐ, ch. iv. 38, &c.—Pl. fem. ܐܚܪ̈ܢܢ, S. Matt. xii. 45, &c.—Def. ܐܚܪ̈ܢܝܬܐ, S. John vi. 23, &c.

Heb. אַחֵר, Gen. iv. 25.—Chald. אָחֳרָן, Dan. ii. 11, &c.; and the fem. form אָחֳרִי (for אָחֳרִית), ver. 39, &c.

— ܘܬܪܝܢ, *and two*—καὶ δύο—Cardinal numb. masc. Pref. ܘ with ܼ before a vowelless consonant. See note, ch. vi. 7.

— ܡܢ ܬܠܡܝ̈ܕܘܗܝ, *of his disciples*—ἐκ τῶν μαθητῶν αὐτοῦ—Pl. (with affixed pron.) of ܬܠܡܝܕ, noun masc. *A disciple, one who learns from another.* Def. ܬܠܡܝܕܐ, ch. xviii. 15.—Pl. ܬܠܡܝ̈ܕܝܢ, def. ܬܠܡܝ̈ܕܐ, in the same verse. Root ܠܡܕ, Heb. לָמַד, *taught.*

Heb. תַּלְמִיד, 1 Chron. xxv. 8.

36. ܘܚܪ, *and he looked*—Gr. καὶ ἐμβλέψας—Verb pret. 3. sing. (pref. ܘ) ܚܪ ܚܘܪ. *Gazed earnestly upon, expected, waited for*, with ܒ of the object.—Pret. 3. fem. ܚܪܬ, S. Mark xiv. 67; S. Luke xxii. 56.—1. sing. ܚܪܬ, Acts xi. 6; xxii. 13.—3. pl. ܚܪܘ, S. John xiii. 22; S. Mark ix. 8:—Fem. ܚܪ̈ܝ, S. Mark xvi. 4.—Fut. ܢܚܘܪ, Acts vii. 32.—3. pl. ܢܚܘܪܘܢ, S. John xix. 37.—2. pl. ܬܚܘܪܘܢ, S. James ii. 3.—1. pl. ܢܚܘܪ, Hebr. x. 24; xii. 2.—Imperat. ܚܘܪ, Acts iii. 4; iv. 29.—Pl. ܚܘܪܘ, S. Matt. vi. 1, 26.—Part. ܚܐܪ (pron. *Khōyar*), S. Mark v. 32, &c.—Pl. masc. ܚܝܪܝܢ, with ܠ of the object, Gr. προσδοκῶντες, S. Luke viii. 40:—coalescing with ܚܢܢ, ܚܝܪܝܢܢ, 2 Cor. iv. 18.—Fem. ܚܝܪ̈ܢ, S. Luke iv. 20.

— ܟܕ ܡܗܠܟ, *walking, as He walked*—Gr. περιπατοῦντι—Participles,

S. JOHN I. 36, 37.

Ver. 36. used as such (i.e. not forming a tense) have commonly before them ܡܿ or ܕ. See above, ver. 32, note.

Pael Part. of ܗܠܟ (not used in Peal). Pa. ܡܗܰܠܶܟ (ch. v. 9). *Walked, journeyed.* Pret. 3. pl. ܗܰܠܶܟܘ, Acts xvi. 6; Hebr. xiii. 9. —2. pl. ܗܰܠܶܟܬܘܢ, Col. iii. 7; ܗܰܠܶܟܗܘܰܝܬܘܢ (pluperf.), Eph. ii. 2.—1. pl. ܗܰܠܶܟܢ, 2 Cor. xii. 18; 2 Thess. iii. 7.—Fut. ܢܗܰܠܶܟ, S. John xi. 10.—1. sing. ܐܗܰܠܶܟ, 2 Cor. vi. 16.—3. pl. ܢܗܰܠܟܘܢ, S. Mark xii. 38.—2. pl. ܬܗܰܠܟܘܢ, Eph. iv. 1, &c.—1. pl. ܢܗܰܠܶܟ, Rom. vi. 4, &c.—Imperat. ܗܰܠܶܟ, S. John v. 8, 11, 12, &c.—Pl. ܗܰܠܶܟܘ, ch. xi. 15, &c.—Inf. ܠܡܗܰܠܟܘ, ch. vii. 1; S. Luke xx. 46.—Part. fem. ܡܗܰܠܟܐ, S. Mark v. 42. — Pl. masc. ܡܗܰܠܟܝܢ, S. John vi. 66, &c.;—with ܥܰܡ, ܡܗܰܠܟܝܢܰܢ, Rom. viii. 4, &c.

Heb. הָלַךְ, Ps. i. 1, and very frequently.—Pi. הִלֵּךְ, 1 Kings xxi. 27; elsewhere always in poetry, as Ps. xxxviii. 7, &c.—Chald. Pa. הַלֵּךְ, Dan. iv. 26.—Aph. אַהְלֵךְ, part. ch. iii. 25; iv. 34.

37. ܘܫܡܥܘ, *and they heard*—καὶ ἤκουσαν—Pret. 3. pl. (pref. ܘ with ܿ before a vowelless consonant) of ܫܡܰܥ (ch. iii. 32). *Heard.*—Pret. 2. sing. ܫܡܰܥܬ, Rev. iii. 3:—with aff. S. John xi. 41.—1. sing. ܫܡܰܥܬ, ch. viii. 26, 40; xv. 15.—2. pl. ܫܡܰܥܬܘܢ, ch. v. 37, &c. —1. pl. ܫܡܰܥܢ, ch. iv. 42; xii. 34:—ܫܡܰܥܢܢ, 2 S. Pet. i. 18.— Fut. ܢܫܡܰܥ, S. Matt. xviii. 17, &c.—Fem. ܬܫܡܰܥ, Acts iii. 23. —1. sing. ܐܫܡܰܥ, 3 S. John ver. 4.—3. pl. ܢܫܡܥܘܢ, S. John v. 25, 28.—Imperat. ܫܡܰܥ, pl. ܫܡܰܥܘ, S. Matt. xiii. 18:—with aff. ܫܡܰܥܘܢܝ, S. Mark vii. 14.—Inf. ܠܡܫܡܰܥ, S. Matt. xiii. 17, &c.:—with aff. S. John vi. 60.—Part. ܫܡܰܥ, S. John iii. 8, &c.— Fem. ܫܡܥܐ, ch. x. 3.—Pl. masc. ܫܡܥܝܢ, ch. v. 25, &c.:— coalescing with ܐܢܐ, ܫܡܥܝܢܢ, Phil. i. 30.—Pl. fem. ܫܡܥܢ, S. Matt. xiii. 16.—Part. Peil ܫܡܝܥ, Acts xv. 24; xix. 2.

Heb. שָׁמַע, Ps. vi. 9 (and very frequently).—Chald. שְׁמַע, Dan. v. 14, 16.

S. JOHN I. 37, 38.

Ver. 37. ܗܿܢܘܢ ܬ݁ܪܝܗܘܢ, *the two, those two*—οἱ δύο—The numeral (see note, ver. 35) with pl. affix. See Phillips' Gr. § 31.

— ܘܐܙܠܘ, *and they went*, (with ܒܬܪ) *followed*—καὶ ἠκολούθησαν—Pret. 3. pl. (with pref. ܘ, to which the first vowel is remitted) of ܐܙܠ݂ (ch. iv. 47). *Went, went away.*—For the peculiarity of this verb, see Phillips' Gr. § 40 (9); Cowper's Gr. § 108 (6); 111 (1).

    Pret. 3. sing. fem. ܐܙܠܬ݀·, ch. iv. 28, &c.—1. sing. ܐܙܠܬ݂, ch. ix. 11.—3. pl. fem. ܐܙܠ̈ܝܢ, S. Matt. xxv. 10; ܐܙܠ̈ܝܢ, ch. xxviii. 8, 11.—1. pl. ܐܙܠܢ, Acts xxviii. 14; ܐܙܠܢܢ, S. Luke ix. 13.— Fut. ܢܐܙܠ, S. John vii. 35, &c.—2. sing. ܬܐܙܠܼ, S. Mark ix. 43, &c.—1. sing. ܐܙܠ, S. John xvi. 7, &c.—3. pl. ܢܐܙܠܘܢ, S. Matt. viii. 18, &c.—2. pl. ܬܐܙܠܘܢܼ, S. John xv. 16, &c.—1. pl. ܢܐܙܠ, S. John xiv. 31, &c.—Imperat. ܙܠ, S. John iv. 50, &c.—Fem. ܙܠܝ, ver. 16, &c.—Pl. masc. ܙܠܘ, S. Matt. ii. 8, &c.—Fem. ܐܙ̈ܠܢ, ch. xxv. 9, &c.—Inf. ܠܡܐܙܠ, S. John vi. 67, &c. Most of these forms are of very frequent occurrence.

    Heb. אָזַל, Prov. xx. 14.—Chald. אֲזַל, Dan. vi. 19; Ezr. iv. 23; v. 8, 15.

— ܠܗܘܿܢ, pers. pron. dat. pleonastic, after verb of motion. See Cowper's Gr. § 198 (6).

— ܒܬܪܗ ܕܝܫܘܥ, *after Him that (is) Jesus*, i.e. *after Jesus*. For the pleonastic use of pronouns, see Phillips, Gr. § 55: Cowper, § 198.

38. ܘܐܬܦܢܝ, *and He turned Himself*—Gr. στραφεὶς δέ—Ethpeel pret. 3. sing. (pref. ܘ, to which the first vowel is remitted) of ܦܢܐ. *Turned, returned.* Ethpe. *Was turned, turned himself.*—Pret. 3. sing. fem. ܐܬܦܢܝܬ݀·, ch. xx. 14, 16.—1. sing. ܐܬܦܢܝܬ݂, Rev. i. 12.—3. pl. ܐܬܦܢܝܘ, Acts ix. 35; xi. 21.—2. pl. ܐܬܦܢܝܬܘܢ, 1 Thess. i. 9; 1 S. Pet. ii. 25.—Fut. ܢܬܦܢܐ, S. Luke xvii. 4.—3. pl. ܢܬܦܢܘܢ, S. John xii. 40, &c.—2. pl. ܬܬܦܢܘܢ, Acts iii. 26; xiv. 14;— 1 pl. ܢܬܦܢܐ, ch. xv. 36.—Imperat. ܐܬܦܢܝ (the vowel of the second rad. thrown back on the first), S. Luke ix. 38; xxii. 32.—

S. JOHN I. 38.

Ver. 38. Pl. ܐܬܦܢܝܘ, Gr. ἐπιστρέψατε, Acts iii. 19.—Part. ܡܬܦܢܐ, pl. masc. ܡܬܦܢܝܢ, Acts xv. 19;—combined with ܕ, ܕܡܬܦܢܝܢ, ch. xiii. 46.

— ܐܢܘܢ, *them—αὐτούς—*Pers. pron. 3. pl. masc. This pronoun, with its fem. ܐܢܝܢ, is used as an accusative after a transitive verb. The other pers. pronouns are nominatives.

— ܕܐܙܠܝܢ ܒܬܪܗ, *following Him*—Gr. ἀκολουθοῦντας—See note, ver. 7. For the prefixed ܕ, see notes, ver. 32, 36.

— ܒܥܝܢ ܐܢܬܘܢ, (pron. *bo-e-tun*) *seek ye?—Are ye seeking?—*ζητεῖτε;— Part. pl. (with pronoun, forming pres. 2. pl.) of ܒܥܐ (xix. 38). *Sought, begged, demanded, desired.* Pret. 2. sing. ܒܥܝܬ, S. Matt. xviii. 32.—1. sing. ܒܥܝܬ, S. Luke ix. 40.—3. pl. ܒܥܘ, S. John vii. 30; xix. 31, &c.—with aff. ܒܥܘܗܝ, S. Luke ii. 44.—1. pl. ܒܥܝܢ, Acts xxiv. 6; 1 Thess. ii. 6.—Fut. ܢܒܥܐ, S. Luke xix. 10;—Fem. (without final ܐ) ܬܒܥܐ, S. Luke xi. 24.—2. sing. ܬܒܥܐ, 1 Cor. vii. 27.—1. sing. ܐܒܥܐ, S. John xiv. 16; xvi. 26.— 3. pl. ܢܒܥܘܢ, S. Luke xiii. 24.—2. pl. ܬܒܥܘܢ, ch. xii. 29; with aff. S. John vii. 34, 36, &c.—1. pl. ܢܒܥܐ, 2 Cor. viii. 6.— Imperat. ܒܥܝ, Acts viii. 22.—Pl. ܒܥܘ, S. Matt. vi. 33.—Inf. ܡܒܥܐ, Philem. ver. 9.—pref. ܠ, ܠܡܒܥܐ, S. Mark viii. 11;— with aff. pleon. S. Matt. ii. 13.—Part. ܒܥܐ, S. John iv. 27, &c.— Coalescing with ܐܢܐ, ܒܥܢܐ, *I beseech*, Rom. xii. 1; xvi. 17:— Fem. ܒܥܝܐ, S. John xx. 15.—Pl. masc. coalescing with ܕ, ܒܥܝܢܢ, 1 Cor. iv. 13;—with ܐܢܬܘܢ, ܒܥܝܬܘܢ, 2 Cor. xiii. 3.— Pl. fem. ܒܥܝܢ, S. Matt. xxviii. 5.

Heb. בָּעָה, Isa. xxi. 12.—Chald. בְּעָא, *sought*, with acc. Dan. ii. 13; vi. 5, *requested of a person*, מִן, ch. ii. 16;— קֳדָם, ch. vi. 12;— מִן קֳדָם, ch. ii. 18. Whence בָּעוּ n. f. *Petition*, ch. vi. 8, 14. Syr. ܒܥܘܬܐ, noun fem. def. *a prayer, petition*, 2 Cor. viii. 4.—Pl. ܒܥܘܢ, Eph. vi. 18;—Def. ܒܥܘܬܐ, 1 Tim. v. 5.

— ܐܡܪܝܢ, *they say* or *said*—Gr. εἶπον.—Part. for present tense or preterite.—See Cowper's Gr. § 211 (3).

Ver. 38. ܪܒܝ, *Master*, lit. *our Master*—Gr. Ῥαββί...διδάσκαλε—ܪܒ (S. Matt. xi. 11) adj. *Much, great, principal;* often as a subst. *a great one; lord, prince, Master.* Here with affixed pronoun.—Def. ܪܒܐ, S. Matt. xx. 26, &c.—Fem. ܪܒܐ, 1 S. John v. 9; 3 S. John ver. 4.—Def. ܪܒܬܐ, ch. iii. 29, below.—Constr. ܪܒܬ ܟܢܘܫܬܐ, S. Luke xvi. 2, 3, 4; 1 Cor. ix. 17.—Pl. ܪܒܐ, def. ܪܒܐ.—Constr. ܪܒܝ, ch. vii. 32, below.

   Heb. רַב, Ps. xviii. 15; and frequently.—Chald. רַב, Dan. ii. 10, &c.

— ܗܘܐ ܐܢܬ, *art Thou?*—i.e. *dwellest Thou?*—Gr. μένεις;—Part. of ܗܘܐ with pronoun, forming present tense 2. sing.

39. ܬܘ, *come*—ἔρχεσθε—Imperat. pl. of ܐܬܐ, *Came.* See note, ver. 7, above.

— ܘܬܚܙܘܢ, *and see*, lit. *and ye shall see*—Gr. καὶ ἴδετε—Fut. 2. pl. (pref. ܘ) of ܚܙܐ, *Saw.* See note, ver. 14, above.

— ܗܢܘܢ, *they.* Personal pron. pl.—Fem. ܗܢܝܢ.

— ܐܝܟ, *about*—ὡς—Conjunction, *As, about, as it were.* Lat. *circiter, ferè*.

— ܫܥܐ ܥܣܪ, *the tenth hour*, lit. *ten hours*—ὥρα δεκάτη—ܥܣܪ, pl. def. of ܥܣܪܐ (S. Matt. xx. 12) noun fem. *An hour; also a moment of time.* Def. ܫܥܬܐ, S. John iv. 21, &c.—ܒܗ ܒܫܥܬܐ, *in the selfsame hour, immediately*, S. Matt. viii. 3, 13, &c.—ܫܥܬܗ, *the same*, S. John v. 9, &c.—See note, ver. 12, above.—Pl. (of masc. form) ܫܥܝܢ, ch. iv. 6, 52, &c.

   Chald. שָׁעָה, Dan. iv. 16.—Def. שַׁעֲתָא, in the phrase בַּהּ־שַׁעֲתָא, *immediately*, ch. iii. 6, 15, &c.

40. ܚܕ, *one*—εἷς—Numeral masc. *One, one only, a certain one.*—Fem. ܚܕܐ, ver. 3, above. Used in a variety of phrases; as,

  ܚܕ ܚܕ, *every one*, ch. vi. 7, &c.—ܚܕ ܚܕ ܐ, ch. xxi. 25.

  ܚܕ ܚܕ ܡܢܗܘܢ, *each one of them*, 1 Cor. xii. 18, &c.

  ܚܕ ܟܠ or ܟܠܚܕ, *every man*, S. John vii. 53.

  ܚܕ ܥܠ ܚܕ, *one on another*, Gr. εἰς ἀλλήλους, S. John xiii. 22.

  ܚܕ ܕܚܕ, *one of another, one another's*, ver. 14.

Ver. 40. ܚܕ...ܘܚܕ, *the one...and the other*, S. Matt. xx. 21; xxiv. 40. Fem. ver. 41.

ܚܕ ܠܚܕ, *the one to the other*, S. John xi. 56; xii. 19; or *the one the other, one another*, S. Matt. xxiv. 10, &c.

ܚܕ ܠܘܬ ܚܕ, *one to, towards, another*, S. John xiii. 35.

ܚܕ ܡܢ ܚܕ, *one of, or from, another*, S. John v. 44, &c.

ܚܕ ܥܠ ܚܕ, *one toward another*, Rom. i. 27.

ܚܕ ܥܡ ܚܕ, *one with the other, among yourselves, themselves*, S. John vi. 43; S. Mark i. 27, &c.

ܚܕ ܒܡܐܐ, *one in an hundred, an hundredfold*, S. Matt. xix. 29; S. Mark x. 30; S. Luke viii. 8.

ܚܕ ܟܡܐ, *how much more*, S. Matt. x. 25.

ܡܢ ܚܕ, *with one consent*, Gr. ἀπὸ μιᾶς, S. Luke xiv. 18.

ܚܕܐ ܙܒܢ, *at one time, once*, S. Jude ver. 3, 5.

ܡܚܕܐ, ܡܢ ܚܕܐ, *immediately*, S. John xiii. 32.

Heb. אֶחָד, Gen. i. 5.—Chald. חַד, Dan. ii. 31, &c. used in a similar way with the Syr. word.

Transl. *But one of those who heard John, and followed Jesus, was Andrew, the brother of Simon.*

— ܐܚܘܗܝ, *the brother* (aff. pleon.)—Gr. ὁ ἀδελφός—ܐܚ, def. ܐܚܐ (S. Matt. x. 21) noun masc. *A brother.* Takes affixes after the manner of ܐܒܐ (see ver. 14, above), e.g. ܐܚܝ, *my brother*, S. John xi. 21; ܐܚܘܟ, *thy brother*, S. Matt. v. 23, 24; ܐܚܘܗ (fem.) S. John xi. 23; ܐܚܘܗܝܢ, *their* (fem.) *brother*, ver. 19.—Pl. ܐܚ̈ܝܢ, def. ܐܚ̈ܐ, ch. xxi. 23.

Heb. אָח, Gen. iv. 2 (very frequent).—Chald. אַח, with aff. Ezr. vii. 18.

41. ܠܘܩܕܡ, *first*—Gr. πρῶτος—Adverb, formed by prefixing ܠ to the constr. state of ܩܘܕܡܐ, *the front part* (opp. to ܒܣܬܪܐ, *the back part*) and transposing ܘ.—ܡܢ ܠܘܩܕܡ, *formerly, sometime*, Eph. v. 8.—ܡܢ ܠܘܩܕܡ ܝܕܥ, *He foreknew*, Rom. viii. 29.—ܡܢ ܠܩܘܕܡܝܢ, *first*, Gr. πρῶτον, Acts xxvi. 20.

S. JOHN I. 41, 42.

Ver. 41. ܐܶܫܟ̱ܚܢܰܢ, *we have found* (aff. pleon. and followed by ܠ of the object)—εὑρήκαμεν—Pret. 1. pl. of ܐܶܫܟܚ (ver. 43, 45) equivalent to ܡܫܟܚ with ܐ prosthetic, *Found*. Pret. 2. sing. ܐܫܟܚܬ, Rev. ii. 2:—Fem. ܐܫܟܚܬܝ, S. Luke i. 30.—1. sing. ܐܫܟܚܬ, S. Matt. viii. 10.—3. pl. ܐܫܟܚܘ, S. Matt. xvii. 16; xxvi. 60, &c.—2. pl. ܐܫܟܚܬܘܢ, ch. xxvi. 40—with aff. ch. ii. 8.—1. pl. ܐܫܟܚܢ, ch. xvii. 19.—Fut. ܢܫܟܚ, S. Matt. viii. 28; S. Mark xi. 13:—Fem. (without final ܝ) ܬܫܟܚ, S. Mark iv. 32.—3. pl. ܢܫܟܚܘܢ, S. Luke ix. 12.—Part. ܡܫܟܚ, ver. 46, below:—Fem. ܡܫܟܚܐ, S. Matt. xii. 43, 44; xix. 26.—Pl. masc. ܡܫܟܚܝܢ, S. Matt. ix. 15; xi. 29; S. John viii. 22; coalescing with ܠܢ, ܡܫܟܚܝܢܢ, S. John xiv. 5; with ܐܝܠܝܢ, ܡܫܟܚܝܢ, Eph. iii. 4.—Pl. fem. ܡܫܟܚܢ, S. John iii. 9.

N. B. These forms are by some regarded as an irregular Aphel conjugation.

The part. Peil is regularly ܡܫܟܚ, pl. fem. ܡܫܟܚܢ, *are found, present*, 2 S. Pet. i. 8. ܐܫܟܚ, in the above tenses, with its part. ܡܫܟܚ, also signifies *could, was able;* and is then followed, either

1. By the Inf. with pref. ܠ (S. John iii. 2); or
2. By the Fut. with pref. ܕ (S. John iii. 3); or
3. By the Fut. alone (S. John i. 46); or
4. By the Participle (S. John v. 19).

The first two constructions are by far the most common.

The part. fem. ܡܫܟܚܐ is sometimes used as an adjective, *Possible*, and with ܠܐ, *impossible*, S. Matt. xix. 26; xxiv. 24, &c.

Chald. Aph. הַשְׁכַּח, *found*, Dan. ii. 25; vi. 6, 12; Ezr. vii. 16.

Ver. 42. ܘܐܝܬܝܗ, *and he brought him*—καὶ ἤγαγεν αὐτόν—Aphel pret. 3. sing. (with affixed pronoun, and pref. ܘ, to which the first vowel is remitted) of ܐܬܐ, *Came*.—Aph. ܐܝܬܝ (ch. xix. 39), *Caused to come, led, brought*.—Pret. 3. fem. ܐܝܬܝܬ, with aff. ܐܝܬܝܬܗ,

Ver. 42. S. Matt. xiv. 11.—1. sing. ܐܝܬܝܬ, S. Mark ix. 17.—3. pl. ܐܝܬܝܘ, S. John ii. 8.—Fem. ܐܝܬܝܝ, S. Luke xxiv. 1.—2. pl. ܐܝܬܝܬܘܢ, Acts xix. 37; with aff. S. John vii. 45.—Fut. ܢܝܬܐ, Acts ix. 2, &c.—3. pl. ܢܝܬܘܢ, ch. v. 21, &c.—2. pl. ܬܝܬܘܢ, ver. 28.—Imperat. ܐܝܬܐ, S. John xx. 27.—Pl. ܐܝܬܘ, ch. ii. 8.—Inf. ܠܡܝܬܝܘ, S. John x. 16; S. Mark vi. 55.—Part. ܡܝܬܐ, S. John xv. 5.—Fem. ܡܝܬܝܐ, ch. xii. 24; S. Mark iv. 28.—Pl. masc. ܡܝܬܝܢ, Acts iii. 2.—

Chald. Aph. הַיְתִי, Dan. v. 3, 23; vi. 17, 25.

— ܐܢܬ ܬܬܩܪܐ, *thou shalt be called*—σὺ κληθήσῃ—Ethpeel fut. 2. sing. of ܩܪܐ, *Called.*

Ethpe. ܐܬܩܪܝ (ch. ii. 2), *Was called, read.* Pret. 3. fem. ܐܬܩܪܝܬ, Acts i. 19; Col. iv. 16.—2. sing. ܐܬܩܪܝܬ, 1 Cor. vii. 21.—3. pl. ܐܬܩܪܝܘ, Acts xi. 26.—2. pl. ܐܬܩܪܝܬܘܢ, 1 Cor. i. 9.—Fut. ܢܬܩܪܐ, S. Matt. ii. 23, &c.—Fem. ܬܬܩܪܐ, Col. iv. 16.—1. sing. ܐܬܩܪܐ, 1 Cor. xv. 9.—3. pl. ܢܬܩܪܘܢ, S. Matt. v. 9.—2. pl. ܬܬܩܪܘܢ, S. Matt. xxiii. 8, 10.—Part. ܡܬܩܪܐ, S. John xi. 54, &c.—Fem. ܡܬܩܪܝܐ, ch. v. 2, &c.—Pl. masc. ܡܬܩܪܝܢ, S. Matt. xxiii. 7, &c.

— ܟܐܦܐ, *Cephas—a stone*—Κηφᾶς—Noun, here used as a proper name. See note, ch. ii. 6, below.

43. ܨܒܐ, *willed, would*—ἠθέλησεν—Verb Peal pret. 3. sing. *Willed, desired, was well pleased.*—Pret. 2. sing. ܨܒܝܬ, Hebr. x. 5, 8.—1. sing. ܨܒܝܬ, S. Matt. xxiii. 37, &c.—3. pl. ܨܒܘ, S. John vi. 11, 21, &c.—2. pl. ܨܒܝܬܘܢ, ch. v. 35, &c.—1. pl. ܨܒܝܢ, Acts xvi. 10; ܨܒܝܢܢ, 1 Thess. ii. 18.—Fut. ܢܨܒܐ, S. Luke x. 22.—1. sing. ܐܨܒܐ, Rom. vii. 18.—3. pl. ܢܨܒܘܢ, Rev. xi. 6.—2. pl. ܬܨܒܘܢ, S. John xv. 7; Acts xxiii. 15, Gr. διαγινώσκειν, such is the reading of the Vienna and some other editions; while others read ܬܒܥܘܢ, from ܒܥܐ, *enquired, investigated.*—Inf. ܠܡܨܒܐ,

Ver. 43. 2 Cor. viii. 10, 11; Phil. ii. 13.—Part. ܨܳܒܶܐ, S. John v. 6, 21, &c.—Fem. ܨܳܒܝܳܐ, ch. iii. 8, &c.—Pl. masc. ܨܳܒܶܝܢ, ch. v. 40, &c.—Coalescing with ܐܢ̱ܬ, ܨܳܒܶܝܢܬ, ch. xii. 21, &c.—with ܐܢ̱ܬܘܢ, ܨܳܒܶܝܬܘܢ, S. Matt. vii. 12.—Pl. fem. ܨܳܒ̈ܝܳܢ, 1 Cor. xiv. 35.—
Chald. צְבָא, Dan. iv. 14, 22, 29; v. 19, 21.

— ܠܡܶܦܰܩ, *to go forth*—ἐξελθεῖν—Infin. (with pref. ܠ) of ܢܦܰܩ (ch. iv. 43), *Went out, proceeded forth.* With ܪܽܘܚܳܐ, *defended himself, pleaded his cause,* Acts xix. 33; S. Luke xii. 11 (where some editions, including the Vienna, read ܬܶܦܩܽܘܢ,—others Aph. ܬܰܦܩܽܘܢ.) Pret. 3. fem. ܢܶܦܩܰܬ, S. John xxi. 23, &c.—2. sing. ܢܦܰܩܬ, ch. xvi. 30.—1. sing. ܢܶܦܩܶܬ, ch. viii. 42, &c.—3. pl. ܢܦܰܩܘ, ch. iv. 30, &c.; Fem. ܢܦܰ̈ܩܝ, S. Matt. xxv. 1; S. Mark xvi. 8.—2. pl. ܢܦܰܩܬܘܢ, S. Matt. xi. 7, &c.—1. pl. ܢܦܰܩܢ, Acts xvi. 13, &c.—Fut. ܢܶܦܽܘܩ, S. John x. 9; S. Matt. ii. 6:—Fem. ܬܶܦܽܘܩ, S. Matt. xii. 43.—2. sing. ܬܶܦܽܘܩ, ch. v. 26; S. Luke xii. 59; Fem. ܬܶܦܩܺܝܢ, Acts xvi. 18.—1. sing. ܐܶܦܽܘܩ, S. Luke xiv. 18.—3. pl. ܢܶܦܩܽܘܢ, S. Matt. viii. 12 (Gr. ἐκβληθήσονται); xiii. 49; S. John v. 29.—2. pl. ܬܶܦܩܽܘܢ, S. Matt. xxiv. 26.—1. pl. ܢܶܦܽܘܩ, Heb. xiii. 13.—Imperat. ܦܽܘܩ, S. Mark i. 25, &c. Fem. ܦܽܘܩܝ, ch. ix. 25.—Pl. ܦܽܘܩܘ, S. Matt. xxv. 6, &c.—Part. ܢܳܦܶܩ, S. John xv. 26, &c.—with ܪܽܘܚܳܐ, Acts xxiv. 10 (here ܪ̈ܘܚܳܐ); xxv. 8; xxvi. 1, 2, 24:—Fem. ܢܳܦܩܳܐ, S. Matt. iii. 5, &c.—Pl. masc. ܢܳܦܩܺܝܢ, S. Matt. viii. 28, &c.—with ܪܽܘܚܳܐ, 2 Cor. xii. 19.—Pl. fem. ܢܳܦ̈ܩܳܢ, S. Matt. xv. 19, &c.; with ܪܽܘܚܳܐ, Rom. ii. 15.—Part. Peil ܢܦܺܝܩ, *gone out,* S. Mark vii. 30.
Chald. נְפַק, Dan. ii. 14, &c.

44. ܡܶܢ ܡܕܺܝܢܬܶܗ, *from (of) the city*—(aff. pleon.)—ἐκ τῆς πόλεως—ܡܕܺܝܢܳܐ (S. Matt. xii. 25), noun fem. *A city, state.* Def. ܡܕܺܝܢܬܳܐ, S. John ii. 1.—Constr. ܡܕܺܝܢܰܬ, S. Matt. iv. 5.—Pl. ܡܕܺܝܢܳܢ, S. Luke viii. 4.—Def. ܡܕ̈ܝܢܳܬܳܐ, S. Matt. iv. 25, &c.—

S. JOHN I. 44—46.

Ver. 44. In phrase, ܒܟܠ ܡܕܝܢܐ, *in every city*, Tit. i. 5.—Root ܕ, ܢ, *judged*.

Heb. מְדִינָה, *a province*, Esth. i. 1.—Chald. מְדִינָה, the same, Dan. ii. 48, 49, &c.

45. ܗܘ ܕܟܬܒ ܥܠܘܗܝ, *He of whom...did write*—Gr. ὃν ἔγραψε—Verb Peal pret. (the pref. ܕ taking ܰ before a vowelless consonant), *Wrote.*—Pret. 1. sing. ܟܬܒܬ, ch. xix. 22.—3. pl. ܟܬܒܘ, Acts xv. 23.—2. pl. ܟܬܒܬܘܢ, 1 Cor. vii. 1.—1. pl. ܟܬܒܢ, Acts xxi. 25.—Fut. ܢܟܬܘܒ, 2. sing. ܬܟܬܘܒ, S. John xix. 21.—1. sing. ܐܟܬܘܒ, S. Luke i. 3.—2. pl. ܬܟܬܒܘܢ, 2 Cor. iii. 1.—1. pl. S. Mark x. 4.—Imperat. ܟܬܘܒ, S. Luke xvi. 6, 7.—Inf. ܠܡܟܬܒ, 1 Thess. iv. 9, &c.—Part. ܟܬܒ, S. John viii. 8.—Pl. masc. ܟܬܒܝܢ, coalescing with ܢܢ, ܟܬܒܝܢܢ, 2 Cor. i. 13; 1 S. John i. 4.—Part. Peil ܟܬܝܒ, S. John ii. 17, &c.—Fem. ܟܬܝܒܐ, S. John xv. 25, &c.—Pl. masc. ܟܬܝܒܝܢ, Phil. iv. 3.—Pl. fem. ܟܬܝܒܢ, S. John xii. 16; xx. 30; S. Luke xviii. 31.

Heb. כָּתַב, Exod. xxiv. 4.—Chald. כְּתַב, Dan. v. 5; vi. 26; vii. 1.

Transl. *He of whom Moses did write in the Law, and in the Prophets, —we have found Him that He is* (ܗܘ, used for the Copula) *Jesus, the son of Joseph, who is from Nazareth.*

46. ܢܗܘܐ.... ܡܫܟܚ, *can there....be?*—Gr. δύναται....εἶναι; See note, ver. 41, above.

— ܕܛܒ, *of good, that (is) good*—ἀγαθόν—ܛܒ, adj. *Good*. Used adverbially, *very, exceedingly*, often with pref. ܕ, as S. Matt. ii. 10, 16, &c.—As a comparative, with ܡܢ,—ܛܒ ܡܢ, *more than*, Rom. i. 25.—Def. ܛܒܐ, S. John ii. 10.—Fem. def. ܛܒܬܐ, S. Matt. xiii. 8, 23, &c.—Pl. masc. ܛܒܝܢ, Col. i. 10 :—Def. ܛܒܐ, S. Matt. iii. 10, &c.—Pl. fem. ܛܒܢ, Tit. iii. 8; Philem. ver. 6.—Def. ܛܒܬܐ, S. John v. 29, &c.—R. ܛܐܒ, *was good*.

Heb. טוֹב, Gen. ii. 12, and frequently.

Ver. 47. ܐܰܡܺܝܢ, *truly, indeed*—ἀληθῶς—Adverb, *Rightly, steadfastly*, S. Matt. xiv. 33; 1 Cor. vii. 37.—Formed from ܐܰܡܺܝܢ, *true, firm.*—R. ܐܡܶܢ, *was firm.*

— ܢܶܟܠܳܐ, *guile*—δόλος—Def. of ܟܠܳܐ, noun masc. *Deceit, fraud, subtilty.*—Pl. ܢܶܟܠܶܐ, Acts xiii. 10.—R. ܟܠܳܐ, *was perfidious.*

Heb. נֵכֶל, only in pl. with aff. Numb. xxv. 18.

— ܠܰܝܬ, *there is not*—οὐκ ἔστι—Compounded of ܐܝܬ + ܠܳܐ; see note, ch. i. 1.—

48. ܐܶܡܰܬܝ ܡܶܢ, *whence?*—πόθεν—Adverb, compounded of ܐܰܝ and ܡܶܢ, *hence.* Interrogative or otherwise, and with or without ܡܶܢ. See S. Matt. xiii. 54; xxi. 25; S. Luke xi. 24.

— ܕܠܳܐ, *before that*—πρό—Conjunction compounded of ܠܳܐ + ܕ. The words are sometimes written separately.

— ܢܶܩܪܶܝܟ, *called thee*—Gr. τοῦ σε...φωνῆσαι—Fut. 3. sing. (with aff. 2. sing.) of ܩܪܳܐ, *Called*, (see note, ver. 23).—The Future used as a subjunctive with the preceding conjunction.

— ܬܚܶܝܬ, *under*—ὑπό—Preposition—This word takes three forms, viz. ܬܚܶܝܬ, ܬܚܶܝܬ, and ܬܚܽܘܬ, of which the first two only occur in the N. T.—

ܬܚܶܝܬ is a preposition, followed by nouns, and taking no affixes.

ܬܚܶܝܬ is used with pref. ܠ, and has then the force of an adverb, *Down*, S. John viii. 6; S. Matt. iv. 6, *Under*, Gr. κατωτέρω, S. Matt. ii. 16.—So also when preceded by ܡܶܢ, ܡܶܢ ܠܬܚܶܝܬ, *infrà*, Exod. xx. 4.—ܡܶܢ ܕܰܠܬܚܶܝܬ, *from those who are beneath*, ἐκ τῶν κάτω—answering to ܡܶܢ ܕܰܠܥܶܠ, *from those who are above*, ἐκ τῶν ἄνω, S. John viii. 23.—But when followed by ܡܶܢ it becomes a preposition, *Under*, as ܠܬܚܶܝܬ ܡܶܢ ܐܰܪܥܳܐ, *under the earth*, Phil. ii. 10.

ܬܚܽܘܬ is a preposition, *Under*, and takes affixes of the plural; as ܬܚܽܘܬܰܝ, *under me.*

Heb. תַּחַת, *under*, Ps. x. 7, &c.—Chald. תְּחֵת, תְּחוֹת, Dan. iv. 9, 11.

Ver. 48. ܬܬܐ, *the fig-tree*—τὴν συκῆν—Noun fem. the fuller form of which is ܬܐܢܬܐ, *A fig-tree.* Pl. def. (masc. form) ܬܐܢܐ, S. Mark xi. 13; S. Luke vi. 44; or ܬܐܢܐ, S. Matt. vii. 16. *Figs*, i.e. the fruit.

Heb. תְּאֵנָה, Gen. iii. 7.

49. ܡܠܟܗ, *the King* (aff. pleon.)—ὁ βασιλεύς—ܡܠܟ (Hebr. vii. 1, 2) noun masc. *A King.* Def. ܡܠܟܐ (S. John iv. 46).—Pl. ܡܠܟܝܢ, def. ܡܠܟܐ, S. Matt. ii. 6, &c.—R. ܡܠܟ, *counselled.*

Heb. מֶלֶךְ, Ps. x. 16,—and very frequently.—Chald. def. מַלְכָּא, Dan. ii. 4, &c.

50. ܡܛܠ ܕ, *because*—ὅτι.

— ܡܗܝܡܢ ܐܢܬ, *believest thou?*—πιστεύεις;—Part. with pronoun, forming present tense 2. sing.—See note, ver. 7, above.

— ܕܪܘܪܒܢ, *greater things*—μείζω—Adj. pl. fem. (pref. ܕ, introducing an assertion). The comparative degree expressed by the following ܡܢ. See Phillips, Gr. § 22; Cowper § 188.

ܪܘܪܒ, *Great*, def. ܪܘܪܒܐ, 1 Cor. i. 1.—Chiefly used in the pl. ܪܘܪܒܝܢ, 2 S. Pet. ii. 11. Def. ܪܘܪܒܐ, S. John xxi. 11, &c.—Pl. fem. def. ܪܘܪܒܬܐ, S. Matt. xxiv. 24, &c.

Hence the adv. ܪܘܪܒܐܝܬ, *greatly*, Acts viii. 2, &c. The root ܪܒ (Heb. רָבַב, *became great or many, increased*) occurs only in the reduplicated Pael (Palpel) form ܪܘܪܒ, in which the first ܒ is changed into ܘ; and its pass. Ethpalpal ܐܬܪܘܪܒ, *was magnified.*—Fut. 3. sing. and 1. pl. ܢܬܪܘܪܒ, Phil. i. 20; 2 Cor. x. 15.

51. ܐܡܝܢ, *verily*—ἀμὴν—A particle of asseveration; properly part. Peil of ܐܡܢ, *was constant.* See note, ver. 7, above.

— ܕܡܢ ܗܫܐ, *from henceforth, hereafter*—ἀπ' ἄρτι—Pref. ܕ introducing an assertion.—ܗܫܐ (ch. xi. 8) adv. of time, *Now.* Compounded of ܫܥܐ + ܗܐ (ܗܐ, Chald. הָא is a demonstr. particle, entering into the composition of the pronouns ܗܘ, ܗܝ, ܗܢܘܢ, ܗܢܝܢ, and ܗܪܟܐ, ܗܟܢܐ, &c.—ܥܕܡܐ ܠܗܫܐ, *until now*, S. John ii. 10, &c.

48 S. JOHN I. 51.

Ver. 51. ܦܬܝܚ̈ܐ?, *opened*, sc. ܫܡܝܐ—Gr. (τὸν οὐρανὸν ἀνεῳγότα—Pref. ? (which takes ' before a vowelless consonant) marking a participle used as such.

Part. Peil pl. masc. of ܦܬܚ (S. Matt. v. 2), *Opened*.—Pret. 3. fem. ܦܬܚܬ, Acts xii. 14.—3. pl. ܦܬܚܘ, S. Matt. ii. 11.—1. pl. ܦܬܚܢ, Acts v. 23.—Fut. ܢܦܬܚ, Acts xviii. 14.—1. sing. ܐܦܬܚ, S. Matt. xiii. 35.—3. pl. ܢܦܬܚܘܢ, S. Luke xii. 36.—Imperat. ܦܬܚ, S. Matt. xvii. 27, &c.—Inf. ܠܡܦܬܚ, Rev. v. 2, &c.—Part. ܦܬܚ, S. John x. 3; S. Luke ii. 23.—Part. Peil ܦܬܝܚܐ, 2 Cor. vi. 11. Def. ܦܬܝܚܐ, Rev. iii. 8.—Pl. masc. def. ܦܬܝܚ̈ܐ, Rom. iii. 13.—Pl. fem. ܦܬܝܚ̈ܢ, Acts ix. 8.

Heb. פָּתַח, Ps. xxxix. 10.—Chald. פְּתַח, part. Peil פְּתִיחַ, Dan. vi. 11; vii. 10.

— ܘܡܠܐܟ̈ܘܗܝ, *and the angels* (affix pleon.)—καὶ τοὺς ἀγγέλους—ܡܠܐܟ̈ܐ, def. ܡܠܐܟܐ (ch. v. 4) noun masc. *An Angel*.—Pl. def. ܡܠܐܟ̈ܐ, ch. xx. 12, &c.—The root (ܐܠܟ) exists only in Ethiopic.

Heb. מַלְאָךְ, Ps xxxiv. 8, &c.—Chald. מַלְאַךְ, with aff. Dan. iii. 28; vi. 23.

— ܟܕ ܣܠܩܝܢ, *ascending*—ἀναβαίνοντας—Part. (marked as such by ܟܕ) pl. masc. of ܣܠܩ (ch. ii. 13), *Went up*. This verb in all its forms, except Peal pret. and part. active, and Ethpaal, drops ܠ, as fut. ܢܣܩ, as if from the verb ܢܣܩ. Or, as some Grammarians regard it, a verb defective of all forms but the above mentioned, and borrowing the rest (including Aph. conj.) from ܢܣܩ.

Pret. 3. fem. ܣܠܩܬ, Acts i. 26.—1. sing. ܣܠܩܬ, S. John xx. 17.—3. pl. ܣܠܩܘ, ch. vi. 22, &c. Fem. ܣܠܩ̈ܝܢ, S. Mark xv. 41.—1. pl. ܣܠܩܢ, Acts xxi. 2, 6, 15.—Part. ܣܠܩ, S. John vi. 62, &c.—Fem. ܣܠܩܐ, S. Mark iv. 32.—Pl. fem. ܣܠܩ̈ܢ, S. Luke xxiv. 38.—Ethpaal ܐܣܬܠܩ, *He was raised, taken up*, Acts i. 2, &c.

Chald. סְלֵק, Dan. ii. 29; vii. 3, 8, 20; Ezr. iv. 12.

CHAPTER II.

Ver. 1. ‍ܰܬܠܳܬܳܐ, *the third,*—lit. *which (is) three*—τῇ τρίτῃ—Cardinal number masc. (see ver. 6, below) used for the ordinal.—Fem. ܬܠܳܬ, ch. xiii. 38, &c.

  Heb. שְׁלִישָׁה. fem. שָׁלוֹשׁ, שָׁלֹשׁ.—Chald. תְּלָתָה, masc. Ezr. vi. 15.

— ܡܶܫܬܽܘܬܳܐ, *a banquet*—lit. *a drinking;* specially, *A wedding-feast*—γάμος—Noun fem. def. R. ܐܫܬܝ, *drank.*

  Compare מִשְׁתֶּה, Esth. i. 3, &c.

— ܘܶܐܡܶܗ, *and the mother* (affix pleon.)—καὶ ἡ μήτηρ—ܐܶܡܳܐ (S. Matt. x. 37) noun fem. def. *A mother.* Pl. (irreg.) ܐܶܡܗܳܬܳܐ, S. Mark x. 30.

  Heb. אֵם, Ps. xxvii. 10.

— ܬܰܡܳܢ, *there*—ἐκεῖ—Adverb.—In composition, ܠܬܰܡܳܢ, *thither*, ch. xi. 15; S. Matt. ii. 22.—ܡܶܢ ܬܰܡܳܢ, *from thence,* ch. iv. 21; v. 26.—ܗܳܐ ܬܰܡܳܢ, *lo, there!* S. Mark xiii. 21; S. Luke xvii. 21, 23.

  Heb. שָׁם.—Chald. תַּמָּה, Ezr. v. 17; vi. 1, 6, 12.

2. ܘܳܐܦ, *and also*—δὲ καί—ܐܳܦ, conj. *Also*—The vowel remitted to the prefixed ܘ.—It forms compounds; as ܐܳܦ ܐܶܢ (or ܐܳܦܶܢ), *although*, ch. viii. 14, &c. *but, even, at least,* ch. xiv. 11; S. Mark vi. 56; S. Luke xix. 42. *At least, yet,* 2 Cor. xi. 16.—ܐܳܦܠܳܐ, *not even,* ch. i. 3, above.—ܐܳܦ ܚܢܰܢ, *we also,* 2 S. Pet. i. 18.—ܐܳܦ ܠܰܢ, *to us also; us also,* Rom. iv. 24; 2 Cor. iv. 14.

  N.B. The next word, ܗܘ, may be regarded either as pleonastic, or reciprocal (= *ipse*), or as representing the Gr. art. ὁ.

— ܠܳܗ, *to it,* sc. the feast. ܠ with aff. 3. sing. fem. and here pleonastic, referring to the following noun.

3. ܘܰܚܣܰܪ ܗܘܳܐ, *and there was wanting*—Gr. καὶ ὑστερήσαντος (οἴνου)—ܘ with ܥ before a vowelless consonant.—Verb Peal pret. 3. sing.

Ver. 3. (with ܗܘܐ forming the imperf. or pluperf. tense), *Was deficient, lost, suffered loss.*—Pret. 1. sing. ܚܣܪܬ, Phil. iii. 8.—Fut. ܢܚܣܪ, S. Matt. xvi. 26, &c. Fem. (without final ܬ) ܬܚܣܪ, S. Luke xxii. 32.—2. pl. ܚܣܪܬܘܢ, 2 Cor. vii. 9.—Part. ܚܣܪ, S. Luke xv. 14.

Pael ܚܲܣܸܪ, *wronged, occasioned loss*, with aff. Philem. ver. 18. Heb. חָסֵר, *was lacking, suffered want*, Ps. xxiii. 1; xxxiv. 11. —Pi. חִסֵּר, Ps. viii. 6.—

— ܚܡܪܐ, *wine*—Gr. οἴνου—Noun masc. def.

Heb. חֶמֶר, Deut. xxxii. 14; Isa. xxvii. 2.—R. חָמַר, *fermented.*—Chald. חֲמַר, def. חַמְרָא, Ezr. vi. 9; vii. 22; Dan. v. 1, 2, 4, 23.

— .... ܘܐܡܪܐ, Transl. *and His mother saith to Jesus*, lit. *to Him, to Jesus.* ܐܡܪܐ, part. fem. for present tense; see note, ch. i. 38.—ܠܗ, pleonastic.

4. ܡܐ ܠܝ ܘܠܟܝ, *what have I to do with thee?*—lit. *what to Me and to thee?*—τί ἐμοὶ καὶ σοί;—ܡܐ, interrog. pronoun, used of the thing.

— ܐܢܬܬܐ, *woman*—γύναι—Noun fem. def. *A woman, wife.*—Constr. ܐܢܬܬ, S. Matt. xiv. 3; S. Mark vi. 17, 18. Pl. (anomalous) ܢܫܐ, S. Matt. xi. 11, &c.

Heb. אִשָּׁה for אִנְשָׁה, Gen. ii. 22, 23.—(N.B. In Syr. ܠ takes the place of שׁ; and Nun, which in Heb. is compensated for by Dagesh, is retained with the *linea occultans.*)—Pl. נָשִׁים.—Chald. (not occurring in the Bible) אִתָּא, def. אִתְּתָא or אַנְתְּתָא. Pl. נָשִׁין.

— ܠܐ ܥܕܟܝܠ, *not yet*—οὔπω—ܥܕܟܝܠ, *yet*, ἔτι, Acts ix. 1.—Compound of ܥܕ, *until*, and ܟܝܠ, inseparable particle.

— ܫܥܬܝ, *my hour*—ἡ ὥρα μου—ܫܥܬܐ, see note, ch. i. 39:—with aff. 1. sing.

5. ܠܡܫܡܫܢܐ, *to the servants*—τοῖς διακόνοις—Pl. def. (with pref. prepos.) of ܡܫܡܫܢܐ (S. Matt. xx. 26), noun masc. def. *A servant, minister; Deacon.* Fem. def. form ܡܫܡܫܢܝܬܐ, *a*

S. JOHN II. 5, 6.

Ver. 5. *deaconess*, Rom. xvi. 1.—Root Pa. ܡܫܡ, *ministered*, from the part. of which (ܡܫܡܢܐ) it is formed.

— ܥܒܕܘ, *do—ποιήσατε*—Imperat. pl. masc. of ܥܒܕ (ver. 11, 15), *Did, performed, worked, committed, made* war, *brought forth* fruit, *celebrated* a feast :—a word of very frequent occurrence in these and kindred meanings. Pret. 3. fem. ܥܒܕܬ݂, S. Matt. xxvi. 10, &c.— 2. sing. ܥܒܕܬ, S. Luke ii. 48; iv. 23.—1. sing. ܥܒܕܬ݁, S. John iv. 29, 39, &c.—3. pl. ܥܒܕܘ, ch. v. 29, &c.—2. pl. ܥܒܕܬܘܢ, S. Matt. xxv. 40, 45, &c.—1. pl ܥܒܕܢ, S. Matt. vii. 22, &c.— Fut. ܢܥܒܕ, S. John vii. 17, &c. Fem. ܬܥܒܕ, S. James iii. 12. —2. sing. ܬܥܒܕ, S. Mark x. 35, &c.—1. sing. ܐܥܒܕ, S. John iv. 34, &c.—3. pl. ܢܥܒܕܘܢ, ch. xv. 21, &c.; with aff. ch. vi. 15.— 2. pl. ܬܥܒܕܘܢ, ch. xiii. 15, &c.; with aff. pleon. ver. 16, below.— 1. pl. ܢܥܒܕ, ch. vi. 28, &c.—Imperat. ܥܒܕ, ch. xiii. 27, &c.:— with aff. S. Luke xv. 19.—Infin. ܠܡܥܒܕ, S. John iii. 2, &c.— Part. ܥܒܕ, ver. 18, below. Fem. ܥܒܕܐ, S. Matt. vi. 3, &c.—Pl. masc. ܥܒܕܝܢ, S. John viii. 38, 39, 41, &c. Coalescing with ܠܝ, ܥܒܕܝܢܝ, ch. xiv. 23;—with ܐܝܠܝܢ, ܥܒܕܝܢ ܐܝܠܝܢ, 1 Thess. v. 11.—Constr. ܥܒܕܝ, S. Matt. v. 9, &c.—Pl. fem. ܥܒܕܢ, 1 Cor. xiv. 7.—Part. Peil ܥܒܝܕ, *made*, S. Mark xiv. 58; *Afflicted* with disease, S. Matt. xvii. 15. Fem. ܥܒܝܕܐ, S. Mark v. 23.—Pl. masc. ܥܒܝܕܝܢ, S. John iii. 21; *afflicted*, S. Matt. iv. 24, &c.—Used actively, Acts xv. 36.

N.B. This verb, with a few others, follows the rule of intransitives, which take ܹ or ܼ in the fut. and imperat. instead of the regular vowel ܿ.

Heb. עָבַד, *laboured, served*, Gen. xiv. 4; *tilled* the ground, Gen. ii. 5.—Chald. עֲבַד, *made*, Dan. iii. 1, 15:—*did*, ch. iv. 32; Ezr. vi. 8:—*waged* war, Dan. vii. 21.

6. ܐܝܬ ܗܘܘ, *there were—ἦσαν*—Imperf. 3. pl. fem. of ܗܘܐ. See note, ch. i. 1.

S. JOHN II. 6.

Ver. 6. ܐܓ̈ܢܐ, *waterpots*—ὑδρίαι—Pl. def. (of masc. form) of ܐܓܢܐ, noun fem. *A bowl, basin, pot.* Occurs in the N. T. here and in the next verse, only.

Heb. אַגָּן, pl. אַגָּנוֹת, Isa. xxii. 24.

— ܕܟܐܦܐ, *of stone*—Gr. λίθιναι—Def. of ܟܐܦ (S. Matt. xxiv. 2), noun fem. *A stone, rock.*—Pl. (of masc. form) ܟܐܦ̈ܐ, def. ܟܐܦܐ, S. John viii. 59, &c.

Heb. כֵּף, used only in pl. Jer. iv. 29; Job xxx. 6.

— ܫܬ, *six*—ἕξ—Card. numb. fem.—Masc. ܫܬܐ, S. Matt. xvii. 1.

— ܕܣܝܡܝܢ, *which (were) set, placed*—Gr. κείμεναι—Part. Peil pl. fem. of ܣܡ ܣܐܡ (ch. xix. 19), *Put, placed, imposed; ordained, constituted; destined; gave* a name; *laid* a foundation.—Pret. 2. sing. ܣܡܬ, S. Luke xix. 21; with aff. S. John xx. 15.—1. sing. ܣܡܬ, S. Luke xix. 22; with aff. S. John xv. 16.—3. pl. ܣܡܘ, S. John xix. 2, 29, &c.—Fut. ܢܣܝܡ (as from a verb ܣܝܡ), S. John xv. 13, &c.—2. sing. ܬܣܝܡ, Rom. xiv. 13.—1. sing. ܐܣܝܡ, S. Matt. xii. 18, &c.—3. pl. ܢܣܝܡܘܢ, S. Mark xvi. 18, &c.— 2. pl. ܬܣܝܡܘܢ, S. Matt. vi. 19.—Imperat. ܣܝܡ, S. John xviii. 11, &c.—Pl. ܣܝܡܘ, S. Matt. vi. 20, &c.—Inf. ܠܡܣܡ, 1 Cor. iii. 11; 2 Cor. xii. 14.—Part. ܣܐܡ, S. Luke iv. 40, &c.— Pl. ܣܝܡܝܢ, S. John xviii. 18, &c.—Part. Peil ܣܝܡ, S. John xix. 29, &c. Fem. ܣܝܡܐ, S. Luke vi. 48; xvi. 26.—Pl. masc. ܣܝܡܝܢ, S. John xx. 5; S. Luke xxiv. 12:—Coalescing with ܠܢ, ܣܝܡܝܢܢ, 1 Thess. iii. 3.

Heb. שׂוּם and שִׂים, Gen. ii. 8.—Chald. שִׂים, Dan. iii. 10, 29; vi. 15, &c.

— ܠܬܕܟܝܬܐ, *for (according to, after the manner of) the purification*—κατὰ τὸν καθαρισμόν—Noun fem. def. (with pref. prepos.) *A cleansing, purification.*—R. ܕܟܐ or ܕܟܝ, *was pure.* Whence also ܕܟܝܘܬܐ, noun fem. def. *Purity, sincerity,* 1 Cor. v. 8; vii. 7, &c. ܠܐ ܕܟܝܘܬܐ, *filthiness,* Rev. xvii. 4.—ܕܘܟܝܐ, noun masc. def.

Ver. 6. *Purgation, purification*, Hebr. i. 3, &c.—ܐܲܕ݂ܟ݁ܵܝܐ?, adv. *Purely, sincerely*, Phil. i. 17; 2 Thess. ii. 10.

— ܐܚܝܕܢ?, *containing*—χωροῦσαι—Part. pl. fem. (pref. ?, which marks the participle as such, and takes the first vowel) of ܐܚܕ (S. Matt. xiv. 3), *Laid hold of, seized, caught, possessed, held, comprehended; shut*, S. Matt. vi. 6;—with aff. S. John viii. 20.—Pret. 3. fem. ܐܚܕܬ, ch. xxi. 6; S. Luke vii. 16; viii. 37.—1. sing. ܐܚܕܬ, Hebr. viii. 9.—3. pl. ܐܚܕܘ, S. Matt. xxi. 35, 39, &c.; with aff. pleon. S. John xviii. 12: Fem. ܐܚܕܢ, S. Matt. xxviii. 9.—2. pl. ܐܚܕܬܘܢ, with aff. S. Matt. xxvi. 55.—1. pl. ܐܚܕܢ, S. Luke v. 5.—Fut. ܢܐܚܘܕ, S. Luke xiii. 25: Fem. ܬܐܚܘܕܝܢ, 1 Cor. vii. 2; 2 Tim. ii. 17.—1. sing. ܐܚܘܕ, with aff. Philem. ver. 13.—3. pl. ܢܐܚܕܘܢ, 1 Tim. iii. 9; with aff. S. John vii. 32, &c.—2. pl. ܬܐܚܕܘܢ, S. John xx. 23; with aff. ܬܐܚܕܘܢܝܗܝ, dropping the first rad. ?, S. Luke xxii. 52.—Imperat. ܐܚܘܕ, S. Matt. vi. 6.—Pl. ܐܚܘܕܘ, ch. xxvi. 48.—Inf. ܠܡܐܚܕ, Gr. βαστάζειν, S. John xvi. 12; with aff. ch. vii. 30.—Part. ܐܚܕ, S. Matt. xii. 11, &c.—Part. Peil ܐܚܝܕ, S. Luke xi. 7; often used actively, S. Mark xvi. 8, &c. ܐܚܝܕ ܟܠ, Gr. φέρων πάντα, Hebr. i. 3; ܐܚܝܕ ܟܠ, *Almighty*, παντοκράτωρ, 2 Cor. vi. 18:—Fem. ܐܚܝܕܐ, (act.) S. Matt. viii. 14.—Pl. masc. ܐܚܝܕܝܢ, S. John xx. 19, 23, 26:—actively, S. Matt. xiv. 5, &c.: coalescing with ܒܢܝ, ܐܚܝܕܝܢܢ, Rom. iii. 9, &c.—Pl. fem. ܐܚܝܕܢ, S. Luke xxiv. 16.

Heb. אחז, Ps. xlviii. 7.

— ܬܪܝܢ ܬܪܝܢ, *two apiece*—Gr. ἀνὰ δύο—Distributive, expressed by repetition of the numeral.

— ܐܘ, *or*—ἤ—Conjunction, distinguished from the interjection ܐܘ, *Oh!* by the point above it.

  N.B. When ܐܘ follows an adjective, it marks the comparative degree; as S. Matt. x. 15; xix. 24; S. Mark vi. 11; x. 25; S. Luke x. 12, 14; xv. 7; 2 S. Pet. ii. 21.—As the Gr. ἤ, it is

S. JOHN II. 6—8.

Ver. 6. used also as an adverb of interrogation, *Num!*; see S. Matt. vii. 9; xii. 29; xx. 15.

Heb. אִן, 2 Kings ii. 16.

— ܐܰܓ̈ܢܶܐ, *firkins*—μετρητάς—Pl. of ܐܰܓܢܳܐ, noun masc. def. *A liquid measure* probably the same as the Jewish בַּת, which is usually reckoned = about 7½ gallons. See 2 Chron. iv. 5 and LXX. there.

7. ܡܰܠܰܘ, *fill*—γεμίσατε—Imperat. pl. of ܡܠܳܐ (S. Mark xv. 36), *Filled, was full; was completed,* of time, S. Luke ii. 21.—Pret. 3. fem. ܡܠܳܬ, S. Matt. xiii. 48.—3. pl. ܡܠܰܘ, in this verse, next clause: —Fem. ܡܠܰܝ̈, Acts vii. 30.—Fut. ܢܶܡܠܶܐ, S. Luke xvi. 21:— Fem. (without final ܐ) ܬܶܡܠܶܐ (to) *draw* i.e. to *fill* her vessel with, water, S. John iv. 7.—2. sing. ܬܶܡܠܶܐ, with aff. Acts ii. 28.—3. pl. ܢܶܡܠܝܳܢ, S. John xi. 19 (where see note).—Infin. ܠܡܶܡܠܳܐ, S. Luke xv. 16.—Part. ܡܳܠܶܐ, Acts xiv. 16.—Pl. masc. ܡܰܠܝ̈ܢ, 1 Thess. ii. 11 (but probably to be referred to ܡܰܠܺܝ, or the reading is faulty.—Part. Peil ܡܠܶܐ, see note, ch. i. 14, above.

Heb. מָלָה or מָלָא, Gen. i. 22.—Chald. מְלָא, Dan. ii. 35.

— ܐܶܢܶܝܢ, accusat. pleonastic. Transl. lit. *Fill them, the waterpots* (*with*) *water*.

— ܥܕܰܡܳܐ ܠ, *up to*—ἕως—ܥܕܰܡܳܐ compounded of ܡܰܐ + ܥܕ;—followed by ܕ, *until*, S. Matt. i. 25.

— ܠܥܶܠ, *to the top, to the brim*—ἕως ἄνω—ܥܶܠ, prop. a noun masc. Only thus used as an adverb with pref. ܠ.

8. ܙܠܽܘܥܘ, *draw out*—ἀντλήσατε—Imperat. pl. of ܙܠܰܥ, *Drew water*. Occurs here only in the N. T.—Cogn. ܠܶܦ, ch. iv. 15.

— ܗܳܫܳܐ, *now*—νῦν—Adverb, compounded of ܫܳܐ + ܗܳ. See note, ver. 4, above.

— ܠܪܺܝܫ ܣܡܳܟܳܐ, *to the head,—governor,—of the feast*—τῷ ἀρχιτρικλίνῳ— ܪܺܝܫ (pref. prepos.) noun masc. *Head, beginning, chief; highest point, extremity* (S. Matt. xxiv. 31).—ܡܶܢ ܪܺܝܫ, *From the beginning, first, again,* or *newly,* S. John iii. 3, 7.—Def. ܪܺܝܫܳܐ, S. Matt. ix. 34, &c.—Constr. ܪܺܝܫ, as here, used in a variety of expressions:—as,

Ver. 8. ܪܝܫ ܐܒ̈ܗܬܐ, *head of the fathers, Patriarch,* Acts ii. 29; Hebr. vii. 4.

ܪܝܫ ܒܪܝܬܐ, *the beginning of the creation,* S. Mark xiii. 19.

ܪܝܫ ܙܘܝܬܐ, *the head of the corner,* 1 S. Pet. ii. 6.

ܪܝܫ ܫܘܩܦܐ, *the top of the staff,* Hebr. xi. 21.

ܪܝܫ ܟܢܘܫܬܐ, *ruler of the synagogue,* S. Luke viii. 41.

ܪܝܫ ܡܘܬܒܐ, *the chief seats,* S. Matt. xxiii. 6; S. Mark xii. 39; S. Luke xi. 43; xx. 46.

ܪܝܫ ܡܠܐܟܐ, *the Archangel,* 1 Thess. iv. 6; S. Jude ver. 9.

ܪܝܫ ܡܠܬܗ ܕܐܠܗܐ, *the beginning—first principles—of the words (oracles) of God,* Hebr. v. 12.

ܪܝܫ ܨܒܥܐ, *the tip of the finger,* S. Luke xvi. 24.

ܪܝܫ ܩܪܢܐ, *the head of the corner,* Acts iv. 11; Eph. ii. 20.

ܪܝܫ ܩܪܢܐ ܕܙܘܝܬܐ, *(the same),* S. Luke xx. 17.

ܪܝܫ ܫܘܠܛܢܐ, *the Prince of the power* of the air, Eph. ii. 2.

Pl. ܪ̈ܝܫܐ. Def. ܪ̈ܝܫܐ, S. John vii. 48, &c.—Constr.

ܪ̈ܝܫܝ ܝܪ̈ܚܐ, *the beginnings of the months,* i.e. *the new moons,* Col. ii. 16.

Heb. רֹאשׁ, Gen. iii. 15, and very frequently. Chald. רֵאשׁ, *the head,* Dan. ii. 38. *The sum, amount,* ch. vii. 1.—Pl. רָאשִׁין, ver. 6; Ezr. v. 10.

— ܣܡܟܐ, *the feast.* Noun masc. def. *A reclining; company of recliners,* Gr. κλισία, S. Luke ix. 14:—*Room or place for reclining,* ch. xiv. 8.—*Stability, stedfastness,* Gr. στηριγμός, 2 S. Pet. iii. 17.—Pl. ܣܡܟ̈ܐ, *repeated with a distributive force, by companies, in ranks,* S. Mark vi. 39, 40.—Def. ܣܡܟܐ, S. Matt. xxiii. 6; S. Luke ix. 14; xiv. 7; xx. 46.—R. ܣܡܟ, *reclined, propped up.*

Ver. 9. ܛܥܶܡ, *he tasted*—Gr. ἐγεύσατο—Verb Peal pret. 3. sing. *Tasted.*—Pret. 3. pl. ܛܥܶܡܘ, Hebr. vi. 4, 5.—2. pl. ܛܥܶܡܬܘܢ, 1 S. Pet. ii. 3.—Fut. ܢܶܛܥܰܡ, S. John viii. 52.—2. sing. ܬܶܛܥܰܡ, Col. ii. 21. —3. pl. ܢܶܛܥܡܘܢ, S. Matt. xvi. 28, &c.—1. pl. ܢܶܛܥܰܡ, Acts xxiii. 14.—Part. Peil ܛܥܺܝܡ, Acts xxvii. 33.

Ethpeel ܐܶܬܛܥܶܡ, *was grafted* q. d. was made to *taste* the sap of the stock.—Pret. 2. sing. ܐܶܬܛܥܶܡܬ, Rom. xi. 17, 24.—Fut. ܢܶܬܛܥܰܡ, 1. sing. ܐܶܬܛܥܶܡ, ver. 19.—3. pl. ܢܶܬܛܥܡܘܢ, ver. 23, 24.—Aphel ܐܰܛܥܶܡ, *grafted.*—Fut. ܢܰܛܥܶܡ, ver. 23.—

Heb. טָעַם, Ps. xxxiv. 9.—Chald. טְעֵם, Ps. Dan. iv. 22; v. 21.—

— ܗܳܢܘ, Demonstrative—here representing the Gr. article.

— ܐܰܝܠܶܝܢ?, *who themselves*—Pl. (pref. relat. ܕ) of ܗܳܢܘ, *he, himself.*

— ܐܶܢܘܢ, Pronoun accus. pl. masc.—Pleonastic, referring to the following ܚܰܬܢܐ.

— ܠܚܰܬܢܐ, *to the bridegroom*—Gr. τὸν νυμφίον—ܚܰܬܢܐ, noun masc. def. (pref. prepos.) *A bridegroom.*

Heb. חָתַן, *one who takes any one's daughter in marriage*, Ps. xix. 6.—R. חָתַן, *gave a daughter in marriage*—Part. חֹתֵן, *father-in-law*, Exod. xviii. 1.

10. ܕ ܟܰܕ, *when, after that*—ὅταν—ܕ taking the vowel of the following word, to which it is prefixed.

— ܐܶܬܪܰܘܺܝܘ?, *they have well, sufficiently, drunk*—μεθυσθῶσι—Aphel pret. 3. pl. of ܪܘܺܝ, *Drank his fill, was intoxicated*—Aph. ܐܰܪܘܺܝ, with the same signification. A MS. reads ܐܶܬܪܘܺܝܘ?, Peal pret. 3. pl.

Heb. Hiph. הִרְוָה, *watered copiously*, Isa. lv. 10.

— ܗܳܝܕܶܝܢ, *then*—τότε—Adverb of time. See note, ch. i. 51.

— ܒܨܺܝܪ?, *which is worse*—τὸν ἐλάσσω—ܒܨܺܝܪ (pref. ܕ) adj. *Small; less in size or value.*—ܒܨܺܝܪ ܡܶܕܶܡ, Gr. ἀπὸ μέρους, (he hath grieved) *in part* (all of you), 2 Cor. ii. 5.—Def. ܒܨܺܝܪܐ, *the least*, S. Matt. v. 19; Fem. ܒܨܺܝܪܬܐ, ch. ii. 6. Form of part. Peil from ܒܨܰܪ,

Ver. 10. *Decreased.* Whence also ܒܨܝܪܘܬܐ, noun fem. def. *A small thing,* 1 Cor. iv. 3; xi. 17.

— ܢܛܪܬܗܝ, *thou hast kept* (pron. pleon.)—τετήρηκας—Pret. 2. sing. of ܢܛܪ (2 S. Pet. ii. 5), *Kept, guarded, watched, reserved.*—Pret. 3. sing. fem. ܢܛܪܬ݁, with aff. S. John xii. 7.—2. sing. ܢܛܪܬ݁, Rev. iii. 8, 10.—1. sing. ܢܛܪܬ, S. John xv. 10; xvii. 12, &c.—3. pl. ܢܛܪܘ, ch. xv. 20; xvii. 6.—2. pl. ܢܛܪܬܘܢ, with aff. Acts vii. 53.—Fut. ܢܛܪ, S. Luke xi. 21: with aff. S. John xii. 25:—Fem. (without final ܢ) ܬܛܪ, Rom. ii. 26.—2. sing. ܬܛܪ, 1 Tim. v. 21.—3. pl. ܢܛܪܘܢ, S. John xv. 20, &c.—2. pl. ܬܛܪܘܢ, ver. 10; S. Matt. xxiii. 3.—1. pl. ܢܛܪ, 1 S. John v. 3; S. Jude ver. 21.—Imperat. ܛܪ, S. John xvii. 11, &c.—Pl. ܛܪܘ, ch. xiv. 15; S. Matt. xxiii. 3.—Inf. ܠܡܛܪ, Eph. iv. 3.—Part. ܢܛܪ, S. John vii. 19, &c.—Fem. ܢܛܪܐ, S. Luke ii. 19, 51:—Constr. ܢܛܪܬ ܬܪܥܐ, *the keeper of the door,* S. John xviii. 16, 17.—Pl. masc. ܢܛܪܝܢ, S. Matt. xxvii. 36, 54, &c.—Coalescing with ܠܝ, ܢܛܪܝܢ ܠܝ, 1 S. John ii. 3; iii. 22;—with ܠܟܘܢ, ܢܛܪܝܢ ܠܟܘܢ, Gal. iv. 10.—Part. Peil ܢܛܝܪ, Rom. iii. 8.—Pl. masc. ܢܛܝܪܝܢ, 1 S. Pet. i. 5; S. Jude ver. 1.

Heb. נָצַר, Ps. ciii. 9.—Chald. נְטַר *kept* in the heart, Dan. vii. 28. Compare S. Luke ii. 19.

— ܥܕܡܐ ܠܗܫܐ, *until now*—ἕως ἄρτι—Compound adverb. See notes, ch. i. 51; ii. 7.

11. ܐܬܐ, *sign, miracle*—Gr. τῶν σημείων—Noun fem. def. *A sign, portent.*—Pl. def. ܐܬܘܬܐ, ver. 23, below.

Heb. אוֹת, Gen. i. 14.—Chald. אָת, pl. אָתִין, def. אָתַיָּא, Dan. iii. 32, 33; vi. 28.

— ܩܕܡܝܬܐ, *the first*—Gr. τὴν ἀρχήν—Ordinal fem. def.—See note, ch. i. 15.

Trans. *This is* (ܗܕܐ ܗܝ) *the first miracle that Jesus did in Cana of Galilee.*

— ܘܐܘܕܥ, *and made known, manifested forth*—καὶ ἐφανέρωσε—Aphel pret. 3. sing. (pref. ܘ, which takes the vowel) of ܝܕܥ, *Knew.*—Aph.

Ver. 11. *Indicated, declared, signified.* Pret. 1. sing. ܐܘܕܥܬ, ch. xvii. 6, 26; with aff. ch. xv. 15.—3. pl. ܐܘܕܥܘ, S. Matt. xviii. 31; S. Luke ii. 17.—Fut. ܢܘܕܥ, Rom. ix. 22; with aff. S. John xvi. 13.—1. sing. ܐܘܕܥ, with aff. Acts xx. 27.—3. pl. ܢܘܕܥܘܢ, with aff. Col. iv. 9.—Part. ܡܘܕܥ, S. John xvii. 26; xviii. 32, &c.

Heb. Hiph. הוֹדִיעַ, Ps. cxlv. 12.—Chald. Aph. הוֹדַע, Dan. ii. 15, &c.

12. ܗܕܐ, *this*—τοῦτο—Demonstr. pron. fem. sing.—Followed by ܗܝ it assumes the form ܗܕܐ ܗܝ, as in the preceding verse, and ch. i. 19.

— ܩܠܝܠ, *a few, not many*—Gr. οὐ πολλάς—Adj. used adverbially, as Lat. *paulùm*. Lit. *light, little*. See note, ch. vii. 33, below.

13. ܘܩܪܝܒ ܗܘܐ, *and...was at hand*—καὶ ἐγγὺς ἦν—ܩܪܝܒ, adj. *Near, nigh at hand, nearest.* Of form part. Peil of ܩܪܒ, *was near.*— Def. ܩܪܝܒܐ, used as a substantive, *One who is near, a neighbour*, S. Luke x. 36; and with affixes, as ver. 27, 29, &c.—Fem. ܩܪܝܒܬܐ, S. John xix. 20, &c.—Pl. masc. ܩܪܝܒܝܢ, Acts ii. 10, &c.: coalescing with ܠܝ, ܩܪܝܒܝܢܠܝ, Gr. παρόντες, 2 Cor. x. 11.—Def. ܩܪܝܒܐ, Eph. ii. 13, 17.—Pl. fem. ܩܪܝܒܢ, S. Mark i. 38, &c.

Heb. קָרוֹב, Ps. xxxiv. 19; xxxviii. 12.

— ܦܨܚܐ, *the Passover*—τὸ πάσχα—Noun masc. def.

Heb. פֶּסַח, Exod. xii. 11.—R. פָּסַח, *passed over*, ver. 13, &c.

14. ܐܙܒܢܝܢ, *those that bought*—Gr. τοὺς πωλοῦντας—Part. pl. masc. (pref. rel. ܕ) of ܙܒܢ (S. Mark xv. 46), *Bought.*—Pret. 2. sing. ܙܒܢܬ, Rev. v. 9.—1. sing. ܙܒܢܬ, S. Luke xiv. 18, 19.—3. pl. ܙܒܢܘ, S. Matt. xxvii. 7:—Fem. ܙܒܢܬ, S. Mark xvi. 1.—1. pl. ܙܒܢܢ, S. Luke ix. 13.—Fut. ܢܙܒܢ, S. John xiii. 29; S. Luke xxii. 36. —3. pl. ܢܙܒܢܘܢ, S. John iv. 8, &c.—1. pl. ܢܙܒܢ, ch. vi. 5.— Imperat. pl. fem. ܙܒܢܝܢ, S. Matt. xxv. 9.—Inf. ܠܡܙܒܢ, ver. 10.—Part. ܙܒܢ, Rev. xviii. 11.—Part. Peil pl. constr. ܙܒܝܢܝ, *redeemed* from the earth, Rev. xiv. 3.

S. JOHN II. 14.   59

Ver. 14.   Chald. זְבַן, *bought, gained for oneself.* Part. pl. masc. זָבְנִין, Dan. ii. 8.

N.B. The Editions vary in their reading of this passage; thus,

1. ܘܐܫܟܚ ܠܗܢܘܢ ܕܙܒܢܝܢ, *and found those that bought,* is the reading of the Vienna Edition, Tremellius, and Hutter:—

2. ܘܐܫܟܚ ܒܗܝܟܠܐ ܠܗܢܘܢ ܕܙܒܢܝܢ, *and found in the temple those that bought,*—De la Boderie, Paris 4to:—

3. ܘܐܫܟܚ ܒܗܝܟܠܐ ܠܗܢܘܢ ܕܡܙܒܢܝܢ, *and found in the temple those that sold,*—Ed. Regia, Plantin, Trostius, and Guthir. This latter reading is adopted by Schaaf and Leusden.

— ܬܘܪܐ, *oxen*—βόας—Pl. def. of ܬܘܪܐ (S. Luke xv. 23.—Gr. τὸν μόσχον), noun masc. def. *A bull, ox.*
Heb. שׁוֹר, Exod. xxi. 28; collectively, Gen. xxxii. 6.—Chald. תּוֹר, pl. תּוֹרִין, Dan. iv. 22, 29, 30; v. 21; Ezr. vi. 9, 17; vii. 17.—So in other languages, as Gr. ταῦρος: Lat. *taurus:* Germ. Thier:—Welsh *tarw.*

— ܘܥܪܒܐ, *and sheep*—καὶ πρόβατα—Pl. def. of ܥܪܒܐ (S. Matt. xii. 11, 12), noun masc. def. *A sheep.* Pl. ܥܪܒܐ, S. Matt. xviii. 12; S. Luke xv. 4.

— ܘܡܥܪܦܢܐ, *and the changers of money*—καὶ τοὺς κερματιστάς—Pl. def. of ܡܥܪܦܢܐ, noun masc. def. *A money-changer.* With pref. ܘ, and ܠ of the accusative, which takes ' before the vowelless consonant.—R. ܚܠܦ, in Arab. *turned, changed money.*

— ܕܝܬܒܝܢ, *sitting*—(Part. as such, marked by pref. ܕ)—καθημένους—Part. pl. masc. of ܝܬܒ (ch. iv. 6), *Sat, inhabited, dwelt.*—Pret. 3. sing. fem. ܝܬܒܬ, S. Luke x. 39.—1. sing. ܝܬܒܬ, Acts xxv. 17.—3. pl. ܝܬܒܘ, S. John vi. 17, &c.—2. pl. ܝܬܒܬܘܢ, *Sat in mourning*—Gr. ἐπενθήσατε, 1 Cor. v. 2.—1. pl. ܝܬܒܢ, Acts xvi. 13.—Fut. ܢܬܒ, S. Matt xiii. 2, &c.—3. pl. ܢܬܒܘܢ, S. Matt. xx. 21.—2. pl. ܬܬܒܘܢ, ch. xix. 28, &c.—Imperat. ܬܒ, S. Matt. xxii. 44, &c.—Pl. ܬܒܘ, ch. xxvi. 36; S. Mark xiv. 32.—Inf. ܠܡܬܒ, Rev. iii. 21.—Part. ܝܬܒ, S. John vi. 3, &c.:—Fem. ܝܬܒܐ, ch. xi. 20.—Pl. fem. ܝܬܒܢ, S. Matt. xxvii. 61.

Ver. 14.   Aphel ܐܘܬܒ, *caused to sit, placed;* with aff. Eph. i. 20; ii. 6; Acts xxvii. 6.—Fut. ܢܘܬܒ, 1. sing. ܐܘܬܒ, Acts ii. 30.—Imperat. pl. ܐܘܬܒܘ, 1 Cor. vi. 4.

Heb. יָשַׁב, Ps. i. 1.—Chald. יְתִב, Dan. vii. 9, 10, 26.

15. ܦܪܓܠܐ, *a scourge*—φραγέλλιον—Some editions read ܦܪܓܠܐ. Noun masc. def.—Pl. def. ܦܪܓܠܐ, S. Matt. xxvii. 26.

— ܡܢ ܚܒܠܐ, *of cord, of small cords*—Gr. ἐκ σχοινίων—Noun masc. def. *A rope, cord.* The singular used collectively.—Pl. ܚܒܠܐ, with aff. pleon. Acts xxvii. 32.

Heb. חֶבֶל, Ps. xvi. 6; xviii. 5.—R. חָבַל, *bound, twisted.*

— ܐܦܩ, *He drove out*—ἐξέβαλεν—Aphel pret. 3. sing. of ܢܦܩ, *went out.*—Aph. *Caused to go out, led out, drove forth: spent.*—Pret. 3. sing. fem. ܐܦܩܬ, S. Mark v. 26; S. Luke viii. 43: with aff. S. Mark i. 12.—2. sing. ܐܦܩܬ, Acts xxi. 38.—1. sing. ܐܦܩܬ, Hebr. viii. 9.—3. pl. ܐܦܩܘ, Acts xiii. 50: with aff. S. John ix. 34, 35, &c.—1. pl. ܐܦܩܢ, S. Matt. vii. 22.—Fut. ܢܦܩ, S. Matt. ix. 38, &c.:—Fem. ܬܦܩ, Hebr. vi. 8.—2. sing. ܬܦܩ, S. Luke x. 35.—1. sing. ܐܦܩ, S. Matt. vii. 4; S. Luke vi. 42:—with aff. S. John vi. 47.—3. pl. ܢܦܩܘܢ, S. Matt. x. 1, &c.—with aff. S. John ix. 22; xvi. 2.—2. pl. ܬܦܩܘܢ with ܢܦܫ, *ye shall answer, defend yourselves,* S. Luke xii. 11,—see note, ch. i. 43, above.—1. pl. ܢܦܩ, 1 Tim. vi. 7.—Imperat. ܐܦܩ, S. Matt. vii. 5; S. Luke vi. 42.—Pl. ܐܦܩܘ, S. Matt. x. 8; S. Luke xv. 22;—with aff. S. Matt. xxii. 13.—Inf. ܠܡܦܩܘ, S. Matt. vii. 5, &c.—Part. ܡܦܩ, S. John x. 3, &c.—Pl. masc. ܡܦܩܝܢ, S. Matt. xii. 27.—Part. pass. ܡܦܩ, plur. masc. ܡܦܩܝܢ, S. Luke xiii. 28.

Chald. Aph. הַנְפֵּק, הַנְפִּק, *brought out,* Dan. v. 2, 3; Ezr. v. 14; vi. 5.—

— ܡܢ ܗܝܟܠܐ, *from, out of, the temple*—ἐκ τοῦ ἱεροῦ—Def. of ܗܝܟܠܐ, noun masc. *A temple, king's palace.*

Heb. הֵיכָל, Ps. v. 8.—Chald. הֵיכַל, def. הֵיכְלָא, *the king's*

Ver. 15. *palace*, Dan. iv. 1, 26: *the temple* of Jerusalem, or at Babylon, Dan. v. 2, 3, 5; Ezr. iv. 14.—

— ܐܫܕ, *and poured out*—καὶ ἐξέχεε—Verb Peal pret. 3. sing. *Shed, poured forth.* Pret. 3. pl. ܐܫܕܘ, Rev. xvi. 6.—Fut. ܢܫܘܕ, 1. sing. ܐܫܘܕ, Acts ii. 17, 18.—Imperat. pl. ܐܫܘܕܘ, Rev. xvi. 1.—Inf. ܠܡܫܕ, Rom. iii. 15.

The verb does not occur in Heb., but its deriv. אֶשֶׁד, *the stream, outpouring* of the brooks, Numb. xxi. 15:—and the fem. form אֲשֵׁדָה, pl. אֲשֵׁדוֹת, Josh. x. 40; xii. 8.—Constr. אַשְׁדוֹת, *the springs, or ravines* of Pisgah, Deut. iii. 17; iv. 49; Josh. xii. 3.

— ܥܘܪܦܢܗܘܢ, *their money*—Gr. τὸ κέρμα—ܥܘܪܦܢܐ, noun masc. (here with aff. 3. pl.), *Money, a piece of money.* Def. ܥܘܪܦܢܐ, Gr. χαλκόν, S. Mark xii. 41.—R. ܚܠܦ, see note, preceding verse.

— ܘܦܬܘܪܝܗܘܢ, *and their tables*—Gr. καὶ τὰς τραπέζας—Plur. (pref. ܘ) with affix, of ܦܬܘܪܐ (S. Matt. xxv. 27), noun masc. def. *A table, table of shew-bread* (S. Matt. xii. 4, &c.); *money-changers' table.*— Pl. def. ܦܬܘܪܐ, S. Matt. xv. 27, &c.

— ܗܦܟ, *He overthrew*—ἀνέστρεψε—Verb Peal pret. 3. sing. *Turned, converted, changed, subverted, returned.*—Pret. 3. sing. fem. ܗܦܟܬ, S. Luke i. 56; viii. 55.—1. sing. ܗܦܟܬ, Acts xxii. 17; Gal. i. 17.—3. pl. ܗܦܟܘ, S. Luke ii. 20, &c.:—Fem. ܗܦܟܝ, ch. xxiii. 56; xxiv. 9.—2. pl. ܗܦܟܬܘܢ, Gal. iv. 9.—Fut. ܢܗܦܘܟ, S. Luke x. 6; xix. 12.—1. sing. ܐܗܦܘܟ, S. Matt. xii. 44; S. Luke xi. 24.—3. pl. ܢܗܦܟܘܢ, S. Matt. ii. 12, &c.— Imperat. ܗܦܘܟ, S. Luke viii. 39.—Part. ܗܦܟ, S. Luke x. 35: —Fem. ܗܦܟܐ, 2 Cor. vii. 10. From this verb are derived

ܗܦܟܬܐ, noun fem. *An overthrow*, 2 S. Pet. ii. 6.

ܗܘܦܟܐ, noun masc. def. *Conversation, manners*, 2 S. Pet. ii. 7.— Pl. def. ܗܘܦܟܐ, S. James iii. 13.—Constr. ܗܘܦܟܝ, Rom. viii. 13.

ܗܦܟܬܐ, noun fem. def. *Opposition.*—Pl. def. ܗܦܟܬܐ, 1 Tim. vi. 20. Heb. הָפַךְ, Gen. xix. 21, 25; Ps. lxxviii. 9.—Deriv. הֲפֵכָה, *overthrow*, Gen. xix. 29.

Ver. 16. ܕܰܡܙܰܒܢܺܝܢ, *that sold*—Gr. τοῖς πωλοῦσιν—Pael part. pl. masc. (pref. relat. ܕ before vowelless consonant) of ܙܒܢ, *Bought.*—Pa. ܙܰܒܶܢ (S. Matt. xiii. 44, 46), *Sold.*—Pret. 2. pl. ܙܰܒܶܢܬܘܢ, Acts v. 8.—Fut. ܬܙܰܒܶܢ, S. Luke xxii. 36.—Imperat. ܙܰܒܶܢ, S. Matt. xix. 21, &c.—Pl. ܙܰܒܶܢܘ, S. Luke xii. 33.—Part. ܡܙܰܒܶܢ;—Fem. constr. ܡܙܰܒܢܰܬ, Acts xvi. 14.—Part. pass. ܡܙܰܒܰܢ, Rom. vii. 14.

— ܡܶܟܳܐ, *hence*—ἐντεῦθεν—Adverb compounded of ܟܳܐ + ܡܶܢ. See note, ch. i. 28.

— ܠܳܐ ܬܶܥܒܕܘܢ, *make not* (pron. aff. pleon.)—μὴ ποιεῖτε—Fut. 2. pl. of ܥܒܰܕ, *Made, did*, with ܠܳܐ used as an imperative, as always in prohibitions. Cowper's Gr. § 213 (3).

— ܒܰܝܬܶܗ, *the house* (pref. ܒ of the object, and aff. pron. pleon.)—τὸν οἶκον—ܒܰܝܬܳܐ (ch. viii. 35), noun masc. def. *A house, habitation.* By apocope, ܒܶܝܬ, S. Matt. xii. 25.—Constr. ܒܶܝܬ, which occurs in this verse, and in the proper name ܒܶܝܬ ܥܰܢܝܳܐ, *Bethany*, ch. i. 28.—Also in the following expressions,

ܒܶܝܬ ܐܰܣܺܝܪܶܐ, *house of the bound, prison*, ch. iii. 24 ; S. Matt. v. 25, &c.

ܒܶܝܬ ܒܶܣܡܶܐ, *the place of spices, censer*—θυμιατήριον—Hebr. ix. 4.

ܒܶܝܬ ܒܰܝ, *from house to house*, 1 Tim. v. 13; 2 Tim. iii. 6.

ܒܶܝܬ ܓܰܙܳܐ, *house of the treasure, treasury*, S. John viii. 20, &c.

ܒܶܝܬ ܕܺܝܢܳܐ, *place of judgment*, Acts xvii. 19, &c.

ܒܶܝܬ ܕܰܝܳܢܶܐ, *house of the judges, council*, S. Matt. x. 17.

ܒܶܝܬ ܙܰܝܬܶܐ, *place of olives*, S. Luke xix. 29, 37 ; xxi. 37.

ܕܒܶܝܬ ܝܗܘܕܐ ܘܣܝܠܐ, *the companions of Judas and Silas*, Acts xv. 32.

ܒܶܝܬ ܟܢܘܫܬܐ, *the synagogue*, S. Luke vii. 5; xxii. 66.

ܒܶܝܬ ܟܬܳܒܶܐ, *a case for containing books*, Gr. φαιλόνην or φελόνην 2 Tim. iv. 13.

ܒܶܝܬ ܡܺܝܬܶܐ, *house of the dead, sepulchre*, S. Matt. xiv. 2.

S. JOHN II. 16, 17.

Ver. 16. ܒܝܬ ܡܟܣܐ, *house of publicans, receipt of custom*, S. Matt. ix. 9, &c.

ܒܝܬ ܡܫܪܝܐ, *place of entertainment, guest-chamber*, S. Mark xiv. 14; S. Luke xxii. 11.

ܒܝܬ ܚܒܘܫܝܐ, *place of custody, prison*, Rev. ii. 10; xx. 7.

ܒܝܬ ܥܝܢܐ, *place of the eyes, forehead*, Rev. vii. 3, &c.

ܒܝܬ ܩܒܘܪܐ, *place of burial, grave*, S. John xi. 17, 38, &c. and pl. form,

ܒܝܬ ܩܒܘܪܐ, the same, S. Matt. viii. 28, &c.

ܒܝܬ ܩܦܣܐ, *house of stores, barn*, S. Luke xii. 24; and with aff. ver. 18.

ܒܝܬ ܩܘܪܒܢܐ, *place of oblation, treasury*, S. Matt. xxvii. 6; S. Luke xxi. 4.—

Pl. def. ܒܬܐ, S. Matt. xix. 29, &c.—R. ܒܬ ܒܡܐ, *passed the night.*—

Heb. בַּיִת, constr. בֵּית, pl. בָּתִּים, Ps. v. 8; xxiii. 6, and of frequent occurrence.—Chald. בַּיִת, constr. בֵּית, def. בֵּיתָא, Dan. ii. 5; iv. 27; Ezr. v. 2, 3, 9, 11.—

— ܬܐܓܘܪܬܐ, *merchandize*—Gr. ἐμπορίον—Noun fem. def. *Business, traffic; Gain, profit*, Acts xvi. 16; *Diligence*, S. Luke xii. 58; *Wages*, Rom. vi. 23.

R. ܐܓܪ, *conducted business.*

17. ܘܐܬܕܟܪܘ, *and they remembered*—ἐμνήσθησαν δέ—Ethpeel pret. 3. pl. (pref. ܘ, taking the first vowel) of ܕܟܪ (Peal not found in N. T.), *Remembered.*—Ethpe. ܐܬܕܟܪ (S. Matt. xxvi. 75, &c.) the same.—Pret. 3. sing. fem. ܐܬܕܟܪܬ, Rev. xvi. 19.—1. sing. ܐܬܕܟܪܬ, Acts xi. 16.—3. pl. fem. ܐܬܕܟܪ, S. Luke xxiv. 8.—1. pl. ܐܬܕܟܪ, S. Matt. xxvii. 63.—Fut. ܢܬܕܟܪ, 2. sing. ܬܬܕܟܪ, S. Matt. v. 23. —1. sing. ܐܬܕܟܪ, Hebr. viii. 12; x. 17.—Imperat. ܐܬܕܟܪ, S. Luke xvi. 25; with aff. xxiii. 42.—Plur. ܐܬܕܟܪܘ, S. Luke xvii. 32.— Part. ܡܬܕܟܪ, Rom. i. 9, &c.—Pl. masc. ܡܬܕܟܪܝܢ, coalescing with ܥܡ, ܥܡܡܬܕܟܪܝܢ, 1 Thess. i. 2.

Ver. 17.　　　Heb. זָכַר, Gen. viii. 1; Ps. xxv. 7, &c. &c.

— ܕܰܟܬܝܒ, *that it was written*—ὅτι γεγραμμένον ἐστίν—Part. Peil of ܟܬܰܒ, *Wrote*—see note, ch. i. 45.—Pref. ܕ before vowelless letter.

— ܛܢܳܢܶܗ, *the zeal* (pref. ܕ of assertion, and aff. pron. pleon.)—ὁ ζῆλος—ܛܢܳܢܐ (Rom. x. 2), noun masc. def. *Zeal, emulation;* with aff. 3. pl. Rom. xi. 11.—Root ܛܢܐ, *Envied, emulated, was zealous.*—Pret. 3. pl. ܛܢܘ, Acts vii. 9.—Fut. ܢܛܰܢ.—Imperat. ܛܰܢ, Rev. iii. 19.—Pl. ܛܰܢܘ, 1 Cor. xiv. 1, 39.—Part. ܛܳܐܶܢ, 2 Cor. xi. 2; Gal. i. 14.—Pl. masc. ܛܰܐܢܝܢ, 1 Cor. xii. 31; S. James iv. 2.—Aph. ܐܛܶܢ, *aroused to zeal.*—Fut. ܢܰܛܶܢ, Rom. xi. 14; with aff. ch. x. 19.—Inf. ܡܛܰܢܳܢܘ, 1 Cor. x. 22.—Part. ܡܛܰܢܶܐ, pl. ܡܛܰܢܢܝܢ, coalescing with ܠܰܢ, ܡܛܰܢܢܝܢܰܢ, 1 Cor. x. 22.—

— ܐܰܟܠܰܢܝ, *hath eaten Me up*—κατέφαγέ με—Peal pret. 3. sing. (with aff. pron. 1. sing.) of ܐܟܠ (S. Matt. xii. 4), *Ate, devoured, consumed;* and followed by ܩܰܪܨܐ, *accused, calumniated*, see note, ch. viii. 44, below.—Pret. 3. sing. fem. ܐܶܟܠܰܬ, Rev. xx. 9:—with aff. S. Matt. xiii. 4; S. Mark iv. 4; S. Luke viii. 5.—1. sing. ܐܶܟܠܶܬ, Acts x. 14.—3. pl. ܐܟܰܠܘ, S. John vi. 13, 23, 31, 49, &c.—2. pl. ܐܟܰܠܬܘܢ, ver. 26.—1. pl. ܐܟܰܠܢ, S. Luke xiii. 26.—Fut. ܢܶܐܟܘܠ, S. John vi. 50, 51, &c.—2. sing. ܬܐܟܘܠ, S. Mark xiv. 12.—1. sing. ܐܟܘܠ, ver. 14; S. John iv. 32, &c.—3. pl. ܢܶܐܟܠܘܢ, S. John vi. 5, &c.: with ܩܰܪܨܘܗܝ, *that they might accuse Him*, S. Matt. xii. 10; S. Luke vi. 7; xii. 54.—2. pl. ܬܐܟܠܘܢ, S. John vi. 53, &c.—1. pl. ܢܶܐܟܘܠ, S. Matt. vi. 31, &c.—Imperat. ܐܟܘܠ, Acts x. 13; xi. 7:—Fem. ܐܟܘܠܝ, S. Luke xii. 19.—Pl. ܐܟܘܠܘ, S. Matt. xxvi. 26, &c.—Inf. ܠܡܶܐܟܰܠ, S. John iv. 33, &c.—Part. ܐܟܠ, S. John vi. 58, &c.—Fem. ܐܟܠܐ, Rev. xi. 5: Def. ܐܟܠܬܐ, Hebr. xii. 29.—Pl. masc. ܐܟܠܝܢ, S. John xii. 28, &c.:—with ܩܰܪܨܘܗܝ, S. Matt. xxvii. 12; S. Mark xv. 3; S. Luke xxiii. 2, 10:—coalescing with ܠܰܢ, ܐܟܠܝܢܰܢ, 1 Cor. viii. 8;—with ܐܢܘܢ, ܐܟܠܝܢܠܗܘܢ, Gal. v. 15.—Constr. masc. ܐܟܠܝ ܩܰܪܨܐ, *accusers,*

Ver. 17. 2 Tim. iii. 3.—Pl. fem. اَخْـبِ صَٰنِيَ, *slanderers*, 1 Tim. iii. 11.

Heb. אָכַל, Ps. xxvii. 2. &c. &c.—Chald. אֲכַל in phrase, like the Syr. as above, Dan. iii. 8; vi. 25.

18. ܐܰܢܬ ܡܚܰܘܶܐ, *shewest Thou*—δεικνύεις—Pael part. (with pronoun forming the pres. 2. sing.) of ܗܘܐ, not used in Peal.—Pa. ܚܰܘܺܝ (ch. xx. 20; xxi. 1.) *Shewed, manifested, proved.*—Pret. 1. sing. ܚܰܘܺܝܬ, Gal. ii. 18; with aff. S. John x. 32.—3. pl. ܚܰܘܺܝܘ, S. Matt. viii. 33; xiv. 12.—2. pl. ܚܰܘܺܝܬܽܘܢ, 2 Cor. vii. 11; Hebr. vi. 10.— Fut. ܢܚܰܘܶܐ, S. John xii. 33; xxi. 19; with aff. ch. xvi. 15.— 1. sing. ܐܶܚܰܘܶܐ, Rom. ix. 17; with aff. S. Luke vi. 47; xii. 5.— 3. pl. ܢܚܰܘܽܘܢ, Acts xxiv. 13.—1. pl. ܢܚܰܘܶܐ, 2 Cor. vi. 4.—Imperat. ܚܰܘܳܐ, S. John vii. 4, &c.: with aff. ch. xiv. 8, 9.—Pl. ܚܰܘܰܘ, S. Luke xvii. 14; with aff. S. Matt. ii. 8, &c.—Inf. ܠܰܡܚܰܘܳܝܽܘ, S. John xiv. 22; S. Matt. xvi. 21.—Part. fem. ܡܚܰܘܝܳܐ, Hebr. ix. 16, &c.—Pl. masc. ܡܚܰܘܶܝܢ, S. Matt. xxiv. 1;—coalescing with ܚܢܰܢ, ܡܚܰܘܶܝܢܰܢ, 2 Cor. iv. 2.—Pl. fem. ܡܚܰܘܝܳܬܳܐ, Acts ix. 39.

Heb. Pi. חִוָּה, Ps. xix. 3.—Chald. Pa. חַוָּא, Dan. ii. 11, 24; v. 7.—Aph. הַחֲוָא, ch. ii. 6, 9, 10, 16, 27.

19. ܣܬܽܘܪܘ, *destroy*—λύσατε—Imperat. pl. of ܣܬܰܪ, *Destroyed*.—Pret. 1. sing. ܣܶܬܪܶܬ, Gal. ii. 18.—Fut. ܢܶܣܬܽܘܪ, 1 sing. ܐܶܣܬܽܘܪ, S. Luke xii. 18.—Part. ܣܳܬܰܪ, S. Matt. xxvii. 40.—Pl. ܣܳܬܪܺܝܢ, coalescing with ܚܢܰܢ, ܣܳܬܪܺܝܢܰܢ, 2 Cor. x. 5.

Heb. סָתַר, *hid, concealed*, once in Kal, Prov. xxii. 3 (קרי Niph).—Chald. Pa. סַתַּר, *covered, concealed*. Part. pass. pl. fem. def. Dan. ii. 22. *Destroyed*, i.e. removed out of sight, Ezr. v. 12.

— ܠܰܬܠܳܬܳܐ ܝܰܘܡܺܝܢ, *in three days*—ἐν τρισὶν ἡμέραις—The prep. ܠ referring to point or measure of time:—διὰ τριῶν ἡμερῶν, S. Matt. xxvi. 61. Compare ܠܝܰܘܡܳܬܳܐ, *after (some) days*—Gr. δι' ἡμερῶν, S. Mark ii. 1.

W. C.   9

S. JOHN II. 19—21.

Ver. 19. ܐܢܐ ܡܩܝܡ ܐܢܐ, *I will raise up*—ἐγερῶ—Aphel part. (forming pres. tense, but pointing to future time) of ܩܡ ܩܐܡ ܩܐܡ, *arose*.

Aph. ܐܩܝܡ (ch. xii. 1, 9), *Erected, confirmed, established, sustained.*—Pret. 1. sing. ܐܩܝܡܬ, with aff. Rom. ix. 17.—3. pl. ܐܩܝܡܘ, S. Matt. xxvi. 15; S. Luke xxii. 5.—Fut. ܢܩܝܡ, S. Matt. xxii. 24; xxv. 33.—2. sing. ܬܩܝܡ, Acts vii. 60.—1. sing. ܐܩܝܡ, ch. xv. 16: with aff. S. John vi. 39, 40, 44, 54.—3. pl. ܢܩܝܡܘܢ, Rom. x. 3.—2. pl. ܬܩܝܡܘܢ, S. Mark vii. 9.—1. pl. ܢܩܝܡ, Acts vi. 3.—Inf. ܠܡܩܡܘ, S. Matt. iii. 9; S. Luke iii. 8.—Part. pl. masc. ܡܩܝܡܝܢ, coalescing with ܚܢܢ, ܡܩܝܡܝܢܢ, Rom. iii. 31.—Pl. fem. ܡܩܝܡܢ, 2 S. Pet. i. 8.

Heb. Hiph. הֵקִים, Ps. xli. 11.—Chald. Aph. אֲקִים, and הֲקִים, Dan. ii. 21; iii. 1, &c.: Ezr. vi. 18.

20. ܠܐܪܒܥܝܢ, *In* or *during forty*—Gr. τεσσαράκοντα—ܐܪܒܥܝܢ, numeral: —remitting its first vowel to ܠ, which marks duration of time.

— ܫܢܝܢ, *years*—Gr. ἔτεσιν—Pl. of ܫܢܐ (S. Luke ii. 41), noun fem. *A year.*—Def. ܫܢܬܐ, S. John xi. 49, 51, &c.—Constr. ܫܢܬ, S. Luke iii. 1.—Pl. def. (masc. form) ܫܢܝܐ, S. Luke xii. 19.—R. ܫܢܐ, *moved, changed*.

Heb. שָׁנָה, pl. שָׁנִים, Gen. i. 14; xvii. 21, &c. &c.—Chald. שְׁנָה, pl. שְׁנִין, Dan. vi. 1.

— ܐܬܒܢܝ, *was built, was in building*—ᾠκοδομήθη—Ethpeel pret. 3. sing. of ܒܢܐ, *Built.*—Ethpe. *Was built.* Pret. 2. pl. ܐܬܒܢܝܬܘܢ, Eph. ii. 20.—Part. ܡܬܒܢܐ, Hebr. iii. 4.—Pl. masc. ܡܬܒܢܝܢ, Eph. ii. 22; Col. ii. 7.

Chald. Ithpeel אֶתְבְּנֵא, Ezr. iv. 13, 21; v. 8, 16; vi. 3.

21. ܐܡܪ ܗܘܐ, *He spake—was speaking*—ἔλεγε—Part. forming imperf. tense.

— ܕܦܓܪܗ, *of His Body*—τοῦ σώματος αὐτοῦ—Noun with pron. aff. and

Ver. 21. pref. ܕ of the genitive. ܦܓܪ (S. Matt. xix. 6), noun masc. *A body*, not necessarily a *dead* body, as in Hebrew—Def. ܦܓܪܐ, S. John vi. 63.—Pl. def. ܦܓܪ̈ܐ, S. John xix. 31.

Heb. פֶּגֶר, *a carcase*, Gen. xv. 11.

22. ܡܢ ܒܝܬ ܡܝ̈ܬܐ, *from the dead*—ἐκ νεκρῶν—(See note, ver. 16, above).—Pl. def. of ܡܝܬ (Acts xx. 9), *Dead;* a participial adj. of form part. Peil of ܡܝܬ, *died.*—Def. ܡܝܬܐ, S. John xi. 39. Fem. ܡܝܬܐ, Acts v. 10;—Def. ܡܝܬܬܐ, 1 Tim. v. 6.—Pl. ܡܝܬܝܢ, Eph. ii. 1, 5; coalescing with ܚܢܢ, ܡܝܬܝܢܢ, 2 Cor. vi. 9: 1 S. Pet. ii. 24.

Compare Heb. מֵת, *dead, the dead*, Gen. xx. 3; xxiii. 4; Ps. lxxxviii. 11; cvi. 28.—

— ܐܡܪ ܗܘܐ, *He had said*—Gr. ἔλεγεν—Pret. followed by ܗܘܐ, forming the pluperf. tense.

— ܠܟܬ̈ܒܐ, *the Scriptures*—Gr. τῇ γραφῇ—Pl. def. (pref. ܠ of the object) of ܟܬܒ (2 Tim. iii. 16), noun masc. *A book, writing.*—Def. ܟܬܒܐ, S. John vii. 42, &c.—Pl. ܟܬ̈ܒܝܢ.—There is also a fem. form, ܟܬܒܐ, 2 S. Pet. i. 20.—Constr. ܟܬܒܬ, 1 Cor. xvi. 21; 2 Thess. iii. 18.—R. ܟܬܒ, *wrote.*

Heb. כְּתָב, Dan. x. 21.—Chald. כְּתָב, *A writing*, Dan. v. 8, &c. *A mandate*, Ezr. vi. 18;—*prescribing* how much, ch. vii. 22.

23. ܒܥܐܕܐ, *in the feast*—ἐν τῇ ἑορτῇ—Noun masc. def. with prefixed preposition. The form ܒܥܐܕܐ occurs, S. Matt. xxvi. 5; 1 Cor. v. 8.

— ܣܓܝ̈ܐܐ, *many*—πολλοί—Pl. masc. def. of ܣܓܝ, adj. *Much, great, abundant.*—Def. ܣܓܝܐܐ, S. Matt. vi. 7, &c.—Fem. ܣܓܝܐܐ, Hebr. iii. 3; v. 11.—Def. ܣܓܝܐܬܐ, S. Luke x. 40:—Constr. ܣܓܝܐܬ, S. Luke i. 18.—Pl. masc. ܣܓܝ̈ܐܝܢ, S. Matt. xx. 16; xxii. 14.—Constr. ܣܓܝ̈ܐܝ.—Pl. fem. ܣܓܝ̈ܐܢ, Acts xxiv. 17.

Ver. 23. —Def. ܣܓ̈ܝܐܝܢ, S. John xiv. 30:—in ch. xi. 47, it is written ܣܓ̈ܝܐܬܐ.—R. ܣܓܐ, ܣܓܝ, *increased, was great*.

Heb. שַׂגִּיא, *great*, Job xxxvi. 26; xxxvii. 23. Chald. שַׂגִּיא, *great*, Dan. ii. 31; *Many, much*, ii. 48; iv. 9. As an adv. *Very, greatly*, ch. ii. 12; v. 9.

— ܕܚܙܘ, *who saw, when they saw*—Gr. θεωροῦντες—Pret. 3. pl. with pref. ܕ, relative.

25. ܣܢܝܩ ܗܘܐ, *He needed*—χρείαν εἶχεν—Part. Peil (forming imperf. tense) of ܣܢܩ, *Was in need*. Occurs in Peal only in this participle, which though of pass. form has an active signification, *Wanting, having need of.* Pl. masc. ܣܢܝܩܝܢ, S. Matt. ix. 12, &c.: coalescing with ܠܢ, ܣܢܝܩܝܢܢ, 2 Cor. iii. 1;—with ܐܢܬܘܢ, ܣܢܝܩܝܬܘܢ, 1 Thess. iv. 9; v. 1.

Deriv. ܣܢܝܩܘܬܐ, noun fem. def. *Poverty, necessity*, Rom. xii. 13.

— ܕܐܢܫ ܢܣܗܕ ܠܗ, *that any* (lit. *man*) *should testify to Him*—Gr. ἵνα τις μαρτυρήσῃ—Fut. 3. sing. preceded by ܕ and having the force of a subjunctive. See note, ch. i. 15.

— ܥܠ ܟܠ ܐܢܫ, *of man*—lit. *concerning all* (any) *man*. Gr. περὶ τοῦ ἀνθρώπου.

CHAPTER III.

1. ܐܪܟܘܢܐ, *a ruler*—ἄρχων—Noun masc. def. derived from the Gr. word. Pl. ܐܪܟܘܢܐ, S. Luke xxiii. 13, 35: *Officers of the Temple*, Gr. ὁ στρατηγὸς τοῦ ἱεροῦ, Acts iv. 1.

2. ܒܠܠܝܐ, *by night*—Gr. νυκτός—Def. of ܠܠܝܐ, noun masc. *Night*.—Pl. (fem. form) ܠܝܠܘܢ, S. Matt. iv. 2; xii. 40.

Heb. לַיִל, Isa. xvi. 3; לַיְלָה, Gen. i. 5.—Chald. לֵילְיָא, Dan. ii. 19, &c.

S. JOHN III. 2—4.

Ver. 2. ܝܳܕܥܺܝܢܰܢ, *we know*—οἴδαμεν—Part. pl. ܝܳܕܥܺܝܢ, coalescing with ܚܢܢ, and forming the present tense. See Cowper's Gr. § 91.

— ܡܰܠܦܳܢܳܐ, *a teacher*—διδάσκαλος—Def. of ܡܰܠܦ (1 Tim. iii. 2), noun masc. *A doctor, teacher, one apt to teach.*—Pl. def. ܡܰܠܦܳܢܶܐ, S. Luke ii. 46.—R. ܝܠܦ *taught*—Pa. part. ܡܰܠܦ.

Transl. *We know that from God Thou wert sent* (Gr. ἐλήλυθας) *a teacher.*

— ܠܳܐ ܡܶܫܟܰܚ ܕܢܶܥܒܶܕ, see note, ch. i. 41.

— ܡܰܢ ܕ, *he who.* Interrog. pronoun forming with ܕ a relative.

Transl. *Unless (or, except) he with whom God is.*

— ܥܰܡܶܗ, *with him*—μετ᾽ αὐτοῦ—Preposition with affixed pronoun.

3. ܡܶܢ ܕܪܺܝܫ, *again*—lit. *from that which (is) the head,* or *beginning*—See note, ch. ii. 8, above.

— ܠܳܐ ܡܶܫܟܰܚ ܕ, *he cannot*—οὐ δύναται—See note, ch. i. 41, above.

— ܡܰܠܟܽܘܬܳܐ, *the kingdom* (aff. pleon.)—τὴν βασιλείαν—ܡܰܠܟܽܘܬܳܐ (S. Matt. xii. 25, &c.) noun fem. *A kingdom.*—Def. ܡܰܠܟܽܘܬܳܐ, ver. 5, below.—Constr. ܡܰܠܟܽܘܬ, S. Matt. xi. 11, &c.—Pl. def. ܡܰܠܟܘܳܬܳܐ, S. Matt. iv. 8; S. Luke iv. 5.—R. ܡܠܟ, *counselled.*

Heb. מַלְכוּת (in later Heb. for the earlier form מַמְלָכָה), *Kingdom, reign,* Dan. i. 1: Ps. cxlv. 11, 13.—Chald. מַלְכוּ, def. מַלְכוּתָא, Dan. ii. 37, 39, &c.

4. ܣܳܒܳܐ, *old*—γέρων—Def. of ܣܳܒ, adj. *Old, aged.* Fem. def. ܣܳܒܬܳܐ, pl. def. ܣܳܒܶܐ 1 Tim. iv. 7.—R. ܣܐܒ, *grew old.*

Heb. שָׂב (part. of שִׂיב), Job xv. 10.—Chald. שָׂב, Ezr. v. 5 (pl. constr.)—Pl. def. שָׂבַיָּא, ver. 9.

— ܕܰܠܡܳܐ, Gr. μή; A particle which varies in its meaning according to the context. Here it is equivalent to *fieri potest ut?—num?—* In ch. v. 14. *lest*—Gr. ἵνα μή.

— ܠܟܰܪܣܳܐ, *into the womb*—εἰς τὴν κοιλίαν—Def. (with pref. prep.) of ܟܰܪܣ (ch. ix. 1), noun fem. *The womb, belly.*—Pl. ܟܰܪܣܶܐ, def. ܟܰܪܣܳܬܳܐ, S. Luke xxiii. 29.

Heb. בֶּרֶשׂ, once, Jer. li. 34.

Ver. 4. ܕܬܪܬܝܢ ܙܒܢܝܢ, *the second time*—δεύτερον—ܬܪܬܝܢ, fem. of ܬܪܝܢ, *two.* See note, ch. vi. 7, below.

ܙܒܢܝܢ, pl. of ܙܒܢ (ch. v. 14), noun masc. when it signifies *Time* (sc. *tempus*); but fem. when it is equivalent to Lat. *vice*,—as ܚܕܐ ܙܒܢ, *unâ vice, once*, Rom. vi. 10, &c. The same applies to the plural.—Def. ܙܒܢܐ, S. John v. 6, &c.—Pl. as a fem. *vices*, ܙܒܢܝܢ ܣܓܝܐܢ, *vicibus multis, oft-times*, S. Mark ix. 22. ܙܒܢܝܢ, when joined to a cardinal, forms a numeral adverb; as ܬܪܬܝܢ ܙܒܢܝܢ, *twice*, Gr. δίς—S. Mark xiv. 30.—ܬܠܬ ܙܒܢܝܢ, *thrice*, Gr. τρίς, S. John xiii. 38, &c.—ܚܡܫ ܙܒܢܝܢ, *five times*, Gr. πεντάκις—2 Cor. xi. 24.—ܫܒܥ ܙܒܢܝܢ, *seven times*, Gr. ἑπτάκις—S. Matt. xviii. 21; S. Luke xviii. 4.—ܫܒܥܝܢ ܙܒܢܝܢ, *seventy times*, Gr. ἑβδομηκοντάκις, S. Matt. xviii. 22.—But when ܕ is prefixed to these cardinals, it expresses *secundâ, tertiâ vice*, &c., as in the text: see also ch. ix. 24; xxi. 16.—ܕܬܠܬ ܙܒܢܝܢ, *the third time*, Gr. ἐκ τρίτου, S. Matt. xxvi. 44: τὸ τρίτον, S. John xxi. 17: S. Mark xiv. 41; τρίτον, S. Luke xxiii. 22.

Pl. def. ܙܒܢܐ (according to some editions—the Vienna reads ܙܒܢܐ), S. Luke xxi. 24.—Pl. fem. ܙܒܢܢ, def. ܙܒܢܬܐ, Hebr. ix. 25, 26.

ܙܒܢ is also used in adverbial expressions; as ܒܙܒܢ, *formerly, in time past*, Philem. ver. 11.—ܒܙܒܢ ܙܒܢ, *from time to time, at a certain season*, S. John v. 4.

ܒܟܠܙܒܢ, *evermore, at all times, always*, S. John vi. 34, &c.

ܒܙܒܢܐ ܘܕܠܐ ܙܒܢܐ, lit. *in time and of no time*, i.e. *in season and out of season*, 2 Tim. iv. 2.

ܟܡܐ ܙܒܢܝܢ, *oft-times*, Gr. πολλάκις, S. Matt. xvii. 15.—Interrog. *How often?* Gr. ποσάκις;—ch. xviii. 21. xxiii. 37; S. Luke xiii. 34. *As often as* (ܕ), Gr. ὁσάκις, Rev. xi. 6.

Heb. זְמָן, Eccles. iii. 1.—Chald. זְמַן or זְמָן, def. זִמְנָא, pl. זִמְנִין, Dan. ii. 16; iii. 7, 8; vii. 25. זִמְנִין תְּלָתָה, *three times*, ch. vi. 11.

S. JOHN III. 4—7.

Ver. 4. ܠܡܥܠ, *to enter*—εἰσελθεῖν—Infin. (with pref. ܠ) of ܥܠ ܥܠܐ (ch. xviii. 1.) *Entered.*—Pret. 3. sing. fem. ܥܠܰܬ, S. Mark vi. 22, 25, &c.—2. sing. ܥܠܬ, S. Matt. xxii. 12.—1. sing. ܥܠܬ, S. Luke vii. 44.—3. pl. ܥܠܘ, S. John iv. 8, &c.: Fem. ܥܠܶܝܢ, S. Matt. xxv. 10: ܥܠܢ, S. Mark xvi. 5.—2. pl. ܥܠܬܘܢ, S. John iv. 38; S. Luke xi. 52.—1. pl. ܥܠܢ, Acts xi. 12, &c.—Fut. ܢܶܥܘܠ, ver. 5, below.—2. sing. ܬܶܥܘܠ, S. Matt. viii. 8, &c.: Fem. ܬܶܥܠܝܢ, Vienna edition—others read ܬܶܥܠܝܢ, S. Mark ix. 25.—1. sing. ܐܶܥܘܠ, Rev. iii. 20.—3. pl. ܢܶܥܠܘܢ, S. Mark x. 23, 24, &c.—2. pl. ܬܶܥܠܘܢ, S. Matt. v. 20, &c.—1. pl. ܢܶܥܘܠ, S. Mark v. 12.—Imperat. ܥܘܠ, S. Matt. vi. 6, &c.—Pl. ܥܘܠܘ, ch. vii. 13.—Part. ܥܐܶܠ, S. John x. 1, 2.—Fem. ܥܐܠܐ, ch. xix. 42.—Pl. masc. ܥܐܠܝܢ, S. Matt. x. 11, &c.—Pl. fem. ܥܐܠܢ, S. Matt. xii. 45: S. Mark iv. 19: S. Luke xi. 26.—Part. Peil ܥܠܝܠܐ, pl. masc. ܥܠܝܠܝܢ, in act. sense, S. Luke viii. 30.

Chald. עלל, על, Dan. ii. 16, 24, &c.

6. ܗܘ ܒܣܪܐ, *is flesh*—σάρξ ἐστι—ܗܘ represents the subst. verb, and the two words are pronounced as one; in which case the last vowel of the noun (ܒܣܪܐ) becomes '. So also ܗܘ ܪܘܚܐ, immediately following. Pron. *besrau, ruchau.*

7. ܠܐ ܬܬܕܡܪ, *marvel not*—μὴ θαυμάσῃς—Ethpaal fut. 2. sing. (with ܠܐ, for imperat.) of ܕܡܪ, used only in Ethpa. ܐܬܕܡܪ (S. Matt. viii. 10, &c.), *Wondered, was astonished.*—Pret. 3. sing. fem. ܐܬܕܡܪܬ, Rev. xiii. 3.—2. sing. ܐܬܕܡܪܬ, ch. xvii. 7.—1. sing. ܐܬܕܡܪܬ, ver. 6.—3. pl. ܐܬܕܡܪܘ, S. Matt. viii. 27, &c.—Fut. ܢܬܕܡܪ, S. Mark xv. 5.—3. pl. ܢܬܕܡܪܘܢ, S. Matt. xv. 31: S. Mark ii. 12.—2. pl. ܬܬܕܡܪܘܢ, S. John v. 20, 28.—Inf. ܠܡܬܕܡܪܘ, S. John ix. 30.—Part. ܡܬܕܡܪ, S. Mark vi. 6, &c.—Pl. masc. ܡܬܕܡܪܝܢ, S. John iv. 27.

— ܕܘܠܐ ܠܟܘܢ, *that it is needful for you*—*that ye must*—Gr. δεῖ ὑμᾶς—(ܕ introducing the assertion), Verb (ܘܠܐ) used only in the part.

Ver. 7. pres. and impersonally. *It is necessary, fitting, just.* Lat. *Oportet.*—ܘܳܠܶܐ ܗ̄ܘܳܐ, *it was necessary*, ver. 30, below. Followed by dat. of the person and ܠ with inf.—as here and in ver. 30:—or by ܕ with the future, as ch. iv. 24. Fem. ܘܳܠܝܳܐ ܗ̄ܝ, Acts i. 21; 1 Cor. vii. 36.—Def. ܘܳܠܺܝܬܳܐ, used as a noun with pref. ܒ, *with propriety, reasonably*, Gr. κατὰ λόγον, Acts xviii. 14.—Pl. masc. ܘܳܠܶܝܢ. Fem. ܘܳܠܝܳܢ.—Pl. fem. def. ܘܳܠܝܳܬܳܐ, as a noun, *Decency, propriety*, Rom. ii. 18.

8. ܐܰܬܪ ܕ, *where*—ὅπου—Noun masc. used with ܕ as an adverb of place. Lit. *the place that.* For ܐܰܬܪ, *a place*, see note, ch. xi. 54.

— ܢܳܫܒܳܐ, *blowing*—*bloweth*—πνεῖ—Part. fem. (used for present tense) of ܢܫܰܒ, *Blew.*—Pret. 3. sing. fem. ܢܶܫܒܰܬ, ch. vi. 18: Acts xxviii. 13.—3. pl. fem. ܢܫܰܒ̈, S. Matt. vii. 25, 27.—Fut. ܢܶܫܽܒ, Rev. vii. 1.

Deriv. ܡܰܫܒܳܐ, noun masc. def. *A wind, blowing*, Acts xxvii. 14.

Heb. נָשַׁב, Isa. xl. 7.

— ܘܰܠܐܰܝܟܳܐ, *and whither*—καὶ ποῦ—ܐܰܝܟܳܐ, *where*, with pref. ܠ of the dat. which takes its first vowel,—and ܘ.—See note, ch. i. 28.

— ܗܳܟܰܢܳܐ, *so*—οὕτως. Adverb, *So, thus, likewise.* Its simpler form is ܗܳܟܰܢ, 1 Thess. ii. 14: 1 S. John iv. 11.

9. ܐܰܝܟܰܢܳܐ, *how?*—πῶς;—Adverb of interrogation. See note, ch. i. 23, above.

11. ܡܡܰܠܠܺܝܢܰܢ, *we speak*—λαλοῦμεν—Pael part. plur. (coalescing with ܚܢܰܢ, and forming the pres. tense) of ܡܠܰܠ, not used in Peal, unless ܢܶܡܠܠܽܘܢ, ch. ix. 19, be the only instance. (See note, ii. 7, above).—Pa. ܡܰܠܶܠ (ch. xii. 29), *Spoke.*—Pret. 3. sing. fem. ܡܰܠܠܰܬ, 2 S. Pet. ii. 16.—2. sing. ܡܰܠܶܠܬ, Acts iv. 25.—1. sing. ܡܰܠܠܶܬ, S. John xii. 48, 49, &c.—3. pl. ܡܰܠܶܠܘ, S. Luke ii. 15; x xiv. 25. —1. pl. ܡܰܠܶܠܢ, 2 Cor. vii. 14; 1 Thess. ii. 2.—Fut. ܢܡܰܠܶܠ, S. Matt. xii. 22, &c.—1. sing. ܐܡܰܠܶܠ, S. John xii. 49, &c.—3. pl. ܢܡܰܠܠܽܘܢ, S. Matt. xii. 47, &c. Fem. ܢܡܰܠܠܳܢ, 1 Cor. xiv. 34, 35,

Ver. 11. &c.—2. pl. ܬܡܠܠܘܢ, S. Matt. x. 19; S. Mark xiii. 11.—1. pl. ܢܡܠܠ, 1 Thess. ii. 16, &c.—Imperat. ܡܠܠ, Acts xviii. 9.—Pl. ܡܠܠܘ, S. Mark xiii. 11.—Inf. ܠܡܡܠܠܘ, S. Matt. xii. 34, &c.—Part. ܡܡܠܠ, S. John iv. 26, &c. Fem. ܡܡܠܠܐ, S. Matt. x. 20, &c.—Pl. masc. ܡܡܠܠܝܢ, S. Matt. x. 20, &c.—Constr. ܡܡܠܠܝ̈, Acts xx. 30.—Pl. fem. ܡܡܠܠ̈ܢ, S. Luke vi. 45.—Derived from this verb is the adj. of form part. Peil masc. def. ܡܠܝܠܐ, *rational, reasonable.* Fem. def. ܡܠܝܠܬܐ, Gr. λογικήν, Rom. xii. 1.

Heb. מִלֵּל, Prov. vi. 13; Pi. Ps. cvi. 2.—Chald. Pa. מַלִּל, Dan. vi. 22; vii. 8, 11, 20, 25.

— ܡܩܒܠܝܢ ܐܢܬܘܢ, *ye receive*—λαμβάνετε—Pael part. pl. masc. forming, with the pronoun, the present tense. The pronoun though written separately, coalesces with the participle in pronunciation, forming one word, *m'kabl'tun.*

12. ܕܒܐܪܥܐ, *that which (is) on the earth, earthly things*—Gr. τὰ ἐπίγεια—Def. (with pref. prep. which takes the first vowel, and rel. pron.) of ܐܪܥ.—Noun fem. *Land, earth, region.*—Pl. def. ܐܪ̈ܥܬܐ, ch. iv. 35.

Heb. אֶרֶץ, Gen. i. 1.—Chald. אֲרַע, def. אַרְעָא—(the צ in Aramaic softened into ע, ܥ,) Dan. ii. 35, &c.—The same form is traceable in the Germ. Erde, and the Eng. *Earth.*

14. ܐܪܝܡ, *lifted up*—ὕψωσε—Aphel pret. 3. sing. of ܪܘܡ ܪܡ (not used in Peal).

Ethpeel ܐܬܬܪܝܡ, *Exalted himself, boasted himself.*—Fut. ܢܬܬܪܝܡ, 1 Tim. iii. 6.—2. sing. ܬܬܬܪܝܡ, Rom. xi. 20.—3. pl. ܢܬܬܪܝܡܘܢ, 1 Tim. vi. 17.—Part. ܡܬܬܪܝܡ, 2 Cor. x. 5, &c.—Pl. masc. ܡܬܬܪܝܡܝܢ, 1 S. Pet. v. 5.

Aph. *Lifted up, raised up, exalted; took off* a roof (S. Mark ii. 4). Pret. 3. sing. fem. ܐܪܝܡܬ, S. Luke xi. 27.—3. pl. ܐܪܝܡܘ, S. Matt. xx. 31; S. Mark ii. 4.—Fut. ܢܪܝܡ, S. Matt. xxiii. 12, &c.: Fem. ܬܪܝܡܝܢ, with aff. ܬܪܝܡܝܢܗ, (*that*) *it*, i. e. the hand

S. JOHN III. 14.

Ver. 14. of God, *may exalt you*, 1 S. Pet. v. 6.—2. pl. ܬܬܪܝܡ, with aff. S. John viii. 28.—Imperat. ܐܪܝܡ, pl. ܐܪܝܡܘ, S. John iv. 35.—Part. ܡܪܝܡ, pl. masc. ܡܪܝܡܝܢ, 1 Cor. iv. 19; 1 Tim. ii. 8.

Heb. רוּם, *rose up, was exalted, triumphed*, Ps. xiii. 3. Hiph. הֵרִים, *lifted up, exalted*, Ps. iii. 4, &c. &c. Chald. רוּם, only in part. Peil רָם, Dan. v. 20.—Aph. אָרִים, part. מָרִים, Dan. v. 19.

— ܚܘܝܐ, *the serpent*—τὸν ὄφιν—Noun masc.—Pl. def. of fem. form ܚܘܘܬܐ, S. Matt. x. 16, &c.

— ܥܬܝܕ, *must*—δεῖ—Adj. of form part. Peil of ܥܬܕ, *was ready*, not occurring otherwise in Peal. *Prepared, ordained, future*, S. Matt. xxv. 34.—Also expressing *necessity, readiness*, or *intention*, as Gr. μέλλω, μέλλων,—either, as here, followed by the infin. with ܠ, or by the fut. with ܕ, as in ch. xviii. 32; see also S. Matt. ii. 13. Fem. ܥܬܝܕܐ, S. Matt. xxv. 34, &c.—Pl. masc. ܥܬܝܕܝܢ, S. John vi. 15, &c.: coalescing with ܠܝ, ܥܬܝܕܝܢܠܝ, Rom. xiv. 10, &c.—Pl. fem. ܥܬܝܕܢ, S. Luke xxi. 9, 36.—Def. ܥܬܝܕܬܐ, S. John xvi. 13.—From this is formed ܥܬܝܕܐܝܬ, adv. *Promptly, without delay*, Acts ii. 41; x. 29.

Pael ܥܬܕ, *Prepared, purposed, disposed*, Eph. iii. 11.—Fut. ܢܥܬܕ, 3. pl. ܢܥܬܕܘܢ, 2 Cor. ix. 5.—Imperat. ܥܬܕ, pl. ܥܬܕܘ, Acts xxiii. 23.—Part. ܡܥܬܕ, 2 Cor. v. 5.—Part. pass. ܡܥܬܕ, pl. masc. ܡܥܬܕܝܢ, Eph. vi. 13.

Heb. Pi. עִתֵּד, *made ready*, Prov. xxiv. 27. and Hithpa. הִתְעַתֵּד, *was ready, destined, to be*, followed by ל, Job xv. 28.

— ܠܡܬܬܪܡܘ, *to be lifted up*—ὑψωθῆναι—Ethtaphal inf. (with pref. ܠ) of ܪܘܡ ܪܘܡ (see note above, in this verse). Ethtaph. ܐܬܬܪܝܡ, *Was exalted*, pass. of Aphel, Acts ii. 33.—Pret. 3. sing. fem. ܐܬܬܪܝܡܬ, S. Matt. xi. 23; S. Luke x. 15.—1. sing. ܐܬܬܪܝܡܬ, S. John xii. 32.—Fut. ܢܬܬܪܝܡ, S. John xii. 34, &c.—2. pl. ܬܬܪܝܡܘܢ, 2 Cor. xi. 7.

N.B. In verbs ܥܥ, the Ethpeel and Ethtaphal conjugations are

S. JOHN III. 14—16. 75

Ver. 14. similar in form, and differ only in signification;—Ethpe. having a reciprocal, and Ethtaph. a passive force.

15. ܢܐܒܕ, *should perish*—ἀπόληται—Fut. 3. sing. (for subjunctive, preceded by ܕ) of ܐܒܕ (ch. xvii. 12), *Perished, was lost.*—Pret. 3. sing. fem. ܐܒܕܬ, Hebr. xi. 31.—3. pl. ܐܒܕܘ, S. Matt. x. 6: Fem. ܐܒܕܝ, Rev. xviii. 14.—Fut. 3. sing. fem. ܬܐܒܕ, S. Luke xxi. 18.—3. pl. ܢܐܒܕܘܢ, S. John x. 28.—2. pl. ܬܐܒܕܘܢ, S. Luke xiii. 3, 5.—Part. ܐܒܕ, S. Luke xv. 17:—Fem. ܐܒܕܐ, S. John vi. 27.—Pl. masc. ܐܒܕܝܢ, 2 Cor. ii. 15:—coalescing with ܠܢ, ܐܒܕܝܢܢ, S. Matt. viii. 25, &c.—Pl. fem. ܐܒܕܢ, S. Matt. ix. 17, &c.—Part. Peil, ܐܒܝܕ, S. Matt. xviii. 11, &c. Def. ܐܒܝܕܐ, S. Luke xv. 24, 32.—Pl. masc. def. ܐܒܝܕܝܢ, 2 Thess. ii. 10.

Heb. אָבַד, Ps. xxxvii. 20.—Chald. אֲבַד, fut. יֹאבַד, Jerem. x. 11.

— ܢܗܘܐ ܠܗ, (that) there should be to him, i.e. (that) he should have— Gr. ἔχῃ—Supply ܕ from the preceding clause. The verb in the plural, agreeing with ܚܝܐ.

16. ܐܚܒ, *loved*—ἠγάπησεν—Aphel pret. 3. sing. of ܢܚܒ ܚܒ, *Cherished, kindled, burned*—(see note, S. Luke xii. 49).—Pael ܚܒܒ, *Loved, cherished.*—Part. ܡܚܒܒ, fem. ܡܚܒܒܐ, 1 Thess. ii. 7.—Pl. masc. ܡܚܒܒܝܢ, coalescing with ܠܢ, ܡܚܒܒܝܢܢ, ver. 8.

Aph. *Loved*—Pret. 3. sing. fem. ܐܚܒܬ, S. Luke vii. 47.— 2. sing. ܐܚܒܬ, S. John xvii. 23; with aff. ver. 24, 26.—1. sing. ܐܚܒܬ, with aff. ch. xiii. 34; xv. 9, 12.—3. pl. ܐܚܒܘ, ver. 19, below.—1. pl. ܐܚܒܢ, 1 S. John iv. 10.—Fut. ܢܚܒ, 1 S. John iv. 20, 21.—2. sing. ܬܚܒ, S. Matt. xix. 19.—3. pl. ܢܚܒܘܢ, Eph. v. 28.—2. pl. ܬܚܒܘܢ, S. John xiii. 34; xv. 12, 17.—1. pl. ܢܚܒ, 1 S. John iii. 18, 23, &c. In 2 S. John ver. 5, the characteristic Olaph is retained, as ܢܐܚܒ.—Imperat. ܐܚܒ, pl. ܐܚܒܘ, S. Matt. v. 44.—Inf. ܠܡܚܒܘ, 1 S. John iv. 11: and ܠܡܚܒܬܐ, Rom. xiii. 8.—Part. ܡܚܒ, ver. 35, below, &c.

Ver. 16. ܡܟܐܢܬ, 2 S. John ver. 1: 3 S. John ver. 1.—Pl. masc. ܡܟܣܒܝ, S. John viii. 42, &c.—Coalescing with ܒܝ, ܡܟܣܢܝ, 1 S. John iii. 14.

— ܟܠ ܡܢ ?, *every one who, whosoever*—πᾶς ὁ—The words are sometimes joined, as ? ܟܠܡܢ.

17. ܕܢܕܝܢܝܘܗܝ, *that He might condemn*—*to condemn* (aff. pleon.)—ἵνα κρίνῃ—Fut. 3. sing. (for subjunctive, with ?) of ܢܕܘܢ (Acts xii. 19), *Judged, condemned, contended with* (ܥܡ).—Pret. 2. sing. ܕܢܬ, S. Luke vii. 43.—1. sing. ܕܢܬ, 1 Cor. ii. 2, &c.—3. pl. ܕܢܘ, S. Mark xiv. 64.—Fut. ܢܕܘܢ, S. Matt. v. 40:—Fem. ܬܕܘܢ, for ܬܕܘܢܝܢ, Rom. ii. 27.—1. sing. ܐܕܘܢ, S. John xii. 47.—3. pl. ܢܕܘܢܘܢ, Acts xix. 38.—2. pl. ܬܕܘܢܘܢ, S. Matt. vii. 1, &c.— Imperat. ܕܘܢ, pl. ܕܘܢܘ, S. John vii. 24.—Inf. ܠܡܕܢ, S. John viii. 26.—Part. ܕܐܢ, S. John v. 22, &c.—Fem. ܕܝܢܐ, ch. xii. 48. —Pl. masc. ܕܝܢܝܢ, ch. vii. 24; viii. 15, &c.;—coalescing with ܠܝ, ܕܝܢܝܢܠܝ, 1 Cor. vi. 3.—Part. Peil ܕܝܢ, ver. 18, below; xvi. 11.

Heb. דּוּן or דִּין, Gen. vi. 3.—Chald. דּוּן, דִּין, part. pl. Ezr. vii. 25.

— ܢܚܐ, *might live, have life, be saved*—σωθῇ—Fut. 3. sing. (for subjunct.) of ܚܝܐ (ch. iv. 51), *Lived, was preserved, saved.*—For the anomalies in this verb, see Phillips § 42; and Cowper § 121.

Pret. 3. sing. fem. ܚܝܬ, S. Luke ii. 36.—1. sing. ܚܝܝܬ, Acts xxvi. 5.—3. pl. ܚܝܘ, Rev. xx. 4: Fem. ܚܝܝ, 1 S. Pet. iii. 20.—2. pl. ܚܝܝܬܘܢ, Rom. vi. 13.—1. pl. ܚܝܝܢ, Rom. viii. 24.—Fut. 3. sing. fem. ܬܚܐ, S. Matt. ix. 18.—2. sing. ܬܚܐ, S. Luke x. 28; ܬܚܐ, Rom. x. 9.—1. sing. ܐܚܐ, Acts xvi. 30; Gal. ii. 19.—3. pl. ܢܚܘܢ, S. John v. 25; S. Luke viii. 12, &c. ܒܐܣܐ, 1 Thess. ii. 16: ܢܐܣܐ, 1 Tim. ii. 4.—2. pl. ܬܐܣܘܢ, S. John v. 34; xiv. 19.—1. pl. ܢܚܐ, Acts xv. 11.—Imperat. pl. ܐܣܘ, Acts ii. 40.—Inf. ܠܡܚܐ, S. Mark x. 26; S. Luke

Ver. 17. xviii. 26.—Part. ܚܳܝܶܐ, S. Matt. iv. 4, &c.:—Fem. ܚܳܝܳܐ, S. Mark v. 28; S. Luke viii. 50.—Pl. masc. ܚܳܝܶܝܢ, S. Luke xiii. 23: also ܚܰܝܶܝܢ, S. Matt. xv. 27; Acts ii. 47, &c. and ܚܰܝܺܝܢ, S. Luke xx. 38. Coalescing with ܚܢܰܢ, ܚܳܝܶܝܢܰܢ, Rom. xiv. 8: also ܚܰܝܶܝܢܰܢ, 2 Cor. vi. 9; xiii. 4:—and with ܐܢ̱ܬ݁ܽܘܢ, ܚܰܝܶܝܬ݁ܽܘܢ, Col. ii. 20.

Heb. חָיָה, Gen. v. 3, &c. &c.—Chald. חֲיָה and חַיָּא, Dan. ii. 4, &c.

18. ܡܶܬ݁ܕ݁ܺܝܢ, *condemned, is condemned*—*κρίνεται*—Ethpeel part. (for pres. tense) of ܕ݁ܳܢ ܕ݁ܽܘܢ, *Judged*—Ethpe. ܐܶܬ݁ܕ݁ܺܝܢ, pret. 3. pl. ܐܶܬ݁ܕ݁ܺܝܢܘ, Rev. xx. 12, 13.—Fut. ܢܶܬ݁ܕ݁ܺܝܢ, 2. sing. ܬ݁ܶܬ݁ܕ݁ܺܝܢ, Acts xxv. 20.—1. sing. ܐܶܬ݁ܕ݁ܺܝܢ, 1 Cor. iv. 3.—3. pl. ܢܶܬ݁ܕ݁ܺܝܢܽܘܢ, Rom. ii. 12, &c. —2. pl. ܬ݁ܶܬ݁ܕ݁ܺܝܢܽܘܢ, S. Matt. vii. 2.—Inf. ܠܡܶܬ݁ܕ݁ܳܢܽܘ, Acts xxv. 10.—Part. fem. ܡܶܬ݁ܕ݁ܺܝܢܳܐ, 1 Cor. x. 29.—Pl. masc. ܡܶܬ݁ܕ݁ܺܝܢܺܝܢ, S. Luke vi. 37:—coalescing with ܚܢܰܢ, ܡܶܬ݁ܕ݁ܺܝܢܺܝܢܰܢ, 1 Cor. xi. 32.

— ܡܶܢ ܟ݁ܰܕ݂ܘ, *already*—*ἤδη*—Adverb, sometimes written as one word ܡܶܢܟ݁ܰܕ݂ܘ, *already, now*. ܟ݁ܰܕ݂ܘ occurs without ܡܶܢ, in the sense of *now*, 2 S. Pet. iii. 1.

19. ܕ݁ܺܝܢܳܐ, *the judgment, condemnation*—*ἡ κρίσις*—Def. of ܕ݁ܺܝܢ, noun masc. *Judgment, cause, contention, dispute.*—ܒ݁ܥܶܠ ܕ݁ܺܝܢܳܟ݂, *lord of thy cause*, i.e. *thine adversary*, S. Matt. v. 25: ܒ݁ܥܶܠ ܕ݁ܺܝܢܝ, *my adversary*, S. Luke xviii. 3.—Pl. def. ܕ݁ܺܝܢܶܐ, S. Mark xiii. 9.—R. ܕ݁ܳܢ ܕ݁ܽܘܢ, *judged*.

Heb. דִּין, Ps. lxxvi. 9.—Chald. דִּין, *justice*, Dan. iv. 34; vii. 22. *Judgment, tribunal*, ch. vii. 10.

— ܝܰܬ݁ܺܝܪ ܡܶܢ, *rather than*—*μᾶλλον ἤ*—ܝܰܬ݁ܺܝܪ, adj. *Abounding, excellent*—see note, ch. v. 20:—here used adverbially.

— ܥܒ݂ܳܕ݂ܰܝܗܽܘܢ, *their deeds*—*τὰ ἔργα αὐτῶν*—Pl. with aff. of ܥܒ݂ܳܕ݂ (2 Cor. ix. 8), noun masc. *A work, act, deed.*—Def. ܥܒ݂ܳܕ݂ܳܐ, S. John vi. 29.

Ver. 19. —Constr. ܥܒܳܕ, Acts vii. 41; xvii. 24.—Pl. ܥܒ̈ܳܕܰܝ, Col. i. 10.—
Def. ܥܒ̈ܳܕܶܐ, S. John v. 20, &c. R. ܥܒܰܕ, *performed.*

Heb. עֲבָד, *work, deed,* once, Eccles. ix. 1.

— ܒܺܝ̈ܫܳܬ݂ܳܐ, *evil—πονηρά*—Pl. def. of ܒܺܝܫ (ch. v. 14), adj. often used as a subst. *Evil, an evil, harm.* Def. ܒܺܝܫܳܐ, ch. xvii. 15, &c.—Fem. ܒܺܝܫܳܐ, S. Matt. v. 11, &c.—Def. ܒܺܝܫܬܳܐ, S. John xviii. 23; with aff. S. Matt. vi. 34.—Pl. masc. ܒܺܝ̈ܫܺܝܢ, S. John vii. 7. —Pl. fem. ܒܺܝ̈ܫܳܢ, S. Matt. xii. 45; S. Luke xi. 26.—Def. ܒܺܝ̈ܫܳܬ݂ܳܐ, S. John v. 29, &c.:—with aff. S. Luke xvi. 25. R. ܒܐܶܫ, *was evil.*

Comp. Heb. בְּאֻשִׁים *bad* grapes, Isa. v. 2, 4: and בָּאְשָׁה, *a poisonous weed,* Job xxxi. 40.—Chald. בְּאִישׁ, *bad, wicked,*—fem. def. בְּאִישְׁתָּא, Ezr. iv. 12.

20. ܣܰܢܝ̈ܳܬ݂ܳܐ, *hateful things, evil—φαῦλα*—Pl. fem. def. of ܣܢܺܝܳܐ, part. Peil of ܣܢܳܐ, *hated,* for which see the note following.

— ܣܳܢܶܐ, *hating, hateth—μισεῖ*—Part. act. of ܣܢܳܐ (ch. xv. 18; xvii. 14), *Hated.*—Pret. 2. sing. ܣܢܰܝܬ, Hebr. i. 9.—1. sing. ܣܶܢܺܝܬ, Rom. ix. 13.—3. pl. ܣܢܰܘ, S. John xv. 24; with aff. ver. 25.—Fut. ܢܶܣܢܶܐ, S. Matt. vi. 24: S. Luke xvi. 13.—3. pl. ܢܶܣܢܽܘܢ, S. Matt. xxiv. 10.—Imperat. ܣܢܺܝ, S. Matt. v. 43.—Inf. ܡܶܣܢܳܐ, with pron. aff. and pref. ܠ, ܠܡܶܣܢܝܳܢܟ݂ܽܘܢ, S. John vii. 7. (See Cowper's Gr. § 127 (1, 2), and Paradigm.)—Part. pl. ܣܳܢܶܝܢ, S. Luke vi. 22, 27; with affix, ܣܳܢܰܝܢܰܢ, S. Luke i. 71.—Constr. ܣܳܢܰܝ ܛܳܒ݂ܳܬ݂ܳܐ, *haters of good things,* 2 Tim. iii. 3.—The part. Peil has two forms; one of the form of verbs ל״, ܣܢܶܐ, *odious, hateful,* used of *things,* S. Luke xxiii. 41. Fem. ܣܢܺܝܳܐ, Eph. iv. 29.—Pl. def. ܣܰܢܝ̈ܳܬ݂ܳܐ, as above. The other follows the form of the regular verb, ܣܢܺܝܐ, fem. ܣܢܺܝܐܳ, def. ܣܢܺܝܐܬܳܐ, *hateful,* used of *persons,* or that which represents persons, Rev. xviii. 2.—Pl. masc. ܣܢܺܝܐܺܝܢ, S. Matt. x. 22, &c. Def. ܣܢܺܝ̈ܐܶܐ, Tit. i. 16.

S. JOHN III. 20—24.

Ver. 20. Heb. שָׂנֵא, Ps. v. 6, &c. Chald. שְׂנָא, part. שָׂנֵא *an enemy*, with aff. Dan. iv. 16.

— ܢܬܟܣܣܘܢ, *they should be reproved*—Gr. ἐλεγχθῇ—Ethpeel fut. 3. pl. (with ܕ for subjunctive) of ܟܣܡ ܟܣܣ (not used in Peal).
Ethpe. ܐܬܟܣܣ, *Was accused, reproved*. Part. ܡܬܟܣܣ, S. Luke iii. 19.

21. ܣܥܝܪܝܢ, *are wrought*—ἐστιν εἰργασμένα—Part. Peil pl. (for pres. tense). See note ch. ii. 5. ܣܥܝܪ ܒܝܫܐܝܬ, *badly afflicted*, S. Matt. iv. 24.

22. ܡܬܗܦܟ ܗܘܐ, *He tarried*—διέτριβε—Ethpaal part. (forming imperf. tense) of ܗܦܟ, *Turned*. Ethpa. ܐܬܗܦܟ, *Abode, continued, had his conversation*; followed by ܡܢ, *was removed from*.—Pret. 1. pl. ܐܬܗܦܟܢ, 2 Cor. i. 12; Eph. ii. 3.—Inf. ܠܡܬܗܦܟܘ, 1 Tim. iii. 15.—Part. pl. masc. ܡܬܗܦܟܝܢ, S. Matt. xvii. 22.

23. ܠܘܬ, *near*—ἐγγύς—Compound preposition. ܠܘܬ is properly the constr. state of ܠܘܬܐ, by contraction ܠܘܬ, *A side*: see note, ch. xx. 27.—With aff. ܠܘܬܗ, *by him, near him*, Acts xxiii. 2.

— ܘܥܡܕܝܢ, *and were baptized*—καὶ ἐβαπτίζοντο—Part. pl. masc. (for imperf.; supply ܗܘܘ from the preceding verb) of ܥܡܕ (S. Matt. iii. 16) *Washed, immersed himself, was baptized*.—Pret. 3. sing. fem. ܥܡܕܬ, Acts xvi. 15.—3. pl. ܥܡܕܘ, S. Luke vii. 29.—2. pl. ܥܡܕܬܘܢ, 1 Cor. i. 13.—1. pl. ܥܡܕܢ, Rom. vi. 3.—Fut. ܢܥܡܕ, S. Matt. iii. 13.—1. sing. ܐܥܡܕ, S. Luke xii. 50.—3. pl. ܢܥܡܕܘܢ, Acts x. 47, 48.—2. pl. ܬܥܡܕܘܢ, S. Matt. xx. 22, 23, &c.—Imperat. ܥܡܕ, Acts xxii. 16.—Pl. ܥܡܕܘ, ch. ii. 38.—Inf. ܠܡܥܡܕ, S. Matt. iii. 7; S. Luke iii. 7, 12.—Part. ܥܡܕ, S. Matt. xx. 22, &c.
Heb. עָמַד, *stood, stood firm, endured*, Gen. xxiv. 30, 31: Ps. xxxiii. 11.

24. ܢܦܠ ܗܘܐ, *had fallen, had been cast*—ἦν βεβλημένος—Pret. 3. sing. with ܗܘܐ forming the pluperf. tense.—Verbs neuter or intransitive are often used in a passive sense.

Ver. 24. ܢܦܰܠ, *Fell, fell down,* also *pressed upon,* S. Mark iii. 10: *beat against,* of waves, ch. iv. 37.—Pret. 3. sing. fem. ܢܶܦܠܰܬ݂, S. John xi. 32, &c.: S. Matt. xiii. 47, Gr. βληθείσῃ.—2. sing. ܢܦܰܠܬ, Rev. ii. 5.—1. sing. ܢܶܦܠܶܬ, Acts xxii. 7.—3. pl. ܢܦܰܠܘ, S. John xviii. 6, &c. Fem. ܢܦܰܠܶܝܢ, Acts xii. 7.—2. pl. ܢܦܰܠܬ݁ܘܢ, Gal. v. 4.—1. pl. ܢܦܰܠܢ, Acts xxvi. 14.—Fut. ܢܶܦܶܠ, S. Matt. xxi. 44, &c.: ch. v. 29, 30, Gr. βληθῇ:—Fem. ܬܶܦܶܠ (for ܬܶܦܶܠܝ), S. Matt. xxi. 44.—2. sing. ܬܶܦܶܠ, S. Matt. iv. 9:—ch. v. 25, Gr. βληθήσῃ, —ch. xviii. 8, 9; S. Mark ix. 45, 47, Gr. βληθῆναι.—3. pl. ܢܶܦܠܘܢ, S. Matt. xxiv. 29, &c.—2. pl. ܬܶܦܠܘܢ, 2 S. Pet. iii. 17.—1. pl. ܢܶܦܶܠ, Hebr. ii. 1.—Imperat. ܦܶܠ, Gr. βλήθητι, S. Matt. xxi. 21: S. Mark xi. 23.—Pl. ܦܶܠܘ, S. Luke xxiii. 30.—Inf. ܡܶܦܰܠ, Rom. ix. 6; ܡܶܦܦܰܠ, Hebr. x. 31.—Part. ܢܦܶܠ, S. Matt. xii. 11, &c.: and often in a passive sense, as S. John xii. 6, Gr. τὰ βαλλό- μενα,—S. Matt. iii. 10, Gr. βάλλεται.—Fem. ܢܦܶܠܐ, S. John xii. 24; S. Matt. x. 29.—Pl. masc. ܢܦܠܝܢ, S. Matt. xv. 14, &c. Heb. נָפַל, Ps. v. 11, &c.—Chald. נְפַל, Dan. ii. 46, &c.

— ܒܶܝܬ ܐܰܣܝܪ̈ܶܐ, *into prison;* lit. *house of the bound*—Gr. εἰς τὴν φυλακήν —The prep. ܒ is understood, or coalesces with ܒܶܝܬ. See note, ch. ii. 16.—For ܐܰܣܝܪ̈ܶܐ, see note, ch. xi. 44, below.

25. ܗܘܳܐ ܗܘܳܐ, *there had been*—Gr. ἐγένετο, E.V. *there arose*—Pluperf. of ܗܘܳܐ, formed by the pret. added to its own pret.—Fem. gender, agreeing with the following noun.

— ܫܽܘܐܳܠܐ, *a question*—ζήτησις—Def. of ܫܽܘܐܳܠ, noun fem. *Debate, dispute.* See Phillips, Gr. § 20. Ex. 9: Cowper, § 162, 163 (8). R. ܫܐܠ, *sought, asked.*

Other nouns of this form, derived from verbs ܠ, and occurring in the Gospels, are ܣܘܢܒܐ, ܚܢܳܢܐ, ܟܢܳܢܐ, ܨܠܳܘܐ; and are occa- sionally found pointed ܚܢܳܢܐ, ܒܢܳܝܐ, &c. The pointing in the text is however to be preferred.

26. ܣܰܓ݁ܝ̈ܐܶܐ, *many*—Gr. πάντες.

Ver. 27. ܡܢ ܨܒܘܬ ܢܦܫܗ, *of himself*—(not expressed in the Gr.)—ܨܒܘܬ, constr. of ܨܒܘ, Gr. πρᾶγμα, see note, S. Matt. xviii. 19. —The same phrase occurs, S. John v. 19; vii. 17; xi. 51:—Gr. ἀφ' ἑαυτοῦ, ἀπ' ἐμαυτοῦ.

— ܐܠܐ ܐܢ, *except*, lit. *but if*—ἐὰν μή.

28. ܫܠܝܚܐ ܐܢܐ, *I am sent*—ἀπεσταλμένος εἰμί—Part. Peil def. of ܫܠܝܚ, *Sent;* forming with the pronoun, passive pres. 1. sing. For the verb, see note, ch. v. 36, below.

— ܕܩܕܡܘܗܝ, *before Him*—ἔμπροσθεν ἐκείνου—See note, ch. i. 15.—The rel. ܕ is pleonastic—lit. *One that is before Him.*

29. ܟܠܬܐ, *the bride*—τὴν νύμφην—Noun fem. *A bride*, also *a daughter-in-law*, S. Matt. x. 35; S. Luke xii. 53.

Heb. כַּלָּה, *bride*, Song of Sol. iv. 8, &c. *Daughter-in-law*, Ruth i. 6. R. כָּלַל, *completed, crowned with a chaplet.*

— ܪܚܡܗ, *the friend* (aff. pleon.)—ὁ φίλος—Part. of ܪܚܡ, *Loved dearly* (see note, ch. v. 20, below). Def. ܪܚܡܐ (S. Matt. xi. 19, &c.), used in this form as a noun, *A friend.*—Pl. def. ܪ̈ܚܡܐ, S. Luke xvi. 9; xxiii. 12.—Pl. fem. def. ܪ̈ܚܡܬܐ, with aff. S. Luke xv. 9.

— ܘܨܐܬ, *and hearing*—*and heareth*—καὶ ἀκούων—Part. of ܨܘܬ ܨܬ, *Listened, attended to.* Imperat. pl. ܨܘܬܘ, Acts ii. 14.—Part. pl. ܨܝܬܝܢ, Acts viii. 6.

— ܚܕܘܬܐ, *joy*—Gr. χαρᾷ—Def. of ܚܕܘܐ (Phil. ii. 29; S. James i. 2), noun fem. *Gladness, delight.* With aff. ܚܕܘܬܝ, S. John xv. 11; ܚܕܘܬܗܘܢ, S. Luke xxiv. 41: ܚܕܘܬܟܘܢ, S. John xv. 11; xvi. 22, 24. ܚܕܘܬܗ, S. Matt. xiii. 44.—R. ܚܕܐ, *rejoiced.*

— ܚܕܐ, *rejoicing, rejoiceth*—Gr. χαίρει—Part. of ܚܕܐ or ܚܕܝ (ch. viii. 56), *Was joyful, glad.*—Pret. 3. sing. fem. ܚܕܝܬ, S. Luke i. 47.—1. sing. ܚܕܝܬ, Phil. i. 18, &c.—3. pl. ܚܕܝܘ, S. John xx. 20, &c. —1. pl. ܚܕܝܢ, 2 Cor. vii. 13.—Fut. ܢܚܕܐ, S. John xvi. 20.—3. pl. ܢܚܕܘܢ, ch. iv. 36.—2. pl. ܬܚܕܘܢ, S. Luke x. 20.—1. pl. ܢܚܕܐ, Rev. xix. 7.—Imperat. ܚܕܝ, as ܚܕܝ ܠܟܝ ܘܚܕܝ, a form

Ver. 29. of salutation, 2 S. John ver. 10, and ܚܕܝ alone, ver. 11. Gr. χαίρειν, *God speed you.* Pl. ܚܕܘ, S. Matt. v. 12, &c.: Fem. ܚܕܝܝܢ, S. Luke xv. 9.—Inf. ܠܡܚܕܐ, S. Luke xv. 32.—Part. pl. masc. ܚܕܝܢ, S. Luke i. 58; S. John xiv. 28, ed. Regia,—the Vienna and others have ܚܕܐ ܗܘܝܬܘܢ.—Coalescing with ܚܢܢ, ܚܕܝܢܢ, 2 Cor. vi. 10.

Deriv. ܚܕܘܬܐ, adj. *Cheerful*, 2 Cor. ix. 7. ܚܕܝܐܝܬ, adv. *Cheerfully, willingly*, Acts xvii. 11, &c.

Heb. חָדָה, Exod. xviii. 9.

— ܡܛܠ, *because of*—διά—Prep. *For the sake of*, ἕνεκεν, S. Matt. v. 10: διά, S. Mark iv. 17; Rom. iv. 25. See note, ch. i. 15.

— ܗܐ ܡܫܠܡܐ, *behold, (it is) fulfilled*—Gr. πεπλήρωται—Pael part. pass. fem. of ܡܠܐ, *Was full.*—Pa. ܡܠܝ (Acts iii. 18), *Filled up, fulfilled, supplied.*—Pret. 3. pl. ܡܠܝܘ, 1 Cor. xvi. 17; 2 Cor. xi. 9. —Fut. ܢܡܠܐ, Gal. v. 3, &c.—1. sing. ܐܡܠܐ, S. Matt. v. 17.— 1. pl. ܢܡܠܐ, S. Matt. iii. 15.—Imperat. pl. ܡܠܘ, S. Matt. xxiii. 32.—Part. ܡܡܠܐ, 1 Cor. xiv. 16, &c. — Pl. masc. ܡܡܠܝܢ, coalescing with ܐܢܬܘܢ, ܡܡܠܝܢܬܘܢ, Gal. vi. 2. — Part. pass. ܡܡܠܝܢ.

Heb. Pi. מִלֵּא, Ps. xx. 5, 6.

30. ܠܗ ܗܘ, *for him*—Gr. ἐκεῖνον—ܗܘ, pleonastic.

— ܘܠܐ ܗܘܐ ܠܡܪܒܐ, *it was necessary to increase*—Gr. δεῖ αὐξάνειν—See note, ver. 7, above.

Inf. (with pref. ܠ) of ܪܒܐ (S. Mark iv. 8), *Grew, multiplied, became great.*—Pret. 3. sing. fem. ܪܒܬ, S. Matt. xiii. 32; S. Luke xiii. 19.—Fut. ܢܪܒܐ, S. Mark iv. 27.—2. pl. ܬܪܒܘܢ, Col. i. 10.— Part. ܪܒܐ, S. Luke i. 80; ii. 40, 52:—Fem. ܪܒܝܐ, Acts vi. 7, &c.—Pl. masc. ܪܒܝܢ, S. Matt. xiii. 30:—Pl. fem. ܪܒܝܢ, ch. vi. 28.

Heb. רָבָה, Gen. i. 22; Ps. cxxxix. 18.—Chald. רְבָה, Dan. iv. 8, 19.

Ver. 30. ܠܡܒܨܪܘ, *to decrease*—ἐλαττοῦσθαι—Inf. (pref. ܠ) of ܒܨܪ, *Diminished, became less.* Pa. ܒܨܪ, *Made inferior, was inferior, was deficient in.* Pret. 1. sing. ܒܨܪܬ, 2 Cor. xi. 5; xii. 11.—2. pl. ܒܨܪܬܘܢ, 1 Cor. xvi. 17; Phil. ii. 30.—Fut. ܢܒܨܪ, Rev. xxii. 19.

Ethpa. ܐܬܒܨܪ, *Lacked, was behind, inferior,* 2 Cor. viii. 15.—Pret. 2. pl. ܐܬܒܨܪܬܘܢ, 1 Cor. i. 7; 2 Cor. xii. 13.

Heb. בָּצַר, *cut off, away,* Ps. lxxvi. 13.

31. ܡܢ ܠܥܠ, *from above*—ἄνωθεν—See note, ch. ii. 7.

ܠܥܠ, preceded by ܡܢ is an adverb, and admits no following noun. ܠܥܠ followed by ܡܢ is a preposition, and requires to be followed by a noun or its equivalent, as in this verse, ܠܥܠ ܡܢ ܟܠ, *above all*—ἐπάνω πάντων—See S. Matt. ii. 9; xxiii. 18, 20; S. Luke xxiii. 38; xxiv. 4.

33. ܚܬܡ, *he hath sealed, set to his seal*—ἐσφράγισεν—Verb pret. 3. sing. *Sealed, confirmed.* Pret. 3. pl. ܚܬܡܘ, S. Matt. xxvii. 66.—Fut. ܢܚܬܘܡ, 2. sing. ܬܚܬܘܡ, Rev. xxii. 10.—1. pl. ܢܚܬܘܡ, Rev. vii. 3.—Imperat. ܚܬܘܡ, Rev. x. 4.—Part. Peil ܚܬܝܡ, pl. masc. def. ܚܬܝܡܐ, Rev. vii. 4, 5.

Ethpeel ܐܬܚܬܡ, *Was signed.* Pret. 3. pl. ܐܬܚܬܡܘ, Rev. vii. 4.—2. pl. ܐܬܚܬܡܬܘܢ, Eph. iv. 30. Pael ܚܬܡ, *Signed, sealed*—Pret. 1. sing. ܚܬܡܬ, Rom. xv. 28.—Whence is derived ܚܬܡܐ or ܚܬܡܐ, noun masc. def. *A sign, seal,* Rom. iv. 11: 1 Cor. ix. 2, &c.—Pl. def. ܚܬܡܐ or ܚܬܡܐ, Rev. v. 5, 9.

Heb. חָתַם, *sealed,* 1 Kings xxi. 8.—חוֹתָם, *a signet,* Jerem. xxii. 24 and חֹתֶמֶת, Gen. xxxviii. 25.—Chald. חֲתַם, Dan. vi. 18.

— ܫܪܝܪܐ ܗܘ, *is true*—ἀληθής ἐστιν—See note, ver. 6, above.—ܫܪܝܪܐ, def. of ܫܪܝܪ (ch. viii. 26), adj. *True, firm, sound.* Of form part. Peil of ܫܪ ܫܪܪ, *Became strong.*—Fem. ܫܪܝܪܐ, 2 S. Pet. i. 19; 3 S. John, ver. 12. Def. ܫܪܝܪܬܐ, S. John iv. 18; viii. 40.—Pl. masc. ܗܘܘ ܫܪܝܪܝܢ, *be ye firm* in our Lord, Gr. ἔρρωσθε, Acts xv. 29: *firm* in our love, Gr. ἀληθεύοντες, Eph. iv. 15.—Def. ܫܪܝܪܐ,

Ver. 33. S. John iv. 23.—Pl. fem. ܡܿܢܼܝ, Phil. iv. 8.—Def. ܡܿܢܼܝܬܐ, Rev. xv. 3.—Whence is derived ܡܿܢܼܝܘܬܐ, noun fem. def. *Stedfastness*, Col. ii. 5.

Heb. שָׁרִיר, *strong, firm*, only in pl. def. שָׁרִירֵי, Job xl. 16.—שְׁרִירוּת, *hardness* of heart, Ps. lxxxi. 13.

34. ܗܿܘ ܡܠܐ, *the words*—τὰ ῥήματα—See note, ch. i. 1.—Pronoun pleonastic. See Cowper, Gr. § 198 (1).

— ܒܟܝܠܐ, *by measure*—Gr. ἐκ μέτρου—Noun masc. def. (pref. prepos.) *A measure*. Fem. def. form ܟܝܠܬܐ, S. Matt. vii. 2; S. Mark iv. 24; S. Luke vi. 38.—The masc. is especially spoken of a *greater*, and the fem. of a *lesser;* but not always, as in the last place cited.

Root, Heb. כּוּל, *measured*. Syr. Ethpe. and Aph. S. Matt. vii. 2.

Transl. *For it is not by measure that God hath given*, &c.

35. ܟܠ ܡܕܡ, *every thing, all things*—πάντα—Written as one word, ܟܠܡܕܡ, ch. iv. 25.

36. ܠܐ ܡܬܛܦܝܣ, *believing not, believeth not*—Gr. ἀπειθῶν—Part. of ܐܬܛܦܝܣ (Acts xviii. 20; xxi. 14), a verb used only in Ethpeel (and probably identical with ܐܬܦܝܣ, see note, S. Matt. xxvii. 20), *Obeyed, believed, assented to.*—Pret. 3. pl. ܐܬܛܦܝܣܘ, Acts v. 39, &c.—Fem. ܐܬܛܦܝܣܬ, 1 S. Pet. iii. 20.—2. pl. ܐܬܛܦܝܣܬܘܢ, Acts xxvii. 21.— Fut. ܢܬܛܦܝܣ, 3. pl. ܢܬܛܦܝܣܘܢ, Rom. xv. 21.—2. pl. ܬܬܛܦܝܣܘܢ, Gal. v. 7.— Imperat. pl. ܐܬܛܦܝܣܘ, Hebr. xiii. 17.—Inf. ܠܡܬܛܦܣܘ, Acts v. 29.—Part. pl. masc. ܡܬܛܦܝܣܢܐ, S. Luke i. 17; Acts viii. 6, &c.

Deriv. ܡܬܛܦܝܣܢܘܬܐ, noun fem. def. *Obedience;* with ܠܐ, *Disobedience, unbelief*, Rom. xi. 32, &c.

— ܪܘܓܙܗ, *the wrath* (aff. pleon.)—ἡ ὀργή—ܪܘܓܙܐ (S. Matt. iii. 7), def. of ܪܘܓܙ, noun masc. *Anger, indignation, fury*. R. ܪܓܙ, *Was angry*. Heb. רָגַן, Habak. iii. 2.—Chald. רְגַן, Dan. iii. 13.

CHAPTER IV.

Ver. 1. ......ܝܼܕܰܥ ܕܶܝܢ, Transl. *But Jesus knew that the Pharisees heard (or, had heard) that He made many disciples, and baptized more than John.*

2. ܟܰܡ, *Yet, although*—καίτοιγε.

Transl. *Though it was not Jesus Himself (that) baptized, &c.*

3. ܫܒܰܩܳܗ̇, *He left it* (i. e. ܠܺܝܗܽܘܕ, *Judæa;* the affixed pron. pleonastic) —ἀφῆκε—Pret. 3. sing. of ܫܒܰܩ, *Left, reserved; left behind, deserted; repudiated* or *put away* a wife; *dismissed, sent forth; left out, omitted; permitted; pardoned, remitted.* Pret. 3. sing. fem. ܫܶܒܩܰܬ, ver. 28; with aff. ver. 52, below.—2. sing. ܫܒܰܩܬ, Rev. ii. 4, 20; with aff. S. Matt. xxvii. 46; S. Mark. xv. 34.—1. sing. ܫܶܒܩܶܬ, S. Matt. xviii. 32.—3. pl. ܫܒܰܩܘ, S. Matt. iv. 20, 22, &c.—2. pl. ܫܒܰܩܬܽܘܢ, ch. xxiii. 23; S. Mark vii. 8.—1. pl. ܫܒܰܩܢ, S. Matt. xix. 27, &c.—Fut. ܢܶܫܒܽܘܩ, S. Matt. vi. 14, &c. Fem. ܬܶܫܒܽܘܩܝܼܢ, 1 Cor. vii. 13.—1. sing. ܐܶܫܒܽܘܩ, S. Matt. xviii. 21. —3. pl. ܢܶܫܒܩܽܘܢ, S. Luke xix. 44.—2. pl. ܬܶܫܒܩܽܘܢ, S. John xx. 23, &c.; with aff. ch. xvi. 32.—1. pl. ܢܶܫܒܽܘܩ, Acts vi. 2; Hebr. vi. 1.—Imperat. ܫܒܽܘܩ, S. Matt. iii. 15, &c.: Fem. ܫܒܽܘܩܝ, S. Mark vii. 27.—Pl. ܫܒܽܘܩܘ, S. John xi. 44, &c. —Inf. ܠܡܶܫܒܰܩ, S. Matt. ix. 6, &c.—Part. ܫܳܒܶܩ, S. John x. 12, &c.—Pl. masc. ܫܳܒܩܺܝܢ, S. Matt. xxiii. 14; coalescing with ܚܢܰܢ, ܫܳܒܩܺܝܢܰܢ, S. John xi. 48.—Part. Peil ܫܒܺܝܩ, fem. def. ܫܒܺܝܩܬܳܐ, *a divorced* wife, S. Matt. v. 32; S. Luke xvi. 18.—Pl. masc. ܫܒܺܝܩܺܝܢ, *forgiven* sins, S. Matt. ix. 2, 5, &c.

Chald. שְׁבַק, *Left*, Dan. iv. 12, 20, 23.

4. ܡܰܥܒܕܳܐ ܗܘܳܬ ܠܶܗ, *He must needs—fiebat ei* (Schaaf.)—ἔδει αὐτόν— Aphel part. pass. fem. of ܥܒܰܕ, *Did.*—Aph. ܐܰܥܒܶܕ, *Worked, wrought.* Pret. 3. sing. fem. ܐܰܥܒܕܰܬ, 2 Cor. vii. 11.—Part. ܡܰܥܒܶܕ, 1 Cor. ii. 6.—Part. ܡܰܥܒܰܕ. Lit. *it was done to Him.*—Tremellius (who reads ܡܰܥܒܕܳܐ) and others translate *Opus erat ei.*

Ver. 4. Deriv. ܡܷܥܒ݁ܕܳܢܳܐ, noun masc. def. *A worker*, of wrath, Rom. iv. 15. The same as ܥܳܒܽܘܕܳܐ, S. James i. 25.

ܡܷܥܒ݁ܕܳܢܽܘܬ݂ܳܐ or ܡܷܥܒ݁ܕܳܢܘܳܬ݂ܳܐ, noun fem. def. *A working, operation*, Eph. i. 19; iii. 7, &c.

Heb. Hiph. הֶעֱבִיד, *Caused to work*, Exod. i. 13; vi. 5.

— ܕ݁ܢܷܥܒ݁ܰܪ, *that He should go through; lit. should go, pass through*—Gr. διέρχεσθαι.—ܥܰܒ݂, see note, ch. i. 7.

ܢܷܥܒ݁ܰܪ, fut. 3. sing. of ܥܒܰܪ (ch. viii. 59), *Crossed, passed over, passed by, transgressed.*—Pret. 3. sing. fem. ܥܷܒ݂ܪܰܬ݂, Acts xii. 10; 1 Tim. ii. 14.—1. sing. ܥܷܒ݂ܪܷܬ݂, S. Luke xv. 29.—3. pl. ܥܒܰܪܘ, S. Mark vi. 53;—Fem. ܥܒ݂ܰܪܝ̈ (with paragogic), Rev. xxi. 4.—1. pl. ܥܒ݂ܰܪܢ, Acts xxvii. 5.— Fut. 3. sing. fem. ܬܷܥܒ݁ܰܪ, S. Matt. xxiv. 34; S. Luke xxi. 32; without final ܢ, S. Mark xiii. 30; xiv. 35; S. Luke ii. 35; xvi. 17.—2. sing. ܬܷܥܒ݁ܰܪ, Rom. ii. 25.—1. sing. ܐܷܥܒ݁ܰܪ, 2 Cor. i. 16.—3. pl. ܢܷܥܒ݁ܪܽܘܢ, S. Matt. v. 18, &c.: —Fem. ܢܷܥܒ݁ܪ̈ܢ, ch. xxiv. 35, &c.—1. pl. ܢܷܥܒ݁ܰܪ, S. Mark iv. 35; S. Luke viii. 22.—Imperat. ܥܒ݂ܰܪ, S. Luke xvii. 7.—Inf. ܠܡܷܥܒ݁ܰܪ, 1 Thess. iv. 6.—Part. ܥܳܒ݂ܰܪ, S. John ix. 1, &c.;—Fem. ܥܳܒ݂ܪܳܐ, Hebr. vii. 24.—Pl. masc. ܥܳܒ݂ܪ̈ܝܢ, S. Matt. xv. 2, &c.—Constr. ܥܳܒ݂ܪ̈ܰܝ, 1 Tim. i. 10; S. James ii. 9.

Deriv. ܥܒ݂ܳܪ, noun masc. *Transgression*, Gr. παράβασις, Rom. iv. 15; v. 14.

Heb. עָבַר, Ps. viii. 9, &c. &c.

— ܥܰܠ ܒܶܝܬ݂ ܫܳܡܪ̈ܳܝܶܐ, *on the dwelling-place, territory* (lit. *house*) *of the Samaritans*—Gr. διὰ τῆς Σαμαρείας—Compare note, ch. ii. 16.

5. ܩܪܺܝܬ݂ܳܐ, *the field, parcel of ground*—Gr. τοῦ χωρίου—Fem. def. form of ܩܪܳܐ, noun masc. *A city, town, village*, also *a field, district.*—Pl. def. ܩܘܪ̈ܝܳܐ, S. Luke xiv. 21. (So some Editions: the Vienna and most Editions read ܩܘܪ̈ܝܳܐ).—Strictly, part. Peil of ܩܪܳܐ, Heb. קָרָא, i.q. קָרָה, *met, occurred.* Whence,

Heb. קִרְיָה, *A town, city*, Ps. xlviii. 3.—Chald. קִרְיָה or קַרְיָא, def. קִרְיְתָא, Ezr. iv. 10, &c.

Ver. 6. ܡܥܝܢܐ, *the well*—πηγή—Noun fem. (or com.) def. *A well, fountain.* Derived from ܥܝܢ, *an eye.* Pl. def. ܡܥܝ̈ܢܐ, 2 S. Pet. ii. 17.

Heb. מַעְיָן, *A fountain,* Gen. vii. 11; viii. 2. Metaph. *Joy, delight,* Ps. lxxxvii. 7.

Transl. *And there was there the fount of the waters of Jacob.*

— ܠܐܐ ܗܘܐ, *was wearied*—Gr. κεκοπιακώς—Part. Peil (forming imperf. tense) of ܠܐܐ or ܠܐܝ, *Laboured, toiled, was fatigued.*—Pret. 3. sing. fem. ܠܐܝܬ, Rom. xvi. 6, 12.—2. sing. ܠܐܝܬ, Rev. ii. 3.—1. sing. ܠܐܝܬ, 1 Cor. xv. 10; Gal. iv. 11.—3. pl. ܠܐܝܘ, ver. 38, below;—Fem. ܠܐ̈ܝ, Phil. iv. 3: ܠܐ̈ܝܝܢ (with ܝ paragogic), Rom. xvi. 12.—2. pl. ܠܐܝܬܘܢ, ver. 38, below.—1. pl. ܠܐܝܢ, S. Luke v. 5.—Fut. ܢܠܐܐ, Eph. iv. 28.—Inf. ܠܡܠܐܐ, Acts xx. 35.—Part. ܠܐܐ, 1 Cor. xvi. 16; 2 Tim. ii. 6.—Pl. masc. ܠܐܝܢ, coalescing with ܚܢܢ, ܠܐܝܢܢ, 1 Cor. iv. 12.—Pl. fem. ܠܐ̈ܝܢ, S. Matt. vi. 28; S. Luke xii. 27.—Part. Peil pl. masc. ܠܐܝܢ, 1 Thess. ii. 9; v. 12; 1 Tim. v. 17.—Def. ܠܐ̈ܐ, S. Matt. xi. 28.—From this verb is derived

ܠܐܘܬܐ, noun fem. def. *Labour, hardship,* 2 Cor. vi. 5; xi. 23, 27; 2 Thess. iii. 8.

Heb. לָאָה, *Laboured, was wearied,* Gen. xix. 11.

— ܡܢ ܥܡܠܐ ܕܐܘܪܚܐ, *from, by reason of, the fatigue of the way*—Gr. ἐκ τῆς ὁδοιπορίας—ܥܡܠܐ, def. of ܥܡܠ, noun masc. *Toil, labour.*—Pl. def. ܥܡ̈ܠܐ, Rev. xiv. 13.—R. ܥܡܠ, *Laboured.*

Heb. עָמָל, *Labour, weariness,* Ps. lxxiii. 16; xc. 10.

— ܘܝܬܒ ܗܘܐ ܠܗ, *and He sat, was sitting*—Gr. ἐκαθίζετο—Pret. with ܗܘܐ, forming usually the pluperfect—here the imperfect.—ܠܗ, pleonastic; see Cowper's Gr. § 198 (6).

— ܫܬ ܫܥܝ̈ܢ, *six hours,* i.e. *the sixth hour*—Gr. ὥρα ἕκτη—See note, ch. i. 39.

Ver. 7. ܠܡܺܐܠܐ܂, *that she might draw—to draw*—ἀντλῆσαι—See note, ch. i. 14.—Fut. 3. sing. fem. with pref. ܕ having the force of the infinitive, or Lat. *ut* with the subjunctive.

— ܗܒܝ, *give*—δός—Imperat. sing. fem. of ܝܗܒ, *Gave.*—See note, ch. i. 12.

Transl. *Give Me water (that) I may drink.*

— ܐܶܫܬܶܐ, *(that) I may drink—to drink*—πιεῖν—Fut. 1. sing. (for inf. or subj. but without ܕ) of ܐܫܬܝ, *Drank.*—This verb in Peal pret. and imperat. always has ܐ prosthetic, as will appear from the following forms, occurring in the N.T.:

Pret. 3. sing. masc. ܐܶܫܬܝ, ver. 12, below; Acts ix. 9:—Fem. ܐܶܫܬܝܰܬ, Hebr. vi. 7 (this is the reading of the Par. and Lond. Polyglotts; the Vienna and many other Editions read ܐܶܫܬܝܰܬ, Aph.).—1. sing. ܐܶܫܬܺܝܬ, with aff. S. Matt. xxvi. 42.—3. pl. ܐܶܫܬܝܘ, S. Mark xiv. 23; Acts ii. 13; 1 Cor. x. 4, &c.—1. pl. ܐܶܫܬܝܢ, S. Luke xiii. 26; ܐܶܫܬܝܢ, as if from ܐܫܬܝ, Acts x. 41; 1 Cor. xii. 13 (where the Par. and Lond. Polyglotts read ܐܶܫܬܝܢ).—Fut. ܢܶܫܬܐ, ver. 13, 14, below; vii. 37, &c.—2. sing. ܬܶܫܬܐ, S. Luke xvii. 8; 1 Tim. v. 23.—1. sing. ܐܶܫܬܐ, here, and ver. 10, &c.—3. pl. ܢܶܫܬܘܢ, S. Mark xvi. 18.—2. pl. ܬܶܫܬܘܢ, S. John vi. 53, &c.—1. pl. ܢܶܫܬܐ, S. Matt. vi. 31, &c.—Imperat. fem. ܐܫܬܝ (some read ܐܫܬܝ), S. Luke xii. 19.—Pl. ܐܫܬܘ, S. Matt. xxvi. 27.—Inf. ܠܡܶܫܬܐ, ver. 9, below.—Part. ܫܳܬܶܐ, S. John vi. 54, 56, &c.—Pl. ܫܳܬܶܝܢ, S. Matt. xxiv. 38, &c.

Heb. שָׁתָה, Gen. ix. 21; xxvii. 25.—Chald. שְׁתָה and שְׁתָא, Dan. v. 1, 2, 23.—Pret. with א prosthetic, ver. 3, 4.

8. ܣܝܒܪܬܐ, *food, meat*—Gr. τροφάς—Noun fem. def. derived from ܣܒܪ in its quadriliteral Pael (Paiel) form ܣܰܝܒܰܪ, *bore, sustained, preserved.*

9. ܗܝ ܐܢܬܬܐ, *that woman, the woman*—ἡ γυνή.—ܗܝ, demonstr. pron. fem.—Pl. ܗܳܢܶܝܢ.

S. JOHN IV. 9—11.

Ver. 9. ......ܐܰܝܟܰܢ, Transl. *How (is it that) Thou art a Jew, and askest of me to drink, who am, &c.*

— ܡܶܬܚܰܫܚܺܝܢ, *traffic, have dealings*—Gr. συγχρῶνται—Ethpaal part. pl. masc. of ܚܫܰܚ, *Was useful, fit for, profitable.*

Ethpa. ܐܶܬܚܰܫܰܚ (Acts xxvii. 3), *Conversed, was familiar with, courteous to, made use of.* Pret. 1. sing. ܐܶܬܚܰܫܚܶܬ, 1 Cor. ix. 15. —3. pl. fem. ܐܶܬܚܰܫܰܚ, Rom. i. 26.—1. pl. ܐܶܬܚܰܫܰܚܢ, 1 Cor. ix. 12; 1 Thess. ii. 5.—Fut. ܢܶܬܚܰܫܚܽܘܢ;—1. sing. ܐܶܬܚܰܫܰܚ, 1 Cor. ix. 18.—Part. ܡܶܬܚܰܫܚܺܝܢ, 1 Cor. x. 30.

10. ܐܶܠܳܐ, *if*—*el*—Conjunction. ܐܶܠܳܐ, *except, unless,* S. Matt. xxiv. 22, &c.

Compare Heb. אִלּוּ, Eccles. vi. 6: Esth. vii. 4.

— ܡܰܘܗܰܒܬܳܐ, *the gift*—τὴν δωρεάν—Def. of ܡܰܘܗܰܒܬܳܐ, noun fem. *A gift, supply.*—Constr. ܡܰܘܗܰܒܬ, by enallage for the abs. or def. form, Acts xxv. 11.—Pl. def. ܡܰܘܗܒ̈ܳܬܳܐ, S. Matt. vii. 11, &c. R. ܝܰܗܒ, *Gave.*

— ܚܰܝܳܐ, *living*—Gr. ζῶν—Pl. masc. def. (agreeing with ܡܰܝܳܐ) of ܚܰܝ (ver. 50) adj. *Alive, living.* Def. ܚܰܝܳܐ, ch. vi. 51, 57, 69, &c.— Fem. ܚܰܝܳܐ, Acts ix. 39, &c. Def. ܚܰܝܬܳܐ, Rom. xii. 1; 1 S. Pet. i. 23.—Pl. masc. ܚܰܝܺܝ̈ܢ, Rev. xix. 20;—coalescing with ܡܰܝ̈ܳܐ, ܚܰܝ̈ܶܐ, Acts xvii. 28, &c.—Pl. fem. def. ܚܰܝ̈ܳܬܳܐ, Acts vii. 38; 1 S. Pet. ii. 5.

Heb. חַי, Gen. xliii. 7; Ps. lviii. 10, &c.—Chald. חַי, def. חַיָּא, pl. חַיִּין, def. חַיַּיָּא, Dan. ii. 30, &c.

11. ܡܳܪܝ, *my lord*—E.V. *Sir*—Κύριε—Noun with affix.—ܡܳܪ, def. ܡܳܪܳܐ (S. Matt. xi. 25), noun masc. *Lord, master*—Employed as a title of respect to a master or stranger, and to Christ Himself, by His Disciples, in His character as Man.—Pl. ܡܳܖ̈ܰܝ, def. ܡܳܖ̈ܰܝܳܐ, constr. ܡܳܖ̈ܰܝ, 2 Cor. i. 24.—From this is derived ܡܳܪܳܢܳܝܳܐ or ܡܳܪܳܢܳܝܳܐ, *the Lord's* Day, Rev. i. 10. ܡܳܪܽܘܬܳܐ, noun fem. def. *Government,* 2 S. Pet. ii. 10; S. Jude ver. 8.—Pl. def. ܡܳܖ̈ܘܳܬܳܐ, Eph. i. 21; Col. i. 16.

W. C.

S. JOHN IV. 11—14.

Ver. 11. ܕܠܳܐ, *something to draw with*—ἄντλημα — Noun masc. def. *A vessel for drawing water.* Occurs here only in the N. T.—R. ܕܠܳܐ, *Drew up, or out.*

— ܒܺܪܳܐ, *the well*—τὸ φρέαρ—Noun fem. def. (ܒܺܪܳܐ݀, Rev. ix. 1, 2), *A well.* Heb. בְּאֵר, *A well*, Gen. xxi. 19, &c. *A pit*, Ps. lv. 24; lxix. 16.

— ܥܰܡܺܝܩܳܐ, *deep*—βαθύ—Fem. of ܥܰܡܺܝܩ, def. ܥܰܡܺܝܩܳܐ, adj. *Deep.*— Pl. fem. def. ܥܰܡܺܝܩܳܬܳܐ, Rev. ii. 24.—R. ܥܡܩ, Pa. ܥܰܡܶܩ, *Made deep.*

Heb. עֹמֶק, Ps. lxiv. 7.—Chald. עֲמִיק, pl. fem. def. עֲמִיקָתָא, Dan. ii. 22.

12. ܠܡܳܐ, Gr. μή;—Interrogative particle, answering to the Lat. *Num, ne forte?*—Also, *An*, as in ver. 29, Gr. μήτι οὗτός ἐστιν ὁ Χριστός; which Prof. Scholefield would translate *Is this the Christ?*; and ver. 33, Gr. μήτις, *hath any man?* See also S. Mark ii. 19.—Also Lat. *Ne*, as in S. Matt. viii. 4. Used also in the direct question, *Why, for what purpose?* S. Luke xiii. 9.

— ܥܳܢܶܗ, *his cattle*—τὰ θρέμματα αὐτοῦ—Noun pl. with affix.—ܥܳܢܐ, a collective noun of com. gender, *Sheep, cattle, a flock*, S. John x. 1, and frequently throughout the chapter. It is always marked with Ribui, but is singular (as in ch. x. 16), as well as pl. in signification.

Heb. צֹאן, Gen. iv. 2, &c.

13. ܢܶܨܗܶܐ, *shall thirst*—διψήσει—Fut. 3. sing. of ܨܗܶܐ, *Was thirsty.*—Pret. 1. sing. ܨܗܺܝܬ, S. Matt. xxv. 35, 42.—Fut. 1. sing. ܐܶܨܗܶܐ, ver. 15, below.—3. pl. ܢܶܨܗܽܘܢ, Rev. vii. 16.—Part. Peil ܨܗܶܐ, S. John xix. 28; S. Matt. xxv. 37.—Def. ܨܗܝܳܐ, S. Matt. xxv. 44.—Pl. masc. ܨܗܰܝܳܐ, S. Matt. v. 6; coalescing with ܠܢ, ܨܗܰܝܢ, 1 Cor. iv. 11.

Deriv. ܨܶܗܝܳܐ, noun masc. def. *Thirst*, 2 Cor. xi. 27.

14. ܕܡܰܝܳܐ ܕܢܳܒܥܺܝܢ, *of water, springing up*—Gr. ὕδατος ἁλλομένου—Part. pl. masc. of ܢܒܰܥ, *Bubbled forth.* Occurs in Peal here only in the N. T.

Heb. נָבַע, Prov. xviii. 4.

S. JOHN IV. 15—20. 91

Ver. 15. ܕܳܠܷܐ, *drawing, to draw*—Gr. ἀντλεῖν—Part. fem. of ܕܠܳܐ, *Drew up, drew out.*—Part. ܕܠܳܐ, S. Luke xiv. 5.—Occurs not elsewhere in the N. T.

Heb. דָּלָה, Exod. ii. 16, 19.

— ܡܶܢ ܗܳܪܟܳܐ, *from hence*— Compound adverb.—So ܠܗܳܪܟܳܐ (ver. 16), *hither.*

ܗܳܪܟܳܐ (S. Matt. xii. 6, 42, &c.), adv. *Here, in this very place*—Comp. of ܟܳܐ + ܗܳܪ. ܗܳܪ is a particle of emphasis (by some regarded as the same with ܗܳܐ, *behold*); added to ܟܳܐ, *here*, and ܬܰܡܳܢ, *there*, S. Mark xiii. 21.

Transl. *Give me of these waters, that I thirst not again, neither come to draw from hence.*

16. ܙܶܠܝ, *go*—ὕπαγε—Imperat. fem. of ܐܙܰܠ, *Went.* See note, ch. i. 37.

— ܠܒܰܥܠܶܟܝ, *thy husband*—τὸν ἄνδρα σου—Noun with aff. 2. sing. fem. and pref. ܠ of the object. ܒܰܥܠܳܐ, def. ܒܰܥܠܳܐ (ver. 17, below), noun masc. *Lord, master, husband.* The abs. form occurs only in conjunction (often united) with other words, as ܒܥܶܠܕܒܳܒܳܐ, *enemy,* S. Matt. v. 43; ܒܥܶܠܕܺܝܢܳܐ, *adversary,* S. Matt. v. 25; ܒܥܶܠܕܒܳܒܘܽܬܳܐ, S. Luke xxiii. 12. See notes in these places respectively.—Pl. ܒܰܥܠܶܐ, ver. 18, below.

Heb. בַּעַל, *Lord,* Isa. xvi. 8; *Husband,* Exod. xxi. 3.

17. ܫܰܦܺܝܪ, *rightly, well*—καλῶς—Adj. *Right, handsome, goodly,* here used adverbially. Def. ܫܰܦܺܝܪܳܐ, S. Matt. xxvi. 10; S. Mark xiv. 6.—Fem. ܫܰܦܺܝܪܳܐ, S. Mark vii. 27; ix. 50: Def. ܫܰܦܺܝܪܬܳܐ, S. Luke viii. 8.—Pl. masc. ܫܰܦܺܝܪܶܐ, def. ܫܰܦܺܝܪܶܐ, S. John x. 32, 33, &c. —Pl. fem. ܫܰܦܺܝܪܳܢ, Hebr. vi. 9.—Def. ܫܰܦܺܝܪܳܬܳܐ, S. Luke xxi. 5. —R. ܫܦܰܪ, *Was elegant.*

Chald. שַׁפִּיר, *Fair, beautiful,* Dan. iv. 9, 18.

18. ܚܰܡܫܳܐ, *five*—πέντε—Cardinal numb. masc.—Fem. ܚܰܡܫܳܐ, ch. vi. 9. Heb. חֲמִשָּׁה, masc. Exod. xxi. 37.

20. ܛܽܘܪܳܐ, *mountain*— Gr. τῷ ὄρει—Def. of ܛܽܘܪ (S. Matt. xxvi. 30;

S. JOHN IV. 20—23.

Ver. 20.   S. Mark xiv. 26), noun masc. *A mountain, rock.*—Pl. def. ܛܘܼܪܹ̈ܐ,
S. Mark v. 5, &c.

Heb. צוּר, *Rock*, Ps. xviii. 3.—Chald. טוּר, *Mountain*, Dan.
ii. 35.—Def. טוּרָא, ver. 45.

— ܣܓܸܕܘ, *worshipped*—προσεκύνησαν—Pret. 3. pl. of ܣܓܸܕ (ch. ix. 38),
Adored, worshipped. Pret. 3. sing. fem. ܣܸܓܕܲܬ̤, S. Matt. xv. 25,
&c.—3. pl. fem. ܣܓܸܕܹ̈ܝܢ, S. Matt. xxviii. 9.—Fut. ܢܸܣܓܘܼܕ,
1 Cor. xiv. 25.—2. sing. ܬܸܣܓܘܼܕ, S. Matt. iv. 9, 10, &c.—1. sing.
ܐܸܣܓܘܼܕ, S. Matt. ii. 8.—3. pl. ܢܸܣܓܕܘܼܢ, ver. 23, 24, below.—
2. pl. ܬܸܣܓܕܘܼܢ, ver. 21, below.—Imperat. ܣܓܘܼܕ, Rev. xxii. 9.
—Pl. ܣܓܘܼܕܘ, ch. xiv. 7; xix. 10.—Inf. ܠܡܸܣܓܲܕ, in this
verse; ch. xii. 20; S. Matt. ii. 2.—Part. ܣܓܸܕ, pl. masc. ܣܓܕܝܼܢ,
ver. 22, 24, below;—coalescing with ܚܢܲܢ, ܣܓܕܝܼܢܲܢ, ver. 22,
below.

Heb. סָגַד, *Worshipped idols*, Isa. xliv. 15, 17, 19; xlvi. 6.—
Chald. סְגִד, with לְ of the object, Dan. ii. 46.—Fut. יִסְגֻד,
ch. iii. 5, 6, &c.

22. ...... ܐܲܢ̄ܬܘܢ, Transl. *Ye worship what (something) ye know not; but
we worship that which we know.*

— ܠܡܸܕܸܡ, *that which, what*—ܡܵܐ ܕ, relative, with pref. ܠ of the
object.

23. ܐܸܡܲܬܝ ܕ, *when*—ὅτε—Adverb of time. When not followed by ܕ, it
is interrogative *When?* Gr. πότε;—ch. vi. 25.—Other combina-
tions are ܥܕܲܡܵܐ ܠܐܸܡܲܬܝ, *how long?*, S. Matt. xvii. 17, &c.—ܟܠ
ܐܸܡܲܬܝ ܕ, *as often as*, S. Mark v. 4.

ܣܵܓܘܿܕܹ̈ܐ, *the worshippers*—οἱ προσκυνηταί—Pl. def. of ܣܵܓܘܿܕܵܐ, def.
ܣܵܓܘܿܕܵܐ, noun masc. *A worshipper.*—Occurs in this verse only in
the N. T.—R. ܣܓܸܕ, *Worshipped*.

— .... ܐܲܒܵܐ ܓܹܝܪ, Transl. *For indeed the Father seeketh worshippers such
as these.*

ܗܘ, pleonastic; Cowper's Gr. § 198 (1).

Ver. 25. ܡܠܦ, *teaching: He will teach, tell*—ἀναγγελεῖ—For ܡܐܠܦ, Pael part. of ܐܠܦ, for which ܝܠܦ is in common use (see note, ch. vi. 45, below), *Learned.*

Pa. ܐܠܦ, *Taught*, S. Luke xi. 1:—with affix, S. John viii. 28. —Pret. 2. sing. ܐܠܦܬ, S. Luke xiii. 26.—1. sing ܐܠܦܬ, S. John xviii. 20.—Fut. ܢܐܠܦ, ch. vii. 35; or ܢܠܦ, S. Matt. v. 19; with aff. S. John xiv. 26.—1. sing. ܐܠܦ, Acts xx. 20.—3. pl. ܢܠܦܘܢ, Acts iv. 18.—2. pl. ܬܠܦܘܢ, ch. v. 28.—Imperat. ܐܠܦ, 1 Tim. iv. 11, &c.:—with aff. S. Luke xi. 1.—Pl. ܐܠܦܘ, S. Matt. xxviii. 20.—Inf. ܠܡܠܦܘ, S. Matt. xi. 1, &c.—Part. fem. ܡܠܦܐ, Rev. ii. 20.—Pl. masc. ܡܠܦܝܢ, S. Matt. xv. 9, &c.:—coalescing with ܚܢܢ, ܡܠܦܝܢܢ, Col. i. 28.—Constr. ܡܠܦܝ, S. Luke v. 17.—Pl. fem. ܡܠܦܢ, Tit. ii. 3.—Part. pass. ܡܠܦ, fem. ܡܠܦܐ, S. Matt. xiv. 8.—Pl. masc. def. ܡܠܦܐ, ch. vi. 45, below.

Heb. אָלַף, *Learned*, once, Prov. xxii. 25.—Pi. אִלֵּף, *Taught*, Job xv. 5, &c.

28. ܩܘܠܬܗ, *her waterpot*—τὴν ὑδρίαν αὐτῆς—ܩܘܠܬܐ, noun fem. def. with aff. 3. sing. fem. Occurs here only.

29. ܟܠ ܡܕܡ ܕ, *all things that, everything that*—Gr. πάντα ὅσα—See note, ch. i. 3 (ܡܕܡ).

— ܗܘܝܘ, *he is—this is,—is this?*—οὗτός ἐστιν—For ܗܘ ܗܘ, the second ܗ changed for ܝ moveable.

31. ܒܝܢܬ ܗܠܝܢ, *in the midst of these things,—in the meanwhile*—Gr. ἐν τῷ μεταξύ—See note, ch. i. 26.

— ܐܟܘܠ, *eat*—φάγε—Imperat. of ܐܟܠ or ܐܟܠ (S. Luke iv. 2), *Ate.* —Fut. ܢܐܟܘܠ, S. Matt. xv. 20; S. Luke vii. 36.—2. sing. ܬܐܟܘܠ, S. Matt. xxvi. 17.—1. sing. ܐܟܘܠ, S. Luke xvii. 8.—1. pl. ܢܐܟܘܠ, ch. xxii. 8.—Imperat. pl. ܐܟܘܠܘ, S. Luke x. 8.—Inf. ܠܡܐܟܠ, S. John xxi. 5, &c.

Ver. 31.   Aph. ܐܰܟ݂ܶܬ݂, *Gnawed*, part. pl. masc. ܡܰܟ݂ܕ݁ܟ݂ܺܝܢ, Rev. xvi. 10.   Another reading is ܡܰܟ݂ܕ݁ܟ݂ܺܝܢ, Pa. part.

32. ܡܶܐܟ݂ܽܘܠܬ݁ܳܐ, *food, meat*—βρῶσιν—Noun fem.—With aff. 1. sing., ver. 34.—Another fem. form is ܡܶܐܟ݂ܠܳܐ, Rom. xiv. 17; Col. ii. 16; Hebr. ix. 10.— Pl. def. ܡܶܐܟ݂ܠܳܬ݂ܳܐ, *Meats*, 1 Tim. iv. 3.— R. ܐܶܟ݂ܰܠ, *Ate*.

Compare Heb. מַאֲכָל, masc. *Food*, Gen. ii. 9:—מַאֲכֶלֶת, fem. *food for fire*, Isa. ix. 4, 18: and by contraction מַכֹּלֶת, 1 Kings v. 25.

—   ܕ݁ܐܰܝܢܳܐ, *such as, that*—ἥν—Relat. pron. fem.

34.   ܕ݁ܺܝܠܝ݂. The possessive pron. ܕ݁ܺܝܠ (see note, ch. i. 11), with its affixes, gives peculiar energy to the noun to which it refers: more especially when, as here, the affix is likewise added to the noun. So ܕ݁ܺܝܠܝ݂ ܡܶܠܰܝ̈, *to My words*, ch. v. 47.—See also S. Mark ii. 18.

—   ܘܶܐܫܰܠܶܡ, *and that I should finish, and to finish* (affix pleon.) —καὶ τελειώσω—Supply ܕ݁ from ܕ݁ܶܐܥܒ݁ܶܕ݂ in the preceding clause, as ἵνα in the Greek.—The first vowel remitted to ܳܐ.

Pael fut. 1. sing. of ܫܠܶܡ or ܫܠܰܡ, *Completed*.—Pa. ܫܰܠܶܡ (S. Matt. vii. 28), *Finished, completed, perfected, bid farewell*.— Pret. 1. sing. ܫܰܠܡܶܬ݂, with aff. S. John xvii. 4.—3. pl. ܫܰܠܶܡܘ, S. Luke ii. 39.—Fut. ܢܫܰܠܶܡ, S. Matt. xvii. 11.—2. sing. ܬ݁ܫܰܠܶܡ, S. Matt. v. 33.—1. sing. ܐܶܫܰܠܶܡ, S. Luke ix. 61.—3. pl. ܢܫܰܠܡܽܘܢ, Rev. xi. 7.—2. pl. ܬ݁ܫܰܠܡܽܘܢ, S. Matt. x. 23.—Imperat. ܫܰܠܶܡ, 2 Tim. iv. 5.—Pl. ܫܰܠܶܡܘ, 2 Cor. viii. 11.—Inf. ܠܰܡܫܰܠܳܡܽܘ, S. Luke xiv. 29, 30.—Part. ܡܫܰܠܶܡ, Acts xiii. 25.—Pl. masc. ܡܫܰܠܡܺܝܢ, Gal. iii. 3; Hebr. ix. 6.— Part. pass. ܡܫܰܠܰܡ, S. John xix. 30; 1 S. John ii. 5.

From this conjugation is derived ܡܫܰܠܡܳܢܳܐ, adj. *Perfect*, 2 Tim. iii. 17.

Heb. Pi. שִׁלֵּם, *Finished*, 1 Kings ix. 25: *Made secure*, Job viii. 6:—*Restored, paid back*, Ps. xxxvii. 21. *Requited, recompensed*, Ps. lxii. 13.

S. JOHN IV. 35, 36.

Ver. 35. ܐܲܪܒܥܵܐ, *four*—Card. numb. masc.—Fem. ܐܲܪܒܲܥ, S. Luke ii. 37.

— ܝܲܪ̈ܚܹܐ, *months*—Pl. of ܝܲܪܚܵܐ, noun masc. *A month*. Def. ܝܲܪܚܵܐ, S. Luke i. 26, 36.—Pl. def. ܝܲܪ̈ܚܹܐ, S. Luke i. 24.

  Heb. יֶרַח, Exod. ii. 2.—Chald. יְרַח, pl. יַרְחִין, Dan. iv. 26; Ezr. vi. 15.

— ܚܨܵܕܵܐ, *the harvest*—ὁ θερισμός—Noun masc. def.—With aff. S. Matt. ix. 38; S. Luke x. 2.—R. ܚܨܲܕ, *Reaped*.

  Transl. *Say ye not, that after four months cometh the harvest?*

— ܕܲܚܘܲܪ̈ܝ, *that they have become white, are white*—ὅτι λευκαί εἰσι—Pret. 3. pl. (pref. conjunct. ܕ with ' before a vowelless consonant) of ܚܘܲܪ, *Was or became white*.

  Pael ܚܲܘܲܪ, *Made white*.—Pret. 3. pl. ܚܲܘܲܪ̈ܘ, Rev. vii. 14.— Part. pass. ܡܚܲܘܲܪ, fem. def. ܡܚܲܘܲܪܬܵܐ, *whited* wall, Acts xxiii. 3.

  Heb. חָוַר, once, Isa. xxix. 22.

— ܘܡܲܛܝܼܘ, *and have arrived, reached*—Pael pret. 3. pl. (pref. ܘ) of ܡܛܵܐ, *Came, found*.

  Pa. ܡܲܛܝܼ (S. Luke xix. 29, &c.) the same as Peal in meaning.—Pret. 2. pl. ܡܲܛܝܼܬܘܿܢ, Hebr. xii. 4.—1. pl. ܡܲܛܝܼܢ, Acts xxi. 3, &c.—Fut. ܢܡܲܛܸܐ, 1. sing. ܐܹܡܲܛܸܐ, Phil. iii. 11.—Part. ܡܡܲܛܝܵܐ, Acts ix. 3; xxii. 6.—Pl. masc. ܡܡܲܛܹܝܢ, ch. xxvii. 13.

  Ethpaal ܐܸܬܡܲܛܝܼ, *Reached*. Part. pl. ܡܸܬܡܲܛܹܝܢ, *coalescing* with ܣܢܝ, ܣܢܲܝܡܸܬܡܲܛܹܝܢ, 2 Cor. x. 14.

  Transl. *That they are white, and have arrived at harvest already.*

36. ܕܚܵܨܸܕ, *that reapeth*—Gr. θερίζων—Part. (pref. rel. ܕ) of ܚܨܲܕ, *Reaped*. —Pret. 3. pl. ܚܨܲܕ̈ܘ, S. James v. 4.—Fut. ܢܸܚܨܘܿܕ, 2 Cor. ix. 6; Gal. vi. 8.—Inf. ܠܡܸܚܨܲܕ, ver. 38, below.—Part. pl. masc. ܚܵܨܘܿܕܹܐ, S. Matt. vi. 26; S. Luke xii. 24.

  Ethpeel ܐܸܬܚܨܸܕ (or Ethpa. ܐܸܬܚܲܨܲܕ), *Was reaped*.—Pret. 3. sing. fem. ܐܸܬܚܲܨܕܲܬ, Rev. xiv. 16.

— ܐܲܓܪܵܐ, *wages*—μισθόν—Noun masc. *Wages, reward*. R. ܐܓܲܪ, *Trafficked*.

Ver. 36. ܟܳܢܶܫ, *and gathering, gathereth*—καὶ συνάγει—Part. (with pref. ܘ) of ܟܢܫ (S. Luke v. 1), *Congregated, collected together, resorted, heaped together.* Pret. 3. sing. fem. ܟܶܢܫܰܬ, Acts xiii. 44.—3. pl. ܟܢܰܫܘ, S. Mark vii. 1:—Fem. ܟܢܰܫܝ̈, Acts ix. 39.—Fut. ܢܶܟܢܽܘܫ.—Part. fem. ܟܳܢܫܳܐ, S. Matt. xxiii. 37; S. Luke xiii. 34.—Part. Peil ܟܢܺܝܫ (actively), S. Luke xiv. 2:—Fem. ܟܢܺܝܫܳܐ, S. Mark i. 33.—Pl. masc. ܟܢܺܝܫܺܝܢ, S. Matt. xviii. 20, &c.—coalescing with ܥܰܡ, ܟܢܺܝܫܺܝܢܰܢ, Acts xv. 25.—Pl. fem. ܟܢܺܝܫܳܢ̈, Acts xvi. 13.—From this is derived ܟܢܽܘܫܬܳܐ, noun masc. def. *An assembly, gathering together*, Acts xix. 39, &c.—Pl. (of fem. form) ܟܢܽܘܫܳܬ̈ܳܐ, Acts xxii. 19.—There is also a pl. masc. def. ܟܢܽܘܫܬܢܳܐ, not occurring in the N. T.

Heb. כָּנַס, Ps. xxxiii. 7.—Chald. כְּנַשׁ, inf. לְמִכְנַשׁ, *to assemble*, Dan. iii. 2.

— ܦܺܐܪܳܐ, *fruits, fruit*—Gr. καρπόν—Pl. def. of ܦܺܐܪܳܐ (S. Mark iv. 28, 29; S. Luke i. 42), noun masc. def. *Produce, fruit, of the earth or trees.* Pl. ܦܺܐܪ̈ܰܝ, 1 Cor. xiv. 14.—R. ܦܪܳܐ, Aph. ܐܰܦܪܺܝ, *Made fertile, produced fruit.*

Heb. פְּרִי, Gen. i. 11, 12.—R. פָּרָה, Gen. i. 22; Ps. cxxviii. 3.—Cogn. פָּרָא, Hiph. Hos. xiii. 15.

— ܙܳܪܽܘܥܳܐ, *the sower, he that soweth*—Gr. ὁ σπείρων—Noun masc. def. *A sower.*—R. ܙܪܰܥ, *Sowed.*

— ܚܳܨܽܘܕܳܐ, *the reaper, he that reapeth*—Gr. ὁ θερίζων—Noun masc. def. *A reaper.*—Pl. def. ܚܳܨܽܘܕ̈ܶܐ, S. Matt. xiii. 30, 39; S. James v. 4.—R. ܚܨܰܕ, *Reaped.*

— ܐܰܟܚܕܳܐ, *together*—ὁμοῦ—Adverb compounded of ܐܰܝܟ + ܚܰܕ, lit. *as one.* Transl. *And he that soweth and he that reapeth shall rejoice together.*

37. ܐܚܪܺܢܳܐ...ܐܚܪܺܢܳܐ, *one...and another*—ἄλλος...καὶ ἄλλος—See note, ch. i. 35.

Transl. *One is the sower, and another (is) the reaper.*

S. JOHN IV. 37—46.

Ver. 37. ܙܳܪܰܥ, *sowing, soweth*—Gr. ὁ σπείρων—Part. of ܙܪܰܥ (S. Matt. xiii. 4), *Sowed, scattered seed, dispersed.*—Pret. 2. sing. ܙܪܰܥܬ, S. Matt. xiii. 27; xxv. 24; S. Luke xix. 21.—1. sing. ܙܶܪܥܶܬ, S. Matt. xxv. 26; S. Luke xix. 22.—1. pl. ܙܪܰܥܢ, 1 Cor. ix. 11.—Fut. ܢܶܙܪܘܽܥ.—Inf. ܠܡܶܙܪܰܥ, S. Matt. xiii. 3, &c.—Part. pl. ܙܳܪܥܺܝܢ, S. Matt. vi. 26; S. Luke xii. 24.—Part. Peil ܙܪܺܝܥ, fem. ܙܪܺܝܥܳܐ, S. Matt. xiii. 19.—Pl. masc. ܙܪܺܝܥܶܐ, 1 S. Pet. i. 1.—Pl. fem. ܙܪܺܝܥܳܢ, S. James i. 1.

Heb. זָרַע, Gen. xlvii. 23.

42. ܡܚܰܝܳܢܐ, *the Saviour*—(aff. pleon.),—ὁ Σωτήρ—ܡܚܰܝܳܢܳܐ, def. ܡܚܰܝܳܢܳܐ (Acts v. 31), noun masc. *A Saviour, Giver, Preserver of life*. Fem. def. ܡܚܰܝܳܢܺܝܬܳܐ, *the life-giving, quickening*, Spirit, 1 Cor. xv. 45.—Formed from the Aph. part. of ܚܝܳܐ, *Lived*, Aph. ܐܰܚܺܝ, *Caused to live*, part. ܡܰܚܶܐ.

44. ܡܶܬܝܰܩܰܪ, *honoured, is honoured, hath honour*—Gr. τιμὴν ἔχει—Ethpaal part. of ܝܩܰܪ, *Was heavy.* Ethpa. ܐܶܬܝܰܩܰܪ, *Was held in honour.*

45. ܟܠ ܐܳܬܘܳܬܳܐ, *all the signs, wonders*—Gr. πάντα, *all the things.*

46. ܥܒܶܕ, *a servant*—Noun masc.—Def. ܥܰܒܕܳܐ, ch. viii. 34, &c.—Pl. ܥܰܒܕܶܐ, def. ܥܰܒܕܶܐ, ch. xv. 15, &c. R. ܥܒܰܕ, *Did, performed.*

Heb. עָבַד, Gen. ix. 25.—Chald. עֲבַד, Dan. iii. 26; vi. 21; Ezr. v. 11.

— ܥܒܶܕ ܡܰܠܟܳܐ, *A King's minister, courtier, nobleman*—Gr. βασιλικός—Compare עֶבֶד־מֶלֶךְ, *Ebedmelech* the Ethiopian in the court of Zedekiah, Jer. xxxviii. 7.

Transl. *And there was in Capernaum a certain* (ܚܰܕ, *one*) *nobleman, &c.*

— ܗܘܳܐ ܟܪܺܝܗ, *was sick*—ἠσθένει—ܟܪܺܝܗ, adj. *Sick, diseased, weak, infirm.*—Def. ܟܪܺܝܗܳܐ, ch. v. 7.—Fem. ܟܪܺܝܗܬܳܐ, 1 Cor. viii. 7.—Pl. ܟܪܺܝܗܶܐ, S. Luke iv. 40; x. 9.—Def. ܟܪܺܝܗܶܐ, S. John v. 3. Of form part. Peil of ܟܪܰܗ, *Was sick* (Peal not used). Ethpeel ܐܶܬܟܪܰܗ (Rom. iv. 19; Phil. ii. 26, 27), *Was sick, infirm.* Pret. 3. sing. fem. ܐܶܬܟܰܪܗܰܬ, Acts ix. 37.—Part. ܡܶܬܟܪܰܗ, 2 Cor. xi. 29.

W. C.

Ver. 46. Whence also is derived

ܟܽܘܪܗܳܢܳܐ, noun fem. def. *Sickness, weakness, infirmity,* Rom. vi. 19, &c.—Constr. ܟܽܘܪܗܳܢ, Gal. iv. 13.

47. ..... ܗܳܢܳܐ. Transl. *This (man) heard that Jesus was come...and went to Him, and besought Him,* &c.

— ܘܢܰܐܣܶܐ, *and that He would heal, and heal*—καὶ ἰάσηται—Pael fut. 3. sing. of ܐܳܣܺܝ, *Cured,* used only in the form of a participial noun, ܐܳܣܝܳܐ, see note, S. Matt. ix. 12.

Pa. ܐܰܣܺܝ (S. Matt. iv. 24, &c.), *Healed, cured.* Fut. 1. sing. ܐܰܣܶܐ, S. Matt. xiii. 15.—3. pl. ܢܰܐܣܘܽܢ, S. Mark iii. 15.—Imperat. ܐܰܣܳܐ, S. Luke iv. 23.—Pl. ܐܰܣܰܘ, S. Matt. x. 8; S. Luke x. 9.— Inf. ܠܡܰܐܣܳܝܽܘ, S. Matt. x. 1, &c.—Part. ܡܰܐܣܶܐ, S. Matt. iv. 23, &c.—Pl. masc. ܡܰܐܣܶܝܢ, S. Mark vi. 13; S. Luke ix. 6.

— ܠܰܡܡܳܬ, *to die*—ἀποθνῄσκειν—Inf. (with pref. ܠ) of ܡܺܝܬ (ch. viii. 52, 53), *Died, was dead.* This verb preserves ܝ in the preterite, and in its other forms follows the paradigm of verbs ܥܰܠ. See Phillips § 42; Cowper § 120 (4). Pret. 3. sing. fem. ܡܺܝܬܰܬ݀, S. Matt. ix. 18, 24, &c.—1. sing. ܡܺܝܬܶܬ, Rom. vii. 10; Gal. ii. 19. —3. pl. ܡܺܝܬܘ, S. John vi. 49, 58, &c.—2. pl. ܡܺܝܬܬܘܽܢ, Rom. vii. 4, &c.—1. pl. ܡܺܝܬܢ, Rom. vi. 2, 8; vii. 6.—Fut. ܢܡܽܘܬ, S. John vi. 50, &c.—1. sing. ܐܶܡܽܘܬ, Acts xxi. 13; 1 Cor. ix. 15.— 3. pl. ܢܡܽܘܬܘܽܢ, S. Matt. xxvi. 52.—2. pl. ܬܡܽܘܬܘܽܢ, S. John viii. 21, 24.—1. pl. ܢܡܽܘܬ, ch. xi. 16.—Inf. ܠܰܡܡܳܬ, S. Matt. xv. 4; 1 Cor. ix. 15.—Part. ܡܳܐܶܬ, ver. 49, below, &c.:—another form is ܡܳܝܶܬ, with the signification of part. Peil, or a verbal adjective, *Dead,* Hebr. xi. 4.—Fem. ܡܺܝܬܳܐ, S. John xii. 24; S. Mark ix. 44, 46, 48.—Pl. masc. ܡܺܝܬܺܝܢ, 1 Cor. xv. 22:—coalescing with ܢܰܢ, ܡܺܝܬܺܝܢܰܢ, Rom. viii. 36, &c.—Part. Peil (used as a participial noun) ܡܺܝܬܳܐ, Acts xx. 9, &c.—Def. ܡܺܝܬܳܐ, S. John xi. 39, 44; see note, ch. ii. 22, above.

Deriv. ܡܳܝܽܘܬܽܘܬܳܐ, noun fem. def. *Mortality,* with ܠܳܐ, *Immor-*

S. JOHN IV. 47—51.

Ver. 47. *tality*, 1 Cor. xv. 53, 54. ܡܺܝܬܽܘܬܳܐ, noun fem. def. *The dying, mortality*, with aff. 2 Cor. v. 4; aff. pleon. ch. iv. 10.
Heb. מָוֶת, Gen. ii. 17.

48. ܬܶܕܡܪ̈ܳܬܳܐ, *wonders*—τέρατα—Pl. def. of ܬܶܕܡܽܘܪܬܳܐ, noun fem. *A wonder, prodigy*.—Def. ܬܶܕܡܽܘܪܬܳܐ, S. Matt. xxi. 42; S. Mark xii. 11.— Pl. ܬܶܕܡܪ̈ܳܢ.—R. ܕܡܰܪ (in Ethpaal only), *Wondered*.

49. ܚܽܘܬ, *come down*—κατάβηθι—Imperat. of ܢܚܶܬ, *Descended*. See note, ch. i. 32.

— ܛܰܠܝܳܐ, *the child*—τὸ παιδίον—Def. of ܛܠܳܐ (ch. xxi. 18), noun masc. *An infant, child, young man.* With aff. ܛܰܠܝܶܗ, S. Matt. viii. 13: ܛܰܠܝܳܐ, ver. 6, 8: S. Luke vii. 7.—Fem. form ܛܠܺܝܬܳܐ, *A girl, maid, damsel*, Def. ܛܠܺܝܬܳܐ, S. Matt. ix. 24, 25, &c.—Pl. masc. ܛܠܳܝ̈ܶܐ, 1 Cor. xiv. 20, &c.—Def. ܛܠܳܝ̈ܶܐ, S. John xxi. 5.—Pl. fem. ܛܠܳܝ̈ܳܬܳܐ, 1 Tim. v. 2, 11, 14; Tit. ii. 4.—Of form part. Peil of ܛܠܳܐ, *Was fresh, recent*.

Heb. טָלֶה, *A young animal, lamb*, 1 Sam. vii. 9; Isa. lxv. 25. Also טְלִי, the same; Pl. טְלָאִים for טְלָיִים, Isa. xl. 11.

51. ܐܰܪܥܽܘܗܝ, *they met him*—ἀπήντησαν αὐτῷ—Pret. 3. pl. (with aff.) of ܐܪܰܥ, *Met, happened, befel*. Pret. 3. sing. with aff. Acts viii. 27; x. 25.—Pret. 3. fem. ܐܶܪܥܰܬ, with aff. ܐܶܪܥܬܶܗ, S. John xi. 30.— Fut. ܢܰܪܥܽܘܢ, 2. pl. ܬܰܪܥܽܘܢ, Eph. vi. 13.—Inf. ܠܡܶܐܪܰܥ, S. Luke xiv. 31.—Part. ܐܳܪܰܥ, Acts xx. 22.

— ܘܣܰܒܰܪܽܘܗܝ, *and they told him*—Gr. καὶ ἀπήγγειλαν—Pael pret. 3. pl. (with aff.) of ܣܒܰܪ, *Thought, supposed, hoped*.

Pa. ܣܰܒܰܪ (Acts x. 36, &c.), *Announced, brought news; trusted, hoped*, S. John v. 45.—Pret. 3. sing. fem. ܣܰܒܪܰܬ, ch. xx. 18; S. Mark xvi. 10.—1. sing. ܣܰܒܪܶܬ, with aff. 1 Cor. xv. 1, 2; Gal. iv. 13.—2. pl. ܣܰܒܰܪܬܽܘܢ, S. John v. 45.—1. pl. ܣܰܒܰܪܢ, Eph. i. 12. —Fut. ܢܣܰܒܰܪ, with aff. Gal. i. 8.—1. sing. ܐܶܣܰܒܰܪ, Rom. i. 15, &c.—3. pl. ܢܣܰܒܪܽܘܢ, S. Matt. xii. 21; Rom. xv. 12.—2. pl. ܬܣܰܒܪܽܘܢ, 1 S. Pet. ii. 9.—1. pl. ܢܣܰܒܰܪ, Acts xvi. 10.—Imperat.

Ver. 51. ܣܰܒܰܪ, S. Luke ix. 60.—Pl. ܣܰܒܰܪܘ, 1 S. Pet. i. 13.—Inf. ܠܡܣܰܒܳܪܽܘ, S. Luke iv. 18.—Part. ܡܣܰܒܰܪ, S. Luke ii. 10:—Fem. ܡܣܰܒܪܳܐ, Rom. viii. 19.—Pl. masc. ܡܣܰܒܪܻܝܢ, S. John v. 39; S. Luke ix. 6:—coalescing with ܚܢܰܢ, ܡܣܰܒܪܻܝܢܰܢ, Acts xiii. 32, &c.—constr. ܡܣܰܒܪܰܝ, Rom. x. 15.—Pl. fem. ܡܣܰܒܪܳܢ, Acts xxvi. 7; 1 S. Pet. iii. 5.

Heb. Pi. שִׂבֵּר, *Waited for, hoped,* Ruth i. 13; Ps. civ. 27; cxix. 166.

52. ܒܰܐܝܢܳܐ, *in what* (hour, or time)?—Interrog. pron. masc. with prefixed preposition, and ܕ introducing the question.

— ܥܶܕܳܢܳܐ, *time, hour*—Gr. τὴν ὥραν—Def. of ܥܶܕܳܢ, noun masc. *Time, point of time, opportunity.*—ܒܟܽܠ ܥܶܕܳܢ, *at every time, always,* S. Luke xviii. 1, 5. The words are joined, S. John vii. 6.—Constr. ܥܶܕܳܢ ܨܰܦܪܳܐ, *in the time of the morning, early in the morning,* Gr. ὑπὸ τὸν ὄρθρον, Acts v. 21.—Pl. def. ܥܶܕܳܢܶܐ, 1 Thess. v. 1.

Chald. עִדָּן, def. עִדָּנָא, *Time,* and specially *a year.* Pl. עִדָּנִין, Dan. ii. 8; iv. 13; vii. 12, &c.

— ܐܶܬܚܠܺܡ, *he was made whole, became well*—Gr. κομψότερον ἔσχε, *began to amend.*—Ethpeel pret. 3. sing. of ܚܠܰܡ, *Was strong, robust; also Dreamed.*—Fut. ܢܶܚܠܽܘܡ, 3. pl. ܢܶܚܠܡܽܘܢ, Acts ii. 17.

Heb. חָלַם, *Was strong, sound,* Job xxxix. 4. *Dreamed,* Gen. xxxvii. 5, &c.

Ethpe. *Was made whole, convalescent.*—Pret. 3. sing. fem. ܐܶܬܚܰܠܡܰܬ, Rev. xiii. 12.—Fut. ܢܶܬܚܠܶܡ, fem. ܬܶܬܚܠܶܡ, S. Mark v. 23.—2. sing. ܬܶܬܚܠܶܡ, S. John v. 6.—3. pl. ܢܶܬܚܰܠܡܽܘܢ, S. Mark xvi. 18.—Part. ܡܶܬܚܠܶܡ, S. John v. 4.—Pl. masc. ܡܶܬܚܰܠܡܻܝܢ, S. Matt. xv. 31; Acts v. 16.

— ܐܶܬܡܳܠܺܝ, *yesterday*—χθές—Adverb of time.—ܐܶܬܡܳܠ, Hebr. xiii. 8.

Compare Heb. אֶתְמוֹל, Ps. xc. 4; אִתְּמוֹל, 1 Sam. x. 11; אֶתְמוּל, Isa. xxx. 33.—Also תְּמוֹל, Exod. v. 8, 14; Job viii. 9.

— ܫܒܰܥ ܫܳܥܻܝܢ, *at seven hours, at the seventh hour*—ὥραν ἑβδόμην—

S. JOHN IV. 52—54. V. 2.   101

Ver. 52. ܬܪܬܝܢ, card. numb. fem. (for Ordinal). Masc. ܬܪܝܢ, S. Matt. xv.
34. See note, ch. i. 39.

Heb. שֶׁבַע, Gen. v. 7, &c., שִׁבְעָה, masc. Numb. xxiii. 1,
&c.—Chald. שִׁבְעָה, masc. Dan. iii. 19, &c.

— ܐܫܬܐ, *the fever*—ὁ πυρετός—Noun fem. def.—so always pointed, though
the more regular form would seem to be ܐܫܬܐ.
Compare Heb. אֵשׁ, *fire*.

53. ...ܘܝܕܥ, Transl. *And his father knew that* this took place *in that hour
in which* &c.

54. ܐܬܐ ܕܬܪܬܝܢ, *the miracle that (is) two,—the second miracle*—δεύτερον
σημεῖον—See note, ch. iii. 4; and vi. 7, below.

CHAPTER V.

[The common prefixes, as ܒ, ܕ, ܘ, ܘ̇, &c. will not hereafter be noticed,
unless necessary.]

2. ܕܘܟܬܐ, *a place*—Def. of ܕܘܟܐ (ch. x. 1, xx. 7, &c.), noun fem. *A place*.
—ܒܕܘܟܐ ܕܘܟܐ, *in divers places*, S. Matt. xxiv. 7; S. Mark xiii. 8;
S. Luke xxi. 11.—Constr. ܕܘܟܬ, Phil. ii. 16. (Transl. *That ye
may be to them in the place of salvation, to my glory in the day of
Christ.*)—Pl. def. ܕܘܟܝܬܐ, S. John xx. 25; S. Luke xiv. 7.
Masc. abs. form ܕܘܟ, S. Luke ix. 6.

•— ܡܥܡܘܕܝܬܐ, *of washing.*—Gr. κολυμβήθρα—Noun fem. def. *A
washing, baptism, place for washing*. Pl. def. ܡܥܡܕܝܬܐ,
S. Mark vii. 8. R. ܥܡܕ, *Immersed*, Aph. part. ܡܥܡܕ.

— ܘܐܝܬ ܗܘܐ ܒܗ, *and there were (was) in it*—Gr. ἔχουσα, *having*—
ܐܝܬ ܗܘܐ used impersonally, referring to a noun in the plural.
Compare the French *il y a*, and Germ. *es giebt*.
For ܐܝܬ ܠܗܘܢ, see note, S. Luke i. 25.

Ver. 2. ܐܶܣܛܘ̈ܳܢܶܐ, *porches*—στοάς—Pl. of ܐܶܣܛܘܳܐ (ch. x. 23; Acts iii. 11), noun masc. *A porch.* Derived from the Greek word in the text.

3. ܪ̈ܳܡܶܝܢ ܗ̄ܘܰܘ, *were lying, lay*—Gr. κατέκειτο—Part. pl. masc. (forming imperf. tense)—agreeing with ܥܰܡܳܐ, a noun of multitude—of ܪܡܳܐ, *Cast, laid, threw down.* The part. act. (if the word be correctly pointed) is used in the sense of the passive (part. Peil) ܪ̈ܡܶܝܢ ܗ̄ܘܰܘ, compare Acts v. 15. Or the passage may be translated, *And in these (porches) they laid down*, or *used to lay down*, Lat. *dejiciebant.* The use of this verb in Peal is confined to its participles.

Part. act. ܪܳܡܶܐ, S. John xx. 25, &c.—Pl. masc. coalescing with ܚܢܰܢ, ܪܳܡܶܝܢܰܢ, S. James iii. 3.—Part. Peil ܪܡܶܐ, S. John v. 6: xiii. 2.—Fem. ܪܡܝܳܐ, S. Matt. viii. 14, &c.—Pl. masc. ܪ̈ܡܶܝܢ, Acts v. 15.

Ethpeel ܐܶܬ݂ܪܡܺܝ (Rev. viii. 8; xii. 9), *Was cast, cast out; yielded himself to.*—Pret. 3. pl. ܐܶܬ݂ܪܡܺܝܘ, Gal. ii. 13.—1. pl. ܐܶܬ݂ܪܡܺܝܢ, ver. 5.—Fut. ܢܶܬ݂ܪܡܶܐ, fem. ܬܶܬ݂ܪܡܶܐ, Rev. xviii. 21.—3. pl. ܢܶܬ݂ܪܡܽܘܢ, 1 Tim. i. 4; Tit. i. 14.

Pael ܪܰܡܺܝ, *Imposed upon, deceived;* whence ܡܪܰܡܝܳܢܳܐ, noun masc. def. *The deceiver, the Devil*, Gr. ὁ Διάβολος, Rev. xii. 9, 12; xx. 2.

Heb. רָמָה, *Cast, threw*, Exod. xv. 1, 21.—Pi. רִמָּה, *Deceived, beguiled*, Gen. xxix. 25.—Chald. רְמָה, or רְמָא, *Cast*, Dan. iii. 20, 21, 24; vi. 17;—*Set, placed* thrones, ch. vii. 9 (Compare θρόνος ἔκειτο, Rev. iv. 2):—*Imposed* tribute, Ezr. vii. 24.—Ithpe. אִתְרְמָא, *Was cast*, Dan. iii. 6, 15.

— ܥܰܡܳܐ, *a multitude*—πλῆθος—Def. of ܥܰܡ (Rom. x. 19), noun masc. *A people, multitude.*—Pl. ܥܰܡ̈ܡܺܝܢ, def. ܥܰܡ̈ܡܶܐ, *the nations, Gentiles*, S. John xii. 20, &c.

Heb. עַם, *People*, Ps. xviii. 44.—Chald. עַם, pl. עַמְמִין, def. עַמְמַיָּא, Dan. iii. 4, 7, 31; v. 19; vi. 26; vii. 14.—R. Heb. עָמַם, *Gathered, collected together.* In Syr. the second radical has in the plural the *linea occultans.*

S. JOHN V. 3, 4.   103

Ver. 3. ܘܲܣܡܲܝܵܐ, *and the blind*—Gr. τυφλῶν—Pl. def. of ܣܡܵܐ (ch. ix. 2, 19, 20), adj. *Blind.* Form of part. Peil of ܣܡܵܐ, *Was blind.*—Def. ܣܡܲܝܵܐ, ch. ix. 1, 6, &c.

— ܚܓܝܼܣܹܐ, *the halt*—Gr. χωλῶν—Pl. def. of ܚܓܝܼܣ (S. Matt. xviii. 8), adj. *Lame.* Form of part. Peil.—Def. ܚܓܝܼܣܵܐ, S. Mark ix. 45.

The same as ܚܓܝܼܣܵܐ, S. Matt. xi. 5.

— ܝܲܒܝܼܫܹܐ, *the withered*—Gr. ξηρῶν—Pl. def. of ܝܲܒܝܼܫ, adj. *Dry.* Form of part. Peil of ܝܒܫ, *Was dry.*—Def. ܝܲܒܝܼܫܵܐ, S. Luke xxiii. 31.—Fem. ܝܲܒܝܼܫܬܵܐ, S. Matt. xii. 10, &c.—Def. ܝܲܒܝܼܫܬܵܐ, Hebr. xi. 29.

Heb. יָבֵשׁ, *Dry*, Job xiii. 25.—יָבֵשׁ, only in fem. יַבָּשָׁה, *the dry* land, as opposed to sea, Gen. i. 9; Exod. xiv. 16.

— ܘܲܡܣܲܟܹܝܢ ܗܘܘ, *and they were waiting for*—Gr. ἐκδεχομένων—Pael part. pl. (forming imperf. tense) of ܣܟܐ (Peal not used), Pa. ܣܲܟܝܼ, *Waited, awaited, expected, hoped for.*—Pret. 3. pl. ܣܲܟܝܼܘ, Acts xxviii. 6: Hebr. xi. 35.—Fut. ܢܣܲܟܹܐ.—Part. ܡܣܲܟܹܐ, S. Mark xv. 43, &c.:—Fem. ܡܣܲܟܝܵܐ, Rom. viii. 19.—Pl. masc. coalescing with ܠܝܼ, ܡܣܲܟܝܼܢܲܢ, S. Matt. xi. 3; S. Luke vii. 19, 20, &c.: with ܐܲܠܗܐ, 1 Thess. i. 10.

— ܙܵܘܥܵܐ, *the moving*—τὴν κίνησιν—Noun masc. def. *Motion, commotion, a troubling, quaking,* of the earth.—Pl. def. ܙܵܘܥܹܐ, S. Matt. xxiv. 7, &c. R. ܙܥ, ܙܵܥ, *Was agitated, trembled.*

Heb. זְוָעָה, *Terror, vexation*, Isa. xxviii. 19.

•4. ܙܒܲܢ ܘܙܒܲܢ, *from time to time, at a certain season*—Gr. κατὰ καιρόν—See note, ch. iii. 4.

— ܡܙܝܼܥ ܗܘܵܐ, *troubled*—ἐτάρασσε—Aphel part. (forming imperf. tense) of ܙܵܥ, ܙܥ, *Trembled.* Aph. ܐܙܝܼܥ (ch. xi. 33), *Moved, troubled, shook, stirred up;—beckoned with the hand,* Acts xxi. 40.—Pret. 2. sing. ܐܙܝܼܥܬ, Acts xxi. 38.—Fut. ܢܙܝܼܥ, with pref. ܕ and aff. pron. S. Luke vi. 48.—Inf. ܠܡܙܵܥܘ, Acts xvii. 13.

S. JOHN V. 4—7.

Ver. 4. ܡܢ ܒܬܪ, *after*—μετά—Compound preposition. See note, ch. i. 15.

— ܟܐܒܐ, *disease*—Gr. νοσήματι—Def. of ܟܐܒ (S. Matt. iv. 23; x. 1), noun masc. *Sickness, disease, pain; affections, motions to sin.* ܟܐܒ ܡܥܝܐ, *disorder of the bowels, bloody flux,* Gr. δυσεντερία, Acts xxviii. 8.—Pl. ܟܐܒܐ̈, S. Matt. ix. 35.—Def. ܟܐܒܐ, Rom. i. 26; vii. 5; Col. iii. 5.—R. ܟܐܒ, *Was in pain.* Whence also ܟܐܒܢܐ, adj. *Painful,* Rev. xvi. 2.

    Heb. כְּאֵב, *Pain, grief,* Job ii. 13; xvi. 6; Isa. lxv. 14.

Transl. *Every disease he had was healed.*

5. ܬܠܬܝܢ, *thirty*—Numeral, of com. gender.

    Heb. שְׁלֹשִׁים, Gen. v. 16.—Chald. תְּלָתִין, Dan. vi. 8, 13.

— ܬܡܢܐ, *eight* (Thirty and eight, Gr. τριακονταοκτώ)—Card. numeral fem.—Masc. ܬܡܢܝܐ, ch. xx. 26.

    Heb. שְׁמֹנֶה, fem. Judg. iii. 8.

— ܒܟܘܪܗܢܐ, *in the infirmity*—ἐν τῇ ἀσθενείᾳ—Def. of ܟܘܪܗܢ (S. Matt. iv. 23; x. 1), noun masc. *A disease,* affecting the whole body, as ܟܐܒ a part or member only.—Pl. ܟܘܪܗܢܐ̈, S. Matt. ix. 35.—Def. ܟܘܪܗܢܐ, S. Matt. iv. 24, &c.—R. ܟܪܗ, *Was sick.* See note, ch. iv. 46.

6. .... ܠܗܢܐ. Transl. *This (man) Jesus saw lying* (or, *that he was laid*), *and knew that he had long time been thus*—(lit. *that he had long time,* Gr. ὅτι πολὺν ἤδη χρόνον ἔχει)—*and said to him, &c.*

7. ܗܘ ܟܪܝܗܐ, *the impotent man*—ὁ ἀσθενῶν—The demonstr. pron. here represents the Gr. Article.

— ܐܝܢ, *truly, yea, indeed.* Particle of asseveration.

    Transl. *Yea, my Lord, but I have no man, &c.*

— ܕܡܬܬܙܝܥܝܢ, *when they* (sc. ܡܝܐ̈) *have been troubled*—Gr. ὅταν ταραχθῇ (τὸ ὕδωρ)—Ethpeel pret. 3. pl. of ܙܥ ܢܝ, *Was agitated.*

    Peal pret. 2. sing. fem. ܙܥܬܝ (ܙܥܬܝ, Par. and Lond. Polygl.), Acts xii. 15.—Fut. ܢܙܘܥ, 1. sing. ܐܙܘܥ, Acts ii. 25.—Inf. ܡܙܥ, Acts ii. 25.—Part. Peil ܙܝܥ, pl. masc. ܙܝܥܝܢ, 2 S. Pet. ii. 10.

S. JOHN V. 7.

Ver. 7. Ethpe. ܐܬܬܙܝܥ (S. Matt. ii. 3; Acts iv. 31), *Was moved, shaken, troubled.* Pret. 3. sing. fem. ܐܬܬܙܝܥܬ, S. Matt. xxi. 10; xxvii. 51.—Fut. ܬܬܙܝܥ, fem. ܬܬܬܙܝܥ, Hebr. vi. 19.—3. pl. ܢܬܬܙܝܥܘܢ, S. Matt. xxiv. 29, &c.—2. pl. ܬܬܬܙܝܥܘܢ, Acts xx. 10; 2 Thess. ii. 2.—Part. ܡܬܬܙܝܥ, S. Matt. xi. 7; S. Luke vii. 24:— Fem. ܠܐ ܡܬܬܙܝܥܢܝܬܐ, *which cannot be moved*, Gr. ἀσάλευτον, Heb. xii. 28.—Pl. masc. ܡܬܬܙܝܥܝܢ, S. Luke xxiv. 38:—coalescing with ܡܢܝ, ܡܬܬܙܝܥܢܢ, Acts xvii. 28;—with ܐܝܕܐ, ܡܬܬܙܝܥܐ, Col. i. 23.—Pl. fem. ܡܬܬܙܝܥܢ, 1 S. Pet. iii. 6.

Pa. redupl. ܙܥܙܥ, *Disturbed, terrified*, whence Ethpa. ܐܙܕܥܙܥ, *Was disturbed, tossed to and fro.* Part. pl. masc. ܡܙܕܥܙܥܝܢ, Eph. iv. 14.

Heb. זוּעַ, pret. זָע, Esth. v. 9.—Fut. יָזוּעַ, pl. Eccles. xii. 3.—Pi. redupl. זִעֲזַע, part. מְזַעֲזֵעַ, Habak ii. 7.—Chald. זוּעַ, part. pl. זָאֲעִין (Keri זָיְעִין) Dan. v. 19; vi. 27.

— ܕܢܪܡܝܢܝ....ܕ, *that he may put me—to put me—*ἵνα...βάλλῃ με— Aphel fut. 3. sing. (with aff.) of ܪܡܐ, *Cast.*

Aph. ܐܪܡܝ (ch. vii. 30, 44, &c.), *Cast, threw, placed.*—Pret. 3. sing. fem. ܐܪܡܝܬ, S. Matt. xxvi. 12, &c.—1. sing. ܐܪܡܝܬ, Acts xxvi. 10.—3. pl. ܐܪܡܝܘ, S. John xix. 24; xxi. 6, &c.— Fut. ܢܪܡܐ, S. Mark iv. 26.—2. sing. ܬܪܡܐ, S. Matt. xxv. 27.— 1. sing. ܐܪܡܐ, S. Matt. x. 34; S. Luke xii. 49, 51.—3. pl. ܢܪܡܘܢ, S. Matt. xiii. 42, &c.—2. pl. ܬܪܡܘܢ, S. Matt. vii. 6.—1. pl. ܢܪܡܐ, S. Mark vii. 27.—Imperat. ܐܪܡܐ, S. Matt. xvii. 27; S. Luke iv. 9.—Pl. ܐܪܡܘ, S. John xxi. 6.—Inf. ܠܡܪܡܝܐ, S. Matt. xv. 26.

Ethtaphal ܐܬܬܪܡܝ, *Was cast forth*, Rev. xii. 9, &c.—Pret. 3. pl. ܐܬܬܪܡܝܘ, same verse.

— ܥܕ, *While*—Gr. ἐν ᾧ—Conjunction, *Whilst, so long as*, S. Matt. xxvi. 36.—*Until*, 1 Tim. iv. 13:—followed by a pres. tense or participle. Preposition, *During*, as S. John xx. 1; S. Luke xxiv. 1, *During darkness, while yet dark*,—followed by a noun.

Ver. 7. Heb. עַד, conjunct. *While*, 1 Sam. xiv. 19. Prepos. *Unto*, Ps. xlvi. 10.—Chald. עַד, conjunct. followed by דִּי, Dan. iv. 30; vi. 25; vii. 22.—Prepos. Dan. iv. 5, 14; vi. 8, 13; Ezr. v. 16.

8. ܥܰܪܣܳܟ, *thy bed*—τὸν κράββατόν σου—Noun with affix. ܥܰܪܣ, noun fem. *A bed, couch.*—Def. ܥܰܪܣܳܐ, S. Matt. ix. 2, &c.—Pl. def. ܥܰܪ̈ܣܳܬܳܐ, S. Mark vi. 55; vii. 4: Acts v. 15.

Heb. עֶרֶשׂ, *A bed*, Ps. vi. 7.

9. ܒܰܪ ܫܳܥܬܶܗ, lit. *son of his hour:—in that very hour, immediately*—εὐθέως—See note, ch. i. 12.

— ܗܰܘ ܗܽܘ ܝܰܘܡܳܐ, *the same day*, or *on the same day*—Gr. ἐκείνῃ τῇ ἡμέρᾳ—Similarly, in the plur. ܒܗܳܢܽܘܢ ܝܰܘ̈ܡܳܬܳܐ ܗܳܢܽܘܢ, *in those days*, Gr. ἐν ταῖς ἡμέραις ἐκείναις, S. Matt. iii. 1.

Note, that ܗܘܳܬ refers to ܫܰܒܬܳܐ, as in the Gr.

— ܫܰܒܬܳܐ, *the Sabbath*—σάββατον—Def. of ܫܰܒܳܐ (S. John xx. 1, 19, &c.) noun fem. *The week.* The def. state is used to express *the Sabbath day*, everywhere except S. Luke xviii. 12, where it means *a week*:—whereas the abs. form means *a week* everywhere in the Gospels, Acts xx. 7; 1 Cor. xvi. 2.—In Acts xiii. 27; xviii. 4 it is *the Sabbath*.—Pl. ܫܰܒ̈ܰܝܢ, *Sabbaths*, Acts xv. 21.—Def. ܫܰܒ̈ܶܐ, S. Mark i. 21; S. Luke iv. 31; Acts xvii. 2; Col. ii. 16.

Heb. שַׁבָּת, *The Sabbath*, Exod. xx. 8. R. שָׁבַת, *Rested*, see Gen. ii. 2, 3.

10. ܠܗܰܘ ܕܶܐܬܐܰܣܺܝ, *to him that was cured*—τῷ τεθεραπευμένῳ—Ethpaal pret. 3. sing. of ܐܶܣܳܐ, Pa. ܐܰܣܺܝ, *Healed.* Ethpa. *Was cured.*—Pret. 3. sing. fem. ܐܶܬܐܰܣܝܰܬ, S. Matt. ix. 22, &c.—3. pl. ܐܶܬܐܰܣܺܝܘ, S. Matt. xiv. 36;—Fem. ܐܶܬܐܰܣ̈ܝܳܝ, S. Luke viii. 2.—2. pl. ܐܶܬܐܰܣܺܝܬܽܘܢ, 1 S. Pet. ii. 24.—Fut. ܢܶܬܐܰܣܶܐ, S. Matt. viii. 8; S. Luke vii. 7:—Fem. ܬܶܬܐܰܣܶܐ, S. Luke viii. 43.—3. pl. ܢܶܬܐܰܣܽܘܢ, S. Luke vi. 18.—2. pl. ܬܶܬܐܰܣܽܘܢ, S. James v. 16.—Inf. ܠܡܶܬܐܰܣܳܝܽܘ, S. Luke v. 15.—Part. ܡܶܬܐܰܣܶܐ, fem. ܡܶܬܐܰܣܝܳܐ, S. Matt. ix. 21.—Pl. masc. ܡܶܬܐܰܣܶܝܢ, S. Mark vi. 56; S. Luke xiii. 14.

Ver. 10. ܫܠܝܛ, *lawful*—Gr. ἔξεστι—Noun masc. *One who has power, a lord, prince.* So ܫܠܝܛ ܐܢܐ, *I am powerful, I have power*, Gr. ἐξουσίαν ἔχω, ch. x. 18. Also, *Permitted, lawful.*—Def. ܫܠܝܛܐ, *a potentate*, Gr., δυνάστης, Acts viii. 27.—Fem. ܫܠܝܛܐ, 1 Cor. vii. 4.—Pl. masc. ܫܠܝܛܝܢ, S. Matt. xx. 25.—R. ܫܠܛ, *Was powerful.*

Heb. שַׁלִּיט, *A ruler, governor*, Gen. xlii. 6. Chald. שַׁלִּיט, *Powerful*, Dan. ii. 10, &c. *A prince*, ch. ii. 15, &c.—*Empowered*, followed by ל with an infin. Ezr. vii. 24.

11. ܚܠܝܡܐ, *sound, whole*—ὑγιῆ—Def. of ܚܠܝܡ (ver. 14), adj. *Safe, well, sound.*—ܗܘܝ ܚܠܝܡ, *farewell*, Gr. ἔῤῥωσο, Acts xxiii. 30. —Fem. ܚܠܝܡܐ, S. Mark v. 34.—Def. ܚܠܝܡܬܐ, Tit. ii. 7.—Pl. masc. ܚܠܝܡܝܢ, Tit. i. 13; ii. 2.—Def. ܚܠܝ̈ܡܐ, S. Matt. ix. 12; S. Mark ii. 17; S. Luke v. 31.—Pl. fem. def. ܚܠܝ̈ܡܬܐ, 1 Tim. vi. 3; 2 Tim. i. 13.—Form of part. Peil of ܚܠܡ, *Was strong;* whence also ܚܠܝܡܘܬܐ, noun fem. def. *Soundness*, Acts iii. 16.

13. ܐܬܛܫܝ ܗܘܐ, *had concealed Himself, conveyed Himself away*, or simply *departed*—ἐξένευσεν—Ethpeel pret. 3. sing. (forming pluperf. tense) of ܛܫܐ, *Reclined, sat at table;* also, *Retired, hid oneself.* —Ethpe. *Was concealed* or *concealed himself.*—The word occurs here only in the N. T.—From it is derived

ܛܘܫܝܐ, noun masc. def. *Slander, evil report*, as arising from a *concealed* source, 2 Cor. vi. 8.

— ܒܟܢܫܐ, *in the crowd*—ܟܢܫܐ, noun masc. def. *A concourse, congregation, multitude.*—Pl. def. ܟܢ̈ܫܐ, ch. vi. 2, &c.—R. ܟܢܫ, *Assembled.*

Transl. *In the great multitude that was in that place.*—Gr. ὄχλου ὄντος ἐν τῷ τόπῳ.

14. ܒܬܪ ܙܒܢ, *after a time, afterwards*—Gr. μετὰ ταῦτα. See notes, ch. i. 15; iii. 4.

Ver. 14. ܠܐ ܬܘܒ ܬܚܛܐ, *sin not again, sin no more*—μηκέτι ἁμάρτανε—ܬܘܒ, see note, ch. i. 21. Fut. 2. sing. (for imperat. in prohibition) of ܚܛܐ (ch. ix. 2, 3), *Sinned, erred, went astray*.—Pret. 1. sing. ܚܛܝܬ, S. Matt. xxvii. 4; S. Luke xv. 18, 21; Acts xxv. 10.—3. pl. ܚܛܘ, Rom. ii. 12, &c.—1. pl. ܚܛܝܢ, Rom. iii. 25; 1 S. John i. 10.—Fut. ܢܚܛܐ, S. Luke xvii. 3.—3. pl. ܢܚܛܘܢ, Hebr. vi. 6.—2. pl. ܬܚܛܘܢ, 1 Cor. xv. 34, &c.—1. pl. ܢܚܛܐ, Rom. vi. 15.—Inf. ܠܡܚܛܐ, 1 S. John iii. 9.—Part. ܚܛܐ, 1 Cor. vi. 18, &c.—Fem. ܚܛܝܐ, ch. vii. 28.—Pl. masc. ܚܛܝܢ, 1 Tim. v. 20; 1 S. John v. 16.

Heb. חָטָא, *Missed the mark, sinned*, Gen. xx. 6, 9, &c.

— .... ܡܢ, Transl. *Something worse than before*—Gr. χεῖρόν τι—Comparative degree expressed by the adjective followed by ܡܢ.

15. ܕܐܚܠܡܗ, *which had made him whole*—ὁ ποιήσας αὐτὸν ὑγιῆ—Aphel pret. 3. sing. (with pref. relat. pronoun, and aff. 3. sing.) of ܚܠܡ, *Was sound*.—Aph. ܐܚܠܡ, *Made sound, restored to health*. Pret. 1. sing. ܐܚܠܡܬ, ch. vii. 23.—Part. ܡܚܠܡ, fem. ܡܚܠܡܐ, S. James v. 15.

Heb. Hiph. הֶחֱלִים, *Made to recover*, Isa. xxxviii. 16.

16. ܪܕܦܝܢ ܗܘܘ, *they persecuted*—ἐδίωκον—Part. pl. masc. (forming imperf. tense) of ܪܕܦ, *Followed after, persecuted, impelled*.—Pret. 1. sing. ܪܕܦܬ, Acts xxii. 4; 1 Cor. xv. 9.—3. pl. ܪܕܦܘ, S. John xv. 20.—Fut. ܢܪܕܘܦ, 3. pl. ܢܪܕܦܘܢ, ch. xv. 20; S. Luke xi. 49.—2. pl. ܬܪܕܦܘܢ, S. Matt. xxiii. 34.—Inf. ܠܡܪܕܦ, Acts xxvi. 11.—Part. ܪܕܦ, Acts viii. 3, &c.—From this verb are derived

ܪܕܘܦ, noun masc. *A persecutor*, 1 Tim. i. 13. Def. ܪܕܘܦܐ, Phil. iii. 6.—Pl. ܪܕܘܦܐ, with aff. Rom. xii. 14.

ܪܕܘܦܝܐ, noun fem. def. *Persecution*. With affixes, 2 Thess. i. 4; 2 Tim. iii. 11.

Heb. רָדַף, *Pursued*, Ps. xxiii. 6; xxxv. 3.

— ܠܡܩܛܠܗ, *to slay Him*—αὐτὸν ἀποκτεῖναι—(Inf. with aff. pron.) of ܩܛܠ (S. Luke xv. 27), *Killed, destroyed*.—Pret. 3. sing. ܩܛܠ,

S. JOHN V. 16—18.

Ver. 16. Acts vii. 28.—3. pl. ܩܛܠܘ, ver. 52; 1 Thess. ii. 15:—with aff. S. Matt. xxi. 35, &c.—2. pl. ܩܛܠܬܘܢ, S. Matt. xxiii. 35.—Fut. ܢܩܛܘܠ, S. John x. 10: S. Matt. v. 21; Acts xvi. 27;—with aff. S. John xvi. 2.—2. sing. ܬܩܛܘܠ, S. Matt. v. 21, &c.—1. sing. ܐܩܛܘܠ, Rev. ii. 23.—3. pl. ܢܩܛܠܘܢ, ch. ix. 5, 15;—with affix, S. John xi. 53; xii. 10, &c.—1. pl. ܢܩܛܘܠ, with aff. S. Matt. xxi. 38, &c.—Imperat. ܩܛܘܠ, pl. ܩܛܘܠܘ, S. Luke xv. 23.—Inf. ܠܡܩܛܠ, S. John vii. 25; xviii. 31; S. Matt. x. 28:—with affixes, S. John vii. 20; viii. 37, 40, &c.—Part. ܩܛܘܠ, S. John viii. 22, 44; S. Luke xii. 5.—Fem. ܩܛܘܠܐ, constr. ܩܛܘܠܬ ܢܒܝܐ, *thou that killest the Prophets*, S. Matt. xxiii. 37; S. Luke xiii. 34.—Pl. masc. ܩܛܘܠܝܢ, S. Matt. x. 28, &c.—Part. Peil ܩܛܝܠܐ, pl. masc. ܩܛܝܠܝܢ, S. Matt. xxii. 4.

Heb. קָטַל, *Killed*, Ps. cxxxix. 19.—Chald. קְטַל, part. act. קָטֵל, Dan. v. 19.—Part. Peil קְטִיל, ch. v. 30; vii. 11.

18. ܝܬܝܪܐܝܬ, *the more*—μᾶλλον—Adverb, *More, more especially, the rather, chiefly.* Formed from ܝܬܝܪ, *Abundant.* R. ܝܬܪ, *Abounded, was over.*

— ܒܠܚܘܕ, *only*—μόνον—Adverb, *Only, alone, separately, by itself* (S. Luke xxiv. 12).—Compounded of ܚܘܕ, *unity*, and the two prepositions ܒ and ܠ. It occurs, though less frequently, without the first prefix, as in ch. viii. 9, below. In either case it takes affixes of the plural, as ܒܠܚܘܕܘܗܝ, *alone, by Himself*, S. John vi. 15, &c.: ܒܠܚܘܕܝܗ, ܠܚܘܕܝܗ, *by herself*, ch. viii. 9; xii. 24:—ܒܠܚܘܕܝܟ, *Thou only*, ch. xvii. 3; S. Luke xxiv. 18.— ܒܠܚܘܕܝ, *I alone*, S. John viii. 16; xvi. 32, ܒܠܚܘܕܝܗܘܢ, *by themselves, apart*, S. Matt. xvii. 1: S. Mark iv. 10; ix. 28.— ܒܠܚܘܕܝܢ, *alone by ourselves*, 1 Thess. iii. 1.

— ܫܪܐ ܗܘܐ, *He was breaking, had broken*—ἔλυε—Part. (forming imperf. tense) of ܫܪܐ, see note, ch. i. 27.

— .... ܐܦ ܥܠ, Transl. *But also because concerning (or, in respect of) God, He had said that He was His Father.*

Ver. 18: ܘܡܫܘܐ ܗܘܐ, *and made* (*Himself*) *equal*—Gr. ἴσον (ἑαυτὸν) ποιῶν—Aphel part. (forming imperf. tense) of ܫܘܐ, *Was worthy.*—See note, ch. i. 23.

19. ܠܐ ܡܫܟܚ ܥܒܕ, *cannot do*—οὐ δύναται ποιεῖν—See note, ch. i. 46.

— ܐܟܘܬܗ, *likewise*—ὁμοίως—ܐܟܘܬ, a particle always used with affixes. It is of the form pl. constr. of a noun fem. in ܘ—, signifying *quality* or *likeness.*—Used as a subst. ܐܟܘܬܗ ܕܢܡܘܣܐ, *form of the law, lawfully*, 1 Tim. i. 8.—ܐܟܘܬܗܘܢ, *like them*, S. Luke xiii. 5:—ܐܟܘܬܟܘܢ, *like unto you*, S. John viii. 55;—ܐܟܘܬܢ, *like us*, Hebr. iv. 15.

20. ܪܚܡ, *loving, loveth*—φιλεῖ—Part. of ܪܚܡ, *Loved dearly.*—Pret. 2. sing. ܪܚܡܬ, Hebr. i. 9.—1. sing. ܪܚܡܬ, Rom. ix. 13.—3. pl. ܪܚܡܘ, S. John xii. 43.—2. pl. ܪܚܡܬܘܢ, with aff. ch. xvi. 27.—Fut. ܢܪܚܡ, S. Matt. vi. 24, &c.:—with aff. S. John xiv. 23.—2. sing. ܬܪܚܡ, S. Matt. xxii. 37, 39, &c.—1. sing. ܐܪܚܡ, Rev. iii. 19;—with aff. S. John xiv. 21.—3. pl. ܢܪܚܡܘܢ, 1 Tim. iii. 8:—Fem. ܢܪܚܡܢ, Tit. ii. 4.—Part. def. used as a noun, see note, ch. iii. 29.—Part. pl. masc. ܪܚܡܝܢ, S. John xiv. 15, 28, &c.—Constr. ܪܚܡܝ, 2 Tim. iii. 2, 4.

Heb. רָחַם, *Loved*, Ps. xviii. 2.

— ܘܕܝܬܝܪܝܢ ܡܢ ܗܠܝܢ, *and* (*works*) *which are greater than these*—Gr. καὶ μείζονα τούτων (ἔργα)—Pl. masc. of ܝܬܝܪ (ch. x. 10), adj. *Excellent*—Used as an adv. *Much, abundantly*, see note, ch. iii. 19.—Comparative expressed by ܡܢ.—Def. ܝܬܝܪܐ, S. Matt. ix. 16, &c.—Fem. ܝܬܝܪܐ, S. Matt. vi. 25, &c.—Def. ܝܬܝܪܬܐ, 2 Cor. ii. 7, &c.—Pl. fem. ܝܬܝܪܢ, S. John vii. 31.—Def. ܝܬܝܪܬܐ, 2 Cor. xi. 28.—R. ܝܬܪ, *Abounded.*

Chald. יַתִּיר, *Excellent*, Dan. ii. 31, &c. Fem. יַתִּירָה, used adverbially, ch. iii. 22; vii. 7, 19.

N.B. This clause, ܘܕܝܬܝܪܝܢ .... ܠܗ, is wanting in the Vienna Ed. but is restored to the text by Tremellius from another MS.

S. JOHN V. 21—24.   111

Ver. 21. ܡܰܚܶܐ, *quickening, quickeneth*—ζωοποιεῖ—Aphel part. of ܚܝܳܐ, *Lived.* Aph. ܐܰܚܺܝ, (S. Matt. xxvii. 42, &c.) *Gave life to, saved.* Pret. 3. sing. fem. ܐܰܚܝܰܬ݂, with aff. S. Matt. ix. 22; S. Mark x. 52, &c.—Fut. ܢܰܚܶܐ, S. Matt. xvi. 25, &c.: Fem. ܬܰܚܶܐ, with aff. S. James ii. 14.—2. sing. ܬܰܚܶܐ, 1 Tim. iv. 16; and ܬܚܶܐ, 1 Cor. vii. 16; fem. ܬܰܚܝܳܢ, same verse.—1. sing. ܐܰܚܶܐ, S. John xii. 47.—Imperat. ܐܰܚܳܐ, S. Luke xxiii. 47.—Inf. ܠܡܰܚܳܝܽܘ, Hebr. vii. 25; and ܠܡܰܚܳܝܽܘ, S. Matt. xxvii. 42, &c.—Part. fem. ܡܰܚܝܳܐ, S. John vi. 63.—Constr. ܟܠ ܡܰܚܝܰܬ݂, *that quickeneth all*, Gr. ἡ σωτήριος, Tit. ii. 11.

Heb. Hiph. הֶחֱיָה, Gen. vi. 19, 20.—Chald. Aph. part. מַחֵא, Dan. v. 19.

23. ܢܝܰܩܪܽܘܢ, *may honour*—Gr. τιμῶσι (πάντες)—Pael fut. 3. sing. of ܝܩܰܪ, *Was heavy.*—Pa. ܝܰܩܰܪ, *Gave honour to.* Pret. 3. pl. ܝܰܩܰܪܘ, with aff. Acts xxviii. 10.—Fut. 3. sing. with aff. S. John xii. 26.— Imperat. ܝܰܩܰܪ, S. Matt. xv. 4, &c.—Pl. ܝܰܩܰܪܘ, 1 S. Pet. ii. 17.— Part. ܡܝܰܩܰܪ, in this verse.—Pl. masc. ܡܝܰܩܪܺܝܢ, Rom. xii. 10.—Part. pass. ܡܝܰܩܰܪ, *honoured, honourable*, used as a noun, S. Luke xiv. 8;—coalescing with ܗܘ, ܡܝܰܩܪܽܘ, *is honourable*, Hebr. xiii. 4.—Def. ܡܝܰܩܪܳܐ, S. Mark xv. 43.—Fem. ܡܝܰܩܰܪܬܳܐ, Rev. xxi. 19;—Def. ܡܝܰܩܰܪܬܳܐ, ver. 11.—Pl. masc. ܡܝܰܩܪܺܝܢ, 1 Cor. xii. 24.—Pl. fem. def. ܡܝܰܩܪܳܬܳܐ, Rev. xvii. 4, &c.

Aph. ܐܰܘܩܰܪ, *Made heavy, dull*—Pret. 3. pl. ܐܰܘܩܰܪܘ, Acts xxviii. 27.

24. ܫܰܢܺܝ ܠܗ, *has passed, is passed*—μεταβέβηκεν—Pael pret. 3. sing. of ܫܢܳܐ, *Was changed, changed in mind, deranged.* Pa. *Changed his place, departed.*—Pret. 3. pl. ܫܰܢܺܝܘ, Acts xiv. 6.—1. pl. ܫܰܢܺܝܢ, 1 S. John iii. 14.—Fut. ܢܫܰܢܶܐ, S. John xiii. 1, &c.—1. sing. ܐܶܫܰܢܶܐ, 1 Cor. xiii. 2.—3. pl. ܢܫܰܢܽܘܢ, Acts xvi. 39.—2. pl. ܬܫܰܢܽܘܢ, S. Luke x. 7.—Imperat. ܫܰܢܳܐ, S. John vii. 3; S. Matt. xvii. 20.— Part. ܡܫܰܢܶܐ, S. Luke v. 16.—Ethpaal ܐܶܬܬܫܰܢܺܝ, *Was carried over, carried about, translated*, Acts vii. 16; Hebr. xi. 5.—Part. pl. ܡܶܬܬܫܰܢܺܝܢ, Eph. iv. 14.

Ver. 24.   Heb. Pi. שָׁנָה, *Changed*, Ps. lxxxix. 35.—Chald. Pa. שְׁנִי, Dan. iii. 28; iv. 13.—Part. pass. fem. מְשַׁנְיָא, *Diverse*, ch. vii. 7. —Ithpa. Dan. ii. 9, &c.

— ܡܰܘܬܳܐ, *death*—Gr. (ἐκ) τοῦ θανάτου—Noun masc. def.—Pl. def. ܡܰܘ̈ܬܶܐ, 2 Cor. i. 10; xi. 23.—R. ܡܺܝܬ, *Died*.

Heb. מָוֶת, Ps. vii. 14; ix. 14, &c.—Chald. מוֹת, Ezr. vii. 26.

•26. ܒܩܢܘܡܗ, *in Himself*—Gr. ἐν ἑαυτῷ—Lit. *in His Person.*— ܩܢܘܡܐ, def. ܩܢܘܡܳܐ (Hebr. x. 1), noun masc. *Substance, being, person.*—Equivalent to the Gr. ὑπόστασις, although in the only passage (Hebr. i. 3), where this word is used of the Divine Person, the Syr. Translator has rendered it by ܐܝܬܘܬܗ, *His Essence, Being.*—It represents, in the N. T., with affixes, the reflexive pronoun (*ipse, ipsa, &c.*), as here, and ch. vi. 53, &c., and refers to things as well as persons, see S. Luke xi. 17.

27. ܘܫܰܠܛܶܗ, *and hath given Him authority*—καὶ ἐξουσίαν ἔδωκεν αὐτῷ— Aphel pret. 3. sing. (with aff.) of ܫܠܛ (not occurring in Peal in the N. T.), *Ruled, had power.*—Aph. ܐܫܠܛ, *Gave power, caused to rule.*—Pret. 2. sing. ܐܫܠܛܬ, with aff. Hebr. ii. 7.

Heb. Hiph. הִשְׁלִים, Ps. cxix. 133.—Chald. Aph. הַשְׁלֵם, Dan. ii. 38, 48.

28. ܕܒܩܒܪ̈ܐ, *that are in the graves*—οἱ ἐν τοῖς μνημείοις—Noun with pref. prep. and rel. pronoun. Pl. def. of ܩܒܪ, def. ܩܒܪܐ (ch. xi. 31), *A grave.* R. ܩܒܰܪ, *Buried.*

Heb. קָבַר, Gen. xxiii. 9, 20.

29. ܠܩܝܳܡܬܳܐ, *to the resurrection*—εἰς ἀνάστασιν—Def. (with pref. prep.) of ܩܝܳܡܬܳܐ (S. Luke ii. 34; xiv. 14), noun fem. *A rising up.*— R. ܩܳܡ, *Rose.*

Heb. קִימָה, *An arising*, Lam. iii. 63.

— ܛܳܒ̈ܬܳܐ .... ܒܝ̈ܫܬܳܐ, *good...evil*—Gr. τὰ ἀγαθά...τὰ φαῦλα—In such abstract expressions, the Syr. having no neuter, the fem. is used. So ܗܕܐ, Gr. τοῦτο, ver. 28, above.

Ver. 30. ܟܐܢ, *just*—δικαία—Adj. *Just, right*—Def. ܟܐܢܐ (ch. vii. 24), the ܢ being dropped.—Pl. ܟܐܢܝܢ, Rom. ii. 13.—Def. ܟܐܢܐ, S. Matt. v. 45, &c. Pl. fem. ܟܐܢܢ, Phil. iv. 8.—Def. ܟܐܢܬܐ, Rev. xv. 3.

Heb. כֵּן, Gen. xlii. 11, &c.

35. ܫܪܓܐ, *the light*—ὁ λύχνος—Noun masc. def. *A lamp, light*—Pl. def. ܫܪ̈ܓܐ, Rev. xxi. 23; with aff. S. Luke xii. 35.

— ܕܝܩܕ, *that burns—burning*—Gr. ὁ καιόμενος—Part. of ܝܩܕ, *Burned, flamed.* Fut. ܢܐܩܕ. Occurs here only in the N. T.

Heb. דָּלַק, Ps. vii. 14.—Chald. דְּלִק, Dan. vii. 9.

— ܕܬܫܬܒܗܪܘܢ, *that ye should rejoice—to rejoice*—ἀγαλλιασθῆναι—Ethpeal fut. 2. pl. of ܫܒܗܪ, Pa. quadriliteral, *Lightened up, commended, extolled.* The triliteral root (to which ܫ is added) exists in Arabic only.—Part. pl. masc. ܡܫܒܗܪܝܢ, 2 Cor. x. 12.

Ethpa. ܐܫܬܒܗܪ, *Rejoiced, boasted.*—Pret. 1. sing. ܐܫܬܒܗܪܬ, 2 Cor. vii. 14; ix. 2.—1. pl. ܐܫܬܒܗܪܢ, ch. ix. 3, 4.—Fut. ܢܫܬܒܗܪ, 1 Cor. i. 29, 31, &c.—2. sing. ܬܫܬܒܗܪ, Rom. xi. 18. —1. sing. ܐܫܬܒܗܪ, 2 Cor. x. 8, &c.—1. pl. ܢܫܬܒܗܪ, Rom. v. 11; 2 Cor. x. 16.—Inf. ܠܡܫܬܒܗܪܘ, 2 Cor. xi. 30; xii. 1.—Part. ܡܫܬܒܗܪ, Rom. ii. 17, 23, &c.—Pl. masc. ܡܫܬܒܗܪܝܢ, 2 Cor. v. 12, &c.:—coalescing with ܚܢܢ, ܡܫܬܒܗܪܝܢܢ, Rom. v. 2, 3, &c.

Deriv. ܫܘܒܗܪܐ, noun masc. def. *Glory, pride, boasting*, Rom. iii. 27; iv. 2, &c.

ܫܒܗܪܢܐ, adj. *Proud.*—Pl. def. ܫܒܗܪ̈ܢܐ, Rom. i. 30;—or ܫܒܗܪ̈ܢܐ, 2 Tim. iii. 2.

— ܕܫܥܬܐ, *for a season*—Gr. πρὸς ὥραν—Or, *for the hour, at that time.*

36. ܫܠܚܢܝ, *hath sent Me*—με ἀπέσταλκε—Pret. 3. sing. (with aff.) of ܫܠܚ (Acts xxiii. 10), *Sent, sent away, took off; stripped of his raiment*, S. Luke x. 30.—Pret. 3. fem. ܫܠܚܬ, S. Matt. xxvii. 19.—3. pl. ܫܠܚܘ, Acts xiii. 15:—with aff. S. Luke x. 30

Ver. 36. (some regard this as Pael). Fut. ܢܶܫܠܰܚ.—Imperat. ܫܠܰܚ, pl. ܫܠܰܚܘ, with aff. Col. iii. 9.—Inf. ܠܰܡܫܰܠܳܚܘ, with aff. 2 Cor. v. 4.—Part. Peil ܡܫܰܠܰܚ, def. ܡܫܰܠܚܳܐ, S. John iii. 28.—(Used as a noun, see note, ch. xiii. 16, below.)—Pl. ܡܫܰܠܚܶܐ, S. Matt. xxiii. 37; S. Luke xiii. 34.—From this verb are derived ܫܠܳܚܳܐ, noun masc. *A putting off*—Constr. Col. ii. 11, &c.

ܫܠܺܝܚܘܬܳܐ, noun fem. def. *A mission, Apostleship*, Acts i. 25, &c.

37. ܚܶܙܘܶܗ, *His appearance, shape*—εἶδος αὐτοῦ—Noun with aff.—ܚܶܙܘܳܐ, noun masc. def. (S. Matt. xiv. 26, &c.), *Something seen, a vision*. Another form is ܚܶܙܘܳܢܳܐ, pl. def. ܚܶܙܘܳܢܶܐ, Acts ii. 17.—R. ܚܙܳܐ, *Saw*.[1]

Chald. חֲזָא, def. חֶזְוָא, Dan. ii. 19, &c.:—and Heb. חָזָה, Ps. lxxxix. 20.

39. ܒܨܰܘ, *search*—ἐρευνᾶτε—Imperat. pl. of ܒܨܳܐ, *Investigated, explored*. Pret. 3. sing. with aff. ܒܨܳܟ, *hath distinguished thee*, Gr. διακρίνει, 1 Cor. iv. 7.—3. pl. ܒܨܰܘ, 1 S. Pet. i. 11.—Fut. ܢܶܒܨܶܐ, 2. pl. ܬܶܒܨܽܘܢ, Acts xxiii. 15.—Imperat. ܒܨܺܝ, S. John vii. 52.—Part. ܒܳܨܶܐ, Rev. ii. 23.—Fem. ܒܳܨܝܳܐ, 1 Cor. ii. 10.

Ethpeel ܐܶܬܒܨܺܝ, *Was searched out*. Part. ܡܶܬܒܰܨܝܳܐ, Gr. ἐλέγχεται, 1 Cor. xiv. 24.

— ܡܣܰܒܪܺܝܢ ܐܰܢܬܘܢ (pron. *m'sabritun*), *ye think*—δοκεῖτε—See note, ch. iv. 51.—ܣܰܒܰܪ in Pa. more usually means *Announced*, or *Trusted*, as ver. 45, below.—The Par. and Lond. Polyglotts read ܡܚܰܡܣܢܺܝܢ, Aphel part.

40. ܚܰܝܶܐ ܕܰܠܥܳܠܰܡ, *life which is for ever, eternal life*—Gr. ζωήν.

42. ܚܘܒܶܗ, *the love* (aff. pleon.)—τὴν ἀγάπην—ܚܽܘܒܳܐ (ch. xiii. 35, &c.) noun masc. *Love, affection, charity*. R. ܚܰܒܶܒ, *Loved*.

44. ܚܰܕ ܡܶܢ ܚܰܕ, Lit. *one from one,—one of another*—Gr. παρὰ ἀλλήλων.

— ܚܰܕ ܡܶܢ ܐܰܠܳܗܳܐ, *from one God*—Gr. παρὰ τοῦ μόνου Θεοῦ.

Ver. 45. ܠܡܐ ܣܒܪܝܢ ܐܢܬܘܢ, *do ye think?*—Gr. μὴ δοκεῖτε—See note, ch. iv. 12.—Part. pl. (forming pres. tense) of ܣܒܪ (Acts vii. 25), *Thought, supposed, was of opinion;* also *Hoped, trusted, expected.* Pret. 3. sing. fem. ܣܒܪܬ, S. John xx. 15.—2. sing. ܣܒܪܬ, Acts viii. 20.—3. pl. ܣܒܪܘ, S. John xi. 13, 31, &c.—Fut. ܢܣܒܪ, 2. pl. ܬܣܒܪܘܢ, S. Matt. x. 34.—Inf. ܠܡܣܒܪ, Acts xvii. 29.—Part. ܣܒܪ, S. John xxi. 25, &c.—Pl. masc. coalescing with ܚܢܢ, ܣܒܪܝܢܢ, 1 Cor. xii. 23.

Heb. שָׂבַר, *Viewed, observed,* Neh. ii. 13, 15.—Chald. סְבַר, *Hoped,* Dan. vii. 25.

— ܡܩܛܪܓ ܐܢܐ, *I accuse, will accuse*—κατηγορήσω—Part. (forming pres. or fut. tense) of ܩܛܪܓ, Pael quadrilit. verb derived from the Greek by metathesis of γ and ρ. Fut. ܢܩܛܪܓ.—1. sing. ܐܩܛܪܓ, Acts xxviii. 19.—3. pl. ܢܩܛܪܓܘܢ, with aff. S. John viii. 6; S. Mark iii. 2.—Part. pl. masc. ܡܩܛܪܓܝܢ, coalescing with ܚܢܢ, ܡܩܛܪܓܝܢܢ, Acts xxiv. 8.

CHAPTER VI.

1. ܠܥܒܪܗ ܕ, *to the other side of, over*—πέραν τῆς—See note, ch. i. 28.

— ܝܡܐ, *the sea*—θαλάσσης—Def. of ܝܡ, noun masc. *The sea.* Pl. def. ܝܡܡܐ, Acts iv. 24; xiv. 14.—There is also a fem. def. form ܝܡܬܐ (S. John vi. 19; S. Luke v. 2, &c.) used more especially of a *lake,* or *inland sea.*

Heb. יָם, Ps. lxxxix. 10.—Chald. יָם, def. יַמָּא, Dan. vii. 2, 3.

5. ܥܝ̈ܢܘܗܝ, *His eyes*—Gr. τοὺς ὀφθαλμούς—Pl. with aff. of ܥܝܢ, def. ܥܝܢܐ (S. Matt. v. 38, &c.), noun fem. *An eye; fountain.*—Pl. when it signifies *eyes,* of masc. form, though fem. in construction, ܥܝ̈ܢܝܢ, S. Matt. xviii. 9. Def. ܥܝ̈ܢܐ, S. John ix. 32, &c.—But of fem. form when signifying *fountains,* ܥܝ̈ܢܢ, def. ܥܝ̈ܢܬܐ (Ephr. Syr. on Gen. i. 9).

S. JOHN VI. 5—7.

Ver. 5.   Compounds formed by ܩܕܡ are ܠܩܕܡ, *Before*, and ܓܠܝܐܝܬ, *Openly*. See notes, S. John xv. 24; xvi. 25.

Heb. עֵין, Exod. xxi. 24, &c.—Chald. עַיִן, Dan. iv. 31; vii. 8, 20; Ezr. v. 5.

— ܠܚܡܐ, *bread*—Gr. ἄρτους—Def. of ܠܚܡܐ, noun masc. *Bread, food.*—Constr. ܠܚܡ, ܠܚܡ ܐܦܐ, *the shew-bread*, Hebr. ix. 2.—Pl. ܠܚܡܝܢ, ver. 13, below.

Heb. לֶחֶם, Ps. xli. 10, &c.—Chald. לְחֵם, *A feast*, Dan. v. 1.

6. ܡܢܣܐ, *proving, to prove*—πειράζων—Pael part. of ܢܣܐ (not used). Pa. ܢܣܝ, *Tempted, made trial of.*—Pret. 2. sing. ܢܣܝܬ, Rev. ii. 2.—3. pl. ܢܣܝܘ, 1 Cor. x. 9.—Fut. ܢܢܣܐ, with aff. S. Luke x. 25.—2. sing. ܬܢܣܐ, S. Matt. iv. 7; S. Luke iv. 12.—1. pl. ܢܢܣܐ, 1 Cor. x. 9.—Inf. ܠܡܢܣܝܘ, Acts v. 9.—Part. pl. ܡܢܣܝܢ, S. Matt. xvi. 1, &c.—Part. pass. ܡܢܣܝ, Hebr. iv. 15; S. James i. 13.   For ܕ, as here used, see note, ch. i. 36.

Heb. Pi. נִסָּה, *Tempted, tried*, Gen. xxii. 1.

— ܥܬܝܕ ܠܡܥܒܕ, *He was about to do, would do*—ἔμελλε ποιεῖν—See note, ch. iii. 14.

7. ܡܐܬܝܢ, *two hundred*—διακοσίων.

Hoc nomen est unum ex quatuor quae apud Hebraeos in dualem terminationem יִם, et apud Syros in ܝܢ finiuntur. Reliqua tria sunt ܡܨܪܝܢ, *Egyptus* (S. Matt. ii. 13, &c.) à מִצְרַיִם;—ܬܪܝܢ, *duo* (S. John i. 35), à שְׁנַיִם; ܬܪܬܝܢ, *duae* (S. John iii. 4), à שְׁתַּיִם. (Schaaf.)

Heb. מָאתַיִם, Gen. xi. 23.

— ܕܝܢܪܝܢ, *denarii*—Gr. δηναρίων—Pl. of ܕܝܢܪ (S. Matt. xx. 9, 10) noun masc. *A Roman silver coin, value 10 asses—whence its name.*—Def. ܕܝܢܪܐ, S. Matt. xx. 2.—Pl. def. ܕܝܢܪܐ, S. Matt. xviii. 28.

— ܠܐ ܣܦܩ, *not sufficing, is not sufficient*—Gr. οὐκ ἀρκοῦσιν—Part. of ܣܦܩ, *Sufficed; was content with, capable of receiving*, Pret. 3. pl. fem. ܣܦܩ (for ܣܦܩܝ) 3 S. John ver. 10.—Fut. ܢܣܦܩ,

Ver. 7. S. Matt. xix. 12; xxv. 9:—Fem. ܬܣܦܩܢ, 1 Tim. v. 16.—1. sing. ܐܣܦܩ, Acts xi. 17.—3. pl. fem. ܢܣܦܩܢ, S. Luke iii. 14.—Part. fem. ܣܦܩܐ, 2 Cor. xii. 9; 1 Tim. vi. 8.—Pl. masc. ܣܦܩܝܢ, S. John viii. 37; S. Luke xxii. 38;—coalescing with ܚܢܢ, ܣܦܩܝܢܢ, 2 Cor. iii. 5.

— ܩܠܝܠ ܩܠܝܠ, *a little*—βραχύ τι—See note, ch. vii. 33.

— ܚܕ ܚܕ, *each*—ἕκαστος—See note, ch. i. 40. The repetition of the words denoting distribution.

9. ܬܢܢ, *here*—ὧδε—Adverb of place.

— ܚܡܫ, *five*—πέντε—Card. numb. fem.—Masc. ܚܡܫܐ, ch. iv. 18, above.

Heb. חָמֵשׁ, fem. Gen. v. 6.

— ܓܪܝܨܢ, *loaves*—ἄρτους—Pl. of ܓܪܝܨܐ, noun fem. *A cake, loaf, baked bread.*—Def. ܓܪܝܨܬܐ, S. Mark viii. 14.

— ܕܣܥܪܐ, *of barley*—Gr. κριθίνους—Pl. def. (of masc. form) of ܣܥܪܐ, noun fem. *Barley,* def. ܣܥܪܬܐ.

Heb. שְׂעֹרָה, fem. *Barley,* Joel i. 11.—Pl. שְׂעֹרִים, Ruth i. 22.—Root שָׂעַר, *Bristled.*

— ܢܘܢܝܢ, *fishes*—Gr. ὀψάρια, a word which, originally meaning *Anything eaten with bread,* is applied in the N. T. exclusively to *fish*—Compare S. John xxi. 10, with 11.—Pl. of ܢܘܢ, def. ܢܘܢܐ (S. John xxi. 9), noun masc. *A fish,* and *fish,* collectively.—Pl. def. ܢܘܢܐ, ver. 11, below. Root Heb. נון (Ps. lxxii. 17), *Increased, grew.*

Compare Heb. דָּג, Jon. ii. 1; דָּגָה f. Exod. vii. 18, 21.—from דָּגָה, *Increased,* Gen. xlviii. 16.

10. ܢܣܬܡܟܘܢ, *that they may sit down, recline*—Gr. ἀναπεσεῖν—Ethpeel fut. 3. pl. of ܣܡܟ, *Leaned, reclined.*—Ethpe. ܐܣܬܡܟ (ch. xiii. 12, &c.), *Seated himself.*—Pret. 3. pl. ܐܣܬܡܟܘ, in this verse.—Fut. ܢܣܬܡܟ, 2. sing. ܬܣܬܡܟ, S. Luke xiv. 8.—

Ver. 10. Imperat. ܐܣܡܟܘ, S. Luke xiv. 10, &c.—Inf. ܠܡܣܡܟܗ,
S. Matt. xiv. 19.—
Transl. *Cause that all the men may recline.*

— ܥܣܒܐ, *grass*—χόρτος—Def. of ܥܣܒ, noun masc. *Green herb.*
Heb. עֵשֶׂב, Gen. i. 11, 12.—Chald. עֲשַׂב, def. עִשְׂבָּא, Dan. iv. 22, 29, 30.

— ܒܡܢܝܢܐ, *in number*—Gr. τὸν ἀριθμόν—Def. of ܡܢܝܢ (Hebr. xi. 12), noun masc. *Number.* R. ܡܢܐ, *Numbered.*
Chald. מִנְיָן, Ezr. vi. 17.

— ܐܠܦܝܢ, *thousand.*—Pl. of ܐܠܦ, Rev. v. 11. or ܐܠܦ 2 S. Pet. iii. 8. *A thousand.*—Def. ܐܠܦܐ, Rev. xi 3, &c.—Pl. def. ܐܠܦܐ̈, S. Matt. xiv. 21. and ܐܠܦܐ̈, Rev. vi. 15, &c.
Heb. אֶלֶף, Ps. l. 10.—Chald. אֱלַף, אֲלַף, pl. (after the Heb. form) אַלְפִים, Keri אלפין, Dan. v. 1; vii. 10.

11. ܘܒܪܟ, *and He blessed*—Gr. καὶ εὐχαριστήσας—Pael pret. of ܒܪܟ, *Bowed the knee, in worship.* Pa. *Blessed, pronounced blessed.*—Fut. ܢܒܪܟ, 1. sing. ܐܒܪܟ, with aff. Hebr. vi. 14.—Imperat. pl. ܒܪܟܘ, S. Matt. v. 44; S. Luke vi. 28.—Inf. ܠܡܒܪܟܗ, Hebr. vi. 14.— Part. ܡܒܪܟ, S. Luke xxiv. 51.—Pl. masc. ܡܒܪܟܝܢ, ver. 53:— coalescing with ܠܢܝ, ܡܒܪܟܝܢܠܢܝ, 1 Cor. iv. 12; S. James iii. 9.—Part. pass. ܡܒܪܟ, S. Luke i. 42, 68;—coalescing with ܗܘ, ܡܒܪܟܗܘ, *blessed be,* 1 S. Pet. i. 3.—Def. ܡܒܪܟܐ, S. Mark xiv. 61.—Fem. def. ܡܒܪܟܬܐ, S. Luke i. 42.
Heb. Pi. בֵּרַךְ, Gen. xxiv. 1.—Chald. Pa. בָּרֵךְ (for בָּרַךְ) Dan. ii. 19, 20; iv. 31.

— ܦܠܓ, *He distributed*—διέδωκε—Pael pret. of ܦܠܓ or ܦܠܓ, *Divided.*—Pa. the same.—Pret. 3. pl. ܦܠܓܘ, ch. xix. 24, &c.— Imperat. pl. ܦܠܓܘ, S. Luke xxii. 17.—Part. ܡܦܠܓ, S. Luke xi. 22.—Pl. m. ܡܦܠܓܝܢ, Acts ii. 45.
Heb. Pi. פִּלַּג, *Divided,* Ps. lv. 10.

S. JOHN VI. 11, 12.   119

Ver. 11. N.B. The words that follow in the Gr. τοῖς μαθηταῖς, οἱ δὲ μαθηταί, are omitted in the Syr. as in many other versions; also in the Alex. Vat. Sin. and other MSS.

— ܠܗܢܘܢ ܕܣܡܝܟܝܢ, *to them that were set down*—τοῖς ἀνακειμένοις—Part. Peil pl. of ܣܡܟ *Reclined, leaned.*—Fut. ܢܣܡܘܟ, S. Matt. viii. 20; S. Luke ix. 58.—Part. Peil ܣܡܝܟ, S. John xiii. 23, &c. Pl. masc. def. ܣܡܝܟܐ, S. Matt. xiv. 6, 9, &c.—Pl. fem. ܣܡܝܟܢ ܠܐ, *not firm, unstable*, 2 S. Pet. ii. 14.

Heb. סָמַךְ, *Rested upon*, Ps. lxxxviii. 8.

— ܗܟܢܐ ܐܦ, *and so also—and likewise*—ὁμοίως καί.

— ܟܡܐ ܕ, *as much as*—ὅσον—Also, *As long as*, ch. ix. 5.—*Inasmuch as, as often as*, S. Matt. xxv. 40, 45.—*The same as*, Rev. xxi. 16.—*According as*, Hebr. x. 25.—*How, in what respect or way*, 2 Tim. i. 18.

12. ܣܒܥܘ, *they were full, were filled*—ἐνεπλήσθησαν—Pret. 3. pl. of ܣܒܥ, *Was satiated.*—Pret. 3. pl. fem. ܣܒܥܢ, Rev. xix. 21.—2. pl. ܣܒܥܬܘܢ, ver. 26, below.—Fut. ܢܣܒܥ, 3. pl. ܢܣܒܥܘܢ, S. Matt. v. 6; S. Mark vii. 27.—2. pl. ܬܣܒܥܘܢ, S. Luke vi. 21.—Imperat. pl. ܣܒܥܘ, S. James ii. 16.—Inf. ܠܡܣܒܥ, Acts vii. 11.

Deriv. ܣܒܥܐ, *Satiety*, Phil. iv. 12.

Heb. שָׂבֵעַ, Ps. xvii. 15, &c.

— ܟܢܫܘ, *gather up*—συναγάγετε—Pael imperat. pl. of ܟܢܫ, *Congregated.*—Pa. ܟܢܫ (S. Matt. ii. 4, &c.), *Gathered together; received hospitably*, S. Matt. xxv. 35.—Pret. 3. sing. fem. ܟܢܫܬ, S. Matt. xiii. 47.—2. pl. ܟܢܫܬܘܢ, S. James v. 3; with aff. S. Matt. xxv. 35, 43.—1. pl. ܟܢܫܢ, with aff. ver. 38.—Fut. ܢܟܢܫ, S. John xi. 52.—1. sing. ܐܟܢܫ, S. Matt. xxiii. 37.—3. pl. ܢܟܢܫܘܢ, ch. xxiv. 31.—Inf. ܠܡܟܢܫܘ, Rev. xvi. 14; xx. 8.—Part. ܟܢܫ, S. Matt. xxv. 24, 26.—Part. pass. ܟܢܝܫ, pl. masc. ܟܢܝܫܝܢ, Acts x. 24.

Heb. Pi. כִּנֵּס, Ps. cxlvii. 2.

Ver. 12. ܩܨܳܝܶܐ, *the fragments*—τὰ κλάσματα—Pl. def. of ܩܨܳܝܳܐ (Acts ii. 42), noun masc. *A breaking, piece broken.*—R. ܩܨܳܐ, *Broke off.*

— ܕܝܰܬܪܘ, *that have remained over, that remain*—Gr. περισσεύσαντα—Pret. 3. pl. of ܝܰܬܰܪ (S. Matt. xxv. 16), *Excelled, was over and above;* also, *Profited, gained, made gain.*—Pret. 2. sing. ܝܰܬܰܪܬ, S. Matt. xviii. 15.—Fut. ܢܐܬܰܪ, S. Mark viii. 36; S. Luke ix. 25. Fem. ܬܐܬܰܪ (for ܬܐܬܪܝܢ), S. Matt. v. 20.—2. sing. ܬܐܬܰܪ, S. Mark vii. 11.—1. sing. ܐܐܬܰܪ, 1 Cor. ix. 19, 20, &c.—Part. ܝܳܬܰܪ, 1 Cor. xiii. 3.—Pl. ܝܳܬܪܝܢ, coalescing with ܚܢܰܢ, ܝܳܬܪܝܢܰܢ, S. James iv. 13.

Heb. יָתַר, only in part. Kal יוֹתֵר, *The remainder*, 1 Sam. xv. 15.

13. ܬܪܶܥܣܰܪ, *twelve*—δώδεκα—Card. numb. masc.—It has a def. form ܬܪܶܥܣܰܪܬܐ, ch. xx. 24; S. Matt. xxvi. 47;—with aff. ver. 67, below.—Fem. ܬܪܬܰܥܣܪܐ, ch. xi. 9, &c.

Heb. שְׁנֵים עָשָׂר, masc. שְׁתֵּים עֶשְׂרֵה, fem. Exod. xxiv. 4.

— ܩܘܦܝܢܝܢ, *baskets*—κοφίνους—Pl. of ܩܘܦܝܢܐ, noun masc. *A wicker basket.* Derived from the Gr.—The following ܕ marks the genitive.

Transl. *And filled twelve baskets of the fragments which remained to those who ate (had eaten) of the five barley loaves.*

15. ܕܥܬܝܕܝܢ ܕܢܐܬܘܢ, *that they were ready to come, would come*—ὅτι μέλλουσιν ἔρχεσθαι—Infin. expressed by the fut. with ܕ.

— ܢܚܛܦܘܢܝܗܝ, *(and) take Him by force*—καὶ ἁρπάζειν αὐτόν—Fut. 3. pl. (with aff.) of ܚܛܰܦ, *Snatched away.* Pret. 3. sing. fem. ܚܶܛܦܰܬ, Acts viii. 39.—3. pl. ܚܛܰܦܘ, ch. vi. 12.—Fut. ܢܶܚܛܘܦ, S. John x. 28, 29; S. Mark iii. 27.—Imperat. pl. ܚܛܘܦܘ, S. Jude ver. 22.—Part. ܚܳܛܶܦ, S. John x. 12; S. Matt. xiii. 19.

Ethpeel ܐܶܬܚܛܶܦ, *Was seized, caught away*, 2 Cor. xii. 2, 4.—Fut. ܢܶܬܚܛܶܦ, 1. pl. 1 Thess. iv. 17.

Heb. חָטַף, Ps. x. 9.

S. JOHN VI. 15—19.

Ver. 15. ܡܢܬ ܠܗ, *He departed*—ἀνεχώρησε—See note, ch. v. 24.

16. ܪܡܫܐ, *evening*—Gr. ὀψία—Def. of ܪܡܫ, noun masc. *Even-tide.*

17. ܘܣܠܩܘ, *and they sat*—Gr. καὶ ἐμβάντες, *and entered into, embarked.*

— ܠܣܦܝܢܬܐ, *in the ship*—Gr. εἰς τὸ πλοῖον—Def. of ܣܦܝܢܬܐ, noun fem. Lit. *A decked vessel.* Pl. def. ܣܦܝܢܐ, S. Mark iv. 36, &c. Heb. סְפִינָה, Jon. i. 5.—R. סָפַן, *Covered with beams or boards.*

— ܚܫܘܟ ܗܘܐ ܠܗ, *it was dark*—Gr. σκοτία ἐγεγόνει—Pret. 3. sing. fem. of ܚܫܟ (S. Luke xxiii. 45), *Was dark, obscured.* Used here impersonally (see also S. Matt. xiv. 23), in which construction the fem. is most commonly used. For an instance of the masc. see S. Matt. xxvi. 8.—Pret. 3. pl. ܚܫܟܘ, Rev. viii. 12.—Fut. ܢܚܫܟ, S. Matt. xxiv. 29; S. Mark xiii. 24.—3. pl. fem. ܢܚܫܟܢ, Rom. xi. 10.—Inf. ܠܡܚܫܟ, S. Luke xxiv. 29.

Ethpaal ܐܬܚܫܟ, *Was darkened*, Rom. i. 21.

Heb. חָשַׁךְ, Exod. x. 15; Ps. lxix. 24.

— ܗܘܐ ܐܬܐ, *was come, had come*—ἐληλύθει—Part. Peil, forming the plup. tense.

18. ܗܘܐ ܐܙܕܩܦ, *had been raised, had arisen, arose*—διηγείρετο—Ethpeel pret. 3. sing. (forming pluperf. tense) of ܙܩܦ, *Lifted up.*

Ethpe. *Was lifted up, was crucified*, ch. xix. 20, &c.—3. pl. ܐܙܕܩܦܘ, S. Matt. xxvii. 38.—Fut. ܢܙܕܩܦ, ch. xxvi. 2, &c.

Transl. *But the sea had been raised against them, because a great wind had blown.*

19. ܘܕܒܪܘ, *and they rowed*—Gr. ἐληλακότες οὖν—Pret. 3. pl. of ܕܒܪ (ch. xviii. 3), *Arranged, set in order*, whence the usual meanings, *Took, received, led, drove, impelled* a ship. Pret. 3. fem. ܕܒܪܬ, with aff. S. Luke iv. 1.—1. sing. ܕܒܪܬ, Gal. ii. 1.—Fut. ܢܕܒܪ, S. Matt. xv. 14.—1. sing. ܐܕܒܪ, with aff. S. John xiv. 3.—3. pl. ܢܕܒܪܘܢ, with aff. S. Luke v. 3.—Imperat. ܕܒܪ, S. Matt. ii. 13, 20, &c.— Pl. ܕܒܪܘ, S. John xix. 6; S. Luke v. 4;—with aff. S. John xviii. 31.—Part. ܕܒܪ, S. Luke xvii. 7 :—Fem. ܕܒܪܐ, S. Matt. xii. 45.—

Ver. 19. Pl. masc. ܪܳܨܶܝܢ, S. Matt. v. 44; S. Luke vi. 28, Gr. τῶν ἐπηρεαζόντων.—Part. Peil pl. masc. (used actively) ܪܕܺܝܦܺܝܢ, Acts xxi. 16.—Pl. fem. ܪܳܨܳܢ, S. James iii. 4.

Heb. דָּבַר, *Spoke* (from the primary idea of *arrangement*) only in part. דֹּבֵר, Ps. v. 7. More frequent in Peil.

— ܐܶܣܛܕ̈ܰܘܳܬܐ, *stadia, furlongs*—σταδίους—Pl. def. of ܐܶܣܛܕܺܝܐ (1 Cor. ix. 24), *A distance, nearly equal to a furlong; also, the Stadium, race-course.* Pl. ܐܶܣܛܕ̈ܰܘܳܢ, Acts i. 12.

— ܥܶܣܪܺܝܢ, *twenty*—Card. Number.

Heb. עֶשְׂרִים, Gen. xxxi. 38.—Chald. עֶשְׂרִין, Dan. vi. 2.

— ܝܰܡܳܐ, *the lake, sea;* see note, ver. 1, above.

— ܩܪܶܒ, *He drew near*—Gr. ἐγγὺς...γινόμενον—Verb Peal pret. *Was near, approached, touched.* 3. sing. fem. ܩܶܪܒܰܬ݀, S. Matt. iii. 2, &c.—3. pl. ܩܪܶܒܘ, S. John xii. 21, &c.:—Fem. ܩܪ̈ܶܒܝ, S. Matt. xxviii. 9.—Fut. ܢܶܩܪܽܘܒ, S. Mark viii. 22, &c.—2. sing. ܬܶܩܪܽܘܒ, Col. ii. 21.—3. pl. ܢܶܩܪܒܘܢ, S. Matt. xiv. 36, &c.—1. pl. ܩܪܶܒܢ, Hebr. x. 22.—Imperat. pl. ܩܪܽܘܒܘ, S. James iv. 8.—Part. ܩܳܪܶܒ, S. Luke xii. 33:—Fem. ܩܳܪܒܳܐ, S. Matt. ix. 21; S. Mark v. 28.—Pl. ܩܳܪ̈ܒܺܝܢ, S. Mark vi. 56; S. Luke xxiii. 36.

Heb. קָרַב, קָרֵב, Ps. xci. 10.—Chald. קְרֵב, Dan. iii. 56; vi. 13.

— ܕܚܶܠܘ, *they were afraid*—ἐφοβήθησαν—Pret. 3. pl. of ܕܚܶܠ (ch. xix. 8), *Feared, showed reverence.* Pret. 1. sing. ܕܶܚܠܶܬ, S. Matt. xxv. 25; S. Luke xix. 21.—Fut. ܢܶܕܚܰܠ, S. John xiv. 27.—2. sing. ܬܶܕܚܰܠ, S. Matt. i. 20, &c.:—Fem. ܬܶܕܚܠܺܝܢ, S. Luke i. 30.—1. sing. ܐܶܕܚܰܠ, Hebr. xiii. 6.—3. pl. ܢܶܕܚܠܽܘܢ, 1 Tim. v. 20.—2. pl. ܬܶܕܚܠܽܘܢ, next ver. below, &c.:—Fem. ܬܶܕܚܠ̈ܳܢ, S. Matt. xxviii. 5, 10; S. Mark xvi. 6.—Imperat. ܕܚܰܠ, Rom. xi. 20.—Pl. ܕܚܰܠܘ, S. Matt. x. 28: S. Luke xii. 5.—Part. ܕܳܚܶܠ, S. John ix. 31, &c.:—Fem. ܕܳܚܠܳܐ, Acts xvi. 14.—Pl. masc. ܕܳܚܠܺܝܢ, S.

S. JOHN VI. 19—27.

Ver. 19. John ix. 22, &c.:—coalescing with ܣܢܝ, ܙܕܒܚܢܝ, S. Matt. xxi. 26. Part. Peil, used as a noun—see note, S. Mark v. 33.

Cogn. Heb. זָחַל, *Crept, was afraid*, Deut. xxxii. 34; Mic. vii. 17; Job xxxii. 6.—Chald. דְּחַל, Dan. v. 19.

22. ܠܐ ܥܠ ܗܘܐ, *had not gone, went not*—Gr. οὐ συνεισῆλθε—Pluperf. tense.—ܚܨܗܘܢ is pleonastic, followed by the same preposition with its case.

N.B. The clause, ἀλλά...ἀπῆλθον, is omitted by the Syr. translator.

23. ܐܬܝ ܗܘܘ, *they (sc. other boats) had come*—Gr. ἦλθε—Pluperf. pl. 3. fem.

— ܐܠܦܐ, *boats*—πλοιάρια—Pl. def. of ܐܠܦ, def. ܐܠܦܐ (S. Matt. iv. 21, 22, &c.) noun fem. *A small vessel, boat.*

— .... ܟܕ ܒܪܟ, Transl. *When Jesus blessed or had blessed, given thanks*— Gr. εὐχαριστήσαντος τοῦ Κυρίου.

25. ܐܡܬܝ, *when?*—πότε;—Adv. interrogative. See note, ch. iv. 23.

27. ܠܐ ܬܦܠܚܘܢ, *labour not for*—ἐργάζεσθε μή—Fut. 2. pl. for imperat. (with ܠܐ) of ܦܠܚ, *Served, laboured, acquired by labour; served in war; served, or worshipped.*—Pret. 3. pl. ܦܠܚܘ, 1 Cor. x. 7. —2. pl. ܦܠܚܬܘܢ, Gal. iv. 8.—Fut. ܢܦܠܘܚ, Eph. iv. 28.— 2. sing. ܬܦܠܘܚ, S. Matt. iv. 10, &c.—1. sing. ܐܦܠܘܚ, Rom. xv. 16.—3. pl. ܢܦܠܚܘܢ, Acts vii. 7.—1. pl. ܢܦܠܘܚ, ver. 28, below; S. Luke i. 74.—Imperat. ܦܠܘܚ, S. Matt. xxi. 28.—Pl. ܦܠܘܚܘ, Phil. ii. 12.—Inf. ܠܡܦܠܚ, S. John ix. 4, &c.— Part. ܦܠܚ, S. Luke xv. 29.—Def. ܦܠܚܐ, Rom. xvi. 21:— and used as a noun, see note, S. Luke xxiii. 11.—Fem. ܦܠܚܐ, S. Luke ii. 37.—Pl. masc. ܦܠܚܝܢ, Acts vii. 42, &c.:—co- alescing with ܣܢܝ, ܦܠܚܝܢܢ, 1 Cor. iii. 9, &c.:—with ܐܝܠܝܢ, ܦܠܚܝܢ, Col. iii. 24.—Constr. ܦܠܚܝ, S. Matt. vii. 23, &c. —Part. Peil. fem. ܦܠܝܚܐ, S. John viii. 33, where see note.

Ethpeel ܐܬܦܠܚ, *Was cultivated, dressed.* Part. fem. ܡܬܦܠܚܐ (referred by some to Ethpa.), Hebr. vi. 7.

Ver. 27. Aphel ܐܦܠܚ, *Waged war.*—Part. ܡܦܠܚ, 1 Cor. ix. 7.—From this verb are derived,

ܦܠܚܘܬܐ, noun fem. def. *Warfare, army*, 1 Cor. ix. 7; 1 Tim. i. 18.—Pl. def. ܦܠܚܘ̈ܬܐ, Rev. xix. 14, 19. ܦܘܠܚܢܐ, noun masc. def. *Occupation, work, worship*, Acts xix. 25; Col. ii. 18, &c.

Heb. פָּלַח, *Cleft, furrowed* the ground, Ps. cxli. 7.—Chald. פְּלַח, *Laboured, worshipped*, Dan. iii. 12, &c.; vii. 14, 27.

— .... ܠܗܢܐ, Transl. *For Him hath the Father sealed (even) God.*

30. ܣܥܪ ܐܢܬ, *dost Thou work?*—ἐργάζῃ;—Part. (forming pres. tense) of ܣܥܪ (S. Luke i. 68; vii. 16), *Visited, inspected, examined; did, effected*, 1 Cor. v. 2; Hebr. ix. 11. The leading idea seems to be *the turning the attention to anything*, either by ocular or mental inspection.—Pret. 2. sing. ܣܥܪܬ, with aff. Hebr. ii. 6.—2. pl. ܣܥܪܬܘܢܝ, with aff. S. Matt. xxv. 36, 43.—Fut. ܢܣܥܘܪ, Acts vii. 23.—2. sing. ܬܣܥܘܪ, 1 Tim. v. 21.—1. sing. ܐܣܥܘܪ, S. Luke xiii. 33.—3. pl. ܢܣܥܪܘܢ, Rom. ix. 11.—1. pl. ܢܣܥܘܪ, Acts xv. 36.—Imperat. pl. ܣܥܘܪܘ, Phil. iv. 9: 1 S. Pet. v. 2.—Inf. ܠܡܣܥܪ, S. Luke xxii. 23; Phil. ii. 13; S. James i. 27.—Part. fem. ܣܥܪܐ, 1 Cor. xii. 11; Hebr. iv. 12.—Pl. masc. ܣܥܪܝܢ, Rom. i. 32, &c.:—coalescing with ܚܢܢ, ܣܥܪܝܢܢ, 1 S. John iii. 22.—Constr. ܣܥܪܝ, 1 Cor. xii. 29.—Part. Peil ܣܥܝܪ, S. Luke xxiii. 15; Acts xxv. 25; actively, Rom. xv. 18.—Pl. fem. ܣܥܝܪܢ, Acts xxvi. 26.

Deriv. ܣܥܘܪܐ, noun masc. def. *A visitor, Bishop*, 1 S. Pet. ii. 25.

31. ܡܢܢܐ, *manna*—τὸ μάννα.

Heb. מָן, Exod. xvi. 15, 31.

34. ܒܟܠܙܒܢ, *in all time—always, evermore*—Gr. πάντοτε. See notes, ch. i. 3; iii. 4.

35. ܠܐ ܢܟܦܢ, *shall not (never) hunger*—οὐ μὴ πεινάσῃ—Fut. 3. sing. of ܟܦܢ (S. Matt. iv. 2, &c.), *Was hungry.*—Pret. 1. sing. ܟܦܢܬ.

S. JOHN VI. 35—43.   125

Ver. 35. S. Matt. xxv. 35, 42.—3. pl. ܟܦܢܘ, S. Matt. xii. 1.—Fut. 3. pl. ܢܟܦܢܘܢ, Rev. vii. 16.—2. pl. ܬܟܦܢܘܢ, S. Luke vi. 25.— For the part. ܟܦܢ is used the participial noun ܟܦܢ, *hungry*, see note, S. Matt. v. 6.

37. ܠܒܪ, *out*—ἔξω—ܒܪ, *The outside*, used as an adverb with pref. ܠ. See note, S. Matt. iii. 4.

39. ܗܢܘ ܕܝܢ ܨܒܝܢܗ ܕܐܒܝ ܕܫܕܪܢܝ. This clause is absent in the Vienna Edition, but restored by Tremellius. Some Editions omit ܕܐܒܝ.

— ܐܘܒܕ, *I should lose*—ἀπολέσω—Aphel fut. 1. sing. of ܐܒܕ, *Perished*. Aph. ܐܘܒܕ (S. Matt. xxii. 7, &c.), *Caused to perish, destroyed, lost.*—Pret. 1. sing. ܐܘܒܕܬ, S. John xviii. 9.—3. pl. ܐܘܒܕܘ, 1 Cor. x. 9.—Fut. ܢܘܒܕ, S. John x. 10, &c.:—Fem. ܬܘܒܕ (for ܬܐܘܒܕ), S. Luke xv. 8.—2. sing. ܬܘܒܕ, Rom. xiv. 15.—3. pl. ܢܘܒܕܘܢ, S. Matt. xxvii. 20.—2. pl. ܬܘܒܕܘܢ, Hebr. x. 35.—Inf. ܠܡܘܒܕܘ, S. Mark iii. 4, &c.—Part. ܡܘܒܕ, S. Luke ix. 24.

Heb. Hiph. הָאֲבִיד, Deut. vii. 10.—Chald. Aph. הוֹבֵד, Dan. ii. 12, 18, 24.

— ܐܚܪܝܐ, *the last*—τῇ ἐσχάτῃ—Def. of ܐܚܪܝ, adj. *The last*.—Fem. def. ܐܚܪܝܬܐ, S. Matt. xxvii. 64; S. Luke xiv. 9.—Constr. ܐܚܪܝܬ, used as an adv. *Afterwards, at length*, S. Matt. iv. 2, &c.—Pl. masc. def. ܐܚܪܝܐ, S. Matt. xix. 30, &c.—Pl. fem. def. ܐܚܪܝܬܐ, Rev. xv. 1; xxi. 9.

40. ܕܐܒܝ, *of My Father*—Gr. τοῦ πέμψαντός με—The Sin. Vat. and some other MSS. read τοῦ πατρός μου.

41. ܪܛܢܝܢ ܗܘܘ, *murmured*—ἐγόγγυζον—Part. pl. (imperf. tense) of ܪܛܢ, *Murmured*. Pret. 3. pl. ܪܛܢܘ, Acts vi. 1; 1 Cor. x. 10.—Fut. 2. pl. ܬܪܛܢܘܢ, ver. 43, below; 1 Cor. x. 10.—Part. ܪܛܢ. Aphel ܐܪܛܢ, same as Peal.—Part. pl. ܡܪܛܢܝܢ, S. Jude ver. 16. Some Editions read ܡܪܛܢܝܢ, Pael part.

43. ܚܕ ܥܡ ܚܕ, Lit. *one with one—among yourselves*—Gr. μετ' ἀλλήλων—in ver. 52. πρὸς ἀλλήλους.

Ver. 44. ܢܓܕܗ, *has drawn him*—Gr. ἑλκύσῃ αὐτόν—Pret. 3. sing. (with aff.) of ܢܓܕ (Gal. ii. 12), *Drew, attracted, withdrew*.—Pret. 3. pl. ܢܓܕܘ, Acts xvi. 19.—Fut. ܢܓܕ, 1. sing. ܐܓܕ, ch. xii. 32, below.—Inf. with aff. fem. pleon. ܠܡܓܕܗ, ch. xxi. 6.—Part. pl. masc. ܢܓܕܝܢ, ch. xxi. 8.

Ethpeel ܐܬܢܓܕ, *Was drawn*.—Part. ܡܬܢܓܕ, S. James i. 14.—Pl. masc. 2 S. Pet. i. 21. From this verb is derived ܢܓܕܐ, noun masc. def. *A blow, stripe*, with aff. Acts xvi. 33.—Pl. def. ܢܓܕܐ, ch. xxii. 24. Compare, for this meaning, note ch. xix. 1.

45. ܒܢܒܝܐ, *in the Prophet*, sc. Isa. liv. 13.—Gr. ἐν τοῖς προφήταις.

— ܡܠܦܐ, *the taught—taught*—διδακτοί—Pael part. pass. pl. def.—see note, ch. iv. 25.

— ܝܠܦ, *learning—hath learned*—μαθών—Part. of ܝܠܦ (ch. vii. 15, &c.), same as ܝܠܦ, *Learned*. Pret. 1. sing. ܝܠܦܬ, Acts xxiii. 27.—2. sing. ܝܠܦܬ, 2 Tim. iii. 14.—2. pl. ܝܠܦܬܘܢ, Rom. xvi. 17, &c.—1. pl. ܝܠܦܢ, Acts xxviii. 1.—Fut. ܢܐܠܦ, 1 Cor. xiv. 31.—2. sing. ܬܐܠܦ, Acts xxiv. 8.—1. sing. ܐܠܦ, Phil. ii. 19.—3. pl. ܢܐܠܦܘܢ, Acts xxiii. 20:—Fem. ܢܐܠܦܢ, 1 Cor. xiv. 35.—2. pl. ܬܐܠܦܘܢ, 1 Cor. iv. 6.—Imperat. pl. ܝܠܦܘ, S. Matt. ix. 13, &c.—Inf. ܠܡܐܠܦ, with aff. Rev. xiv. 3.—Part. fem. ܝܠܦܐ, 1 Tim. ii. 11.—Pl. fem. ܝܠܦܢ, ch. v. 13.—Part. Peil ܝܠܝܦ, Rom. ii. 18.

46. ܚܙܐ, *seeing, seeth*—Gr. ἑώρακεν.

51. ܚܠܦ ܐܦܝ̈, *for the sake of, for*—Gr. ὑπέρ—Lit. *for the face of*.—See note, ch. xi. 44, below.

52. ܢܨܝܢ ܗܘܘ, *strove*—ἐμάχοντο—Part. pl. (forming imperf. tense) of ܢܨܐ, *Contended, disputed*. Part. ܢܨܐ.—From this verb are derived ܢܨܝ, noun masc. *One who is contentious, a brawler*, 1 Tim. iii. 3.

Ver. 52. ܡܨܘܬܐ, noun fem. def. *A quarrel*—Pl. def. ܡܨܘ̈ܬܐ, S. James iv. 1.

Heb. Niph. נִצָּה, *Strove*, Exod. ii. 13.—מַצּוּת, *Strife*, Isa. xli. 12.

55. ܡܫܬܝܐ, *drink*—πόσις—Def. of ܡܫܬܝ, noun masc. *Something to drink, beverage.* Derived from Aph. part. pass. of ܫܬܐ (ܐܫܬܝ), *Drank.* Aph. ܐܫܬܝ.

59. ܒܟܢܘܫܬܐ, *in the synagogue*—ἐν συναγωγῇ—Noun fem. def. *A congregation, place of assembling.*—Pl. def. ܟܢܘ̈ܫܬܐ, S. Matt. vi. 2, &c.—R. ܟܢܫ, *Assembled.*

60. ܩܫܝܐ, *hard*—σκληρός—Fem. of ܩܫܐ (Acts ix. 4), adj. *Severe, difficult, vehement* (of winds). Def. ܩܫܝܐ, S. Matt. xxv. 24, &c.—Pl. def. ܩܫ̈ܝܐ, Acts xxv. 7.—Pl. fem. def. ܩܫ̈ܝܬܐ, S. James iii. 4. Of form part. Peil of ܩܫܐ (not used in Peal). Heb. *Was hard.*—Pa. ܩܫܝ, *Hardened*—Fut. 2. pl. ܬܩܫܘܢ, Hebr. iii. 8, 15; iv. 7.—Part. ܡܩܫܐ, Rom. ix. 18. Ethpa. ܐܬܩܫܝ, *Was hardened*—Fut. ܢܬܩܫܐ, Hebr. iii. 13.—Part. pl. ܡܬܩܫܝܢ, Acts xix. 9.

Heb. קָשָׁה, fem. קָשָׁה, Exod. i. 14.

61. ܡܟܫܠܐ, *offending—offendeth*—σκανδαλίζει—Aphel part. fem. of ܟܫܠ, *Struck against.*

Aph. ܐܟܫܠ, *Caused to stumble.*—Fut. ܢܟܫܠ, S. Matt. xviii. 6, &c.—1. sing. ܐܟܫܠ, 1 Cor. viii. 13.—1. pl. ܢܟܫܠ, S. Matt. xvii. 27.—Part. ܡܟܫܠ.

Heb. Hiph. הִכְשִׁיל, Ps. lxiv. 9; Prov. iv. 16.

62. ܐܢ . . . ܗܟܝܠ, *if then—what and if?*—ἐὰν οὖν, rather, *what then if?*

— ܐܝܟܐ ܕ, *to the place where—where*—Gr. ὅπου. See note, ch. xi. 54, below.

— ܡܢ ܩܕܝܡ, *formerly, before*—Gr. τὸ πρότερον,—in ver. 64, ἐξ ἀρχῆς.—Compound adverb.

63. ܡܘܬܪܐ, *profiting, profiteth*—ὠφελεῖ—Aphel part. of ܝܬܪ, *Was profitable, took pleasure in.* Aph. ܐܘܬܪ, *Profited.*—Part. fem. ܡܘܬܪܐ, Rom. ii. 25.

Ver. 64. ܡܰܫܠܶܡ, *who betrayed, should betray*—ὁ παραδώσων—Aphel part. of ܐܰܫܠܶܡ or ܡܰܫܠܶܡ, *Finished.*

Aph. ܐܰܫܠܶܡ (ch. xix. 30, &c.), *Gave up, delivered up, committed to, betrayed.*—Pret. 1. sing. ܐܰܫܠܶܡܬ݀, S. Matt. xxvii. 4.—3. pl. ܐܰܫܠܶܡܘ, S. Luke i. 2.—2. pl. ܐܰܫܠܶܡܬܘܢ, S. Mark vii. 13.—Fut. ܢܰܫܠܶܡ, S. Matt. x. 21:—with aff. ver. 71, below, &c.—1. sing. ܐܰܫܠܶܡ, 1 Cor. xiii. 3.—3. pl. ܢܰܫܠܡܘܢ, S. Matt. xxiv. 10.—2. pl. ܬܰܫܠܡܘܢ, with aff. 1 Cor. v. 5.—Part. pl. masc. ܡܰܫܠܡܺܝܢ, S. John xviii. 30; S. Matt. x. 17.—Part. pass. ܡܰܫܠܰܡ, S. Luke iv. 6;—Fem. ܡܰܫܠܰܡܬܐ, 1 S. Pet. v. 2.

Heb. Hiph. הִשְׁלִים, *Completed, executed,* Isa. xliv. 26, 28.— Chald. Aph. אַשְׁלֵם, *Finished, restored,* Dan. v. 26; Ezr. vii. 19.

66. ... ܡܶܠܬܐ, Transl. *On account of this word,* or *saying*—Gr. ἐκ τούτου, E.V. *from that time;*—rather, *because of this, on this account.*

— ܠܒܶܣܬܪܗܘܢ, *back*—εἰς τὰ ὀπίσω—ܒܶܣܬܪ (Rev. xiii. 3), adv. Gr. ὀπίσω, *Behind, after.*—Def. ܡܶܢ ܒܶܣܬܪܐ, *on the back,* ὄπισθεν, Rev. v. 1.— ܒܶܣܬܪܝ ܡܶܢ, *behind me,* ὀπίσω μου, Rev. i. 10.—After the form of a noun sing. with affixes, either in its simple form, as ܒܶܣܬܪܗ, *behind Him,* S. Luke vii. 3;—or preceded by ܡܶܢ, S. Matt. ix. 20; S. Mark v. 27;—or by pref. ܠ, as in this verse, and S. Luke xvii. 31.

67. ܠܬܪܶܥܣܰܪܬܗ, *to His twelve*—Gr. τοῖς δώδεκα.

70. ܓܒܺܝܬܟܘܢ, *have I chosen you?*—ὑμᾶς ἐξελεξάμην;—Pret. 1. sing. (with aff.) of ܓܒܳܐ (S. Mark iii. 14. &c.) *Elected, selected.*—Pret. 3. fem. ܓܒܳܬ, S. Luke x. 42.—1. sing. ܓܒܺܝܬ, S. John xiii. 18.—3. pl. ܓܒܰܘ, Acts vi. 5, &c.—2. pl. ܓܒܰܝܬܘܢ, with aff. S. John xv. 16.—1. pl. ܓܒܰܝܢ, Acts xv. 25.—Fut. ܢܶܓܒܶܐ.— 1. sing. ܐܶܓܒܶܐ, Phil. i. 22.—Imperat. ܓܒܺܝ, 1 Cor. vii. 21.—Pl. ܓܒܰܘ, Acts vi. 3.—Inf. ܡܶܓܒܳܐ, 2 Cor. viii. 19;—pref. ܠ, Acts xv. 14.—Part. ܓܳܒܶܐ, 1 Tim. v. 9.—Pl. masc. ܓܳܒܶܝܢ, 1 Cor. xvi. 3.—Part. Peil ܓܒܶܐ, 2 Cor. viii. 19; 1 S. Pet. ii. 4; used actively,

Ver. 70. Acts i. 14.—Def. ܓܒܝܐ, Acts ix. 15, &c. with aff. pleon. S. Luke xxiii. 35.—Fem. def. ܓܒܝܬܐ, 1 S. Pet. ii. 9, &c.—Pl. masc. def. ܓܒܝܐ, S. Matt. xx. 16, &c.

Ethpeel ܐܬܓܒܝ, *Was chosen.*—Pret. 3. pl. ܐܬܓܒܝܘ, 1 S. Pet. i. 2.—1. pl. ܐܬܓܒܝܢ, Acts x. 41; Eph. i. 11.—From this verb are derived,

ܓܒܝܬܐ, noun fem. def. *Election*, Rom. xi. 5, 7, 28.

ܓܒܝܘܬܐ, noun fem. def. *Election*—with aff. Rom. ix. 11, &c.

ܓܒܝܬܐ, fem. def. pl. *Gatherings*—1 Cor. xvi. 2.

— ܣܛܢܐ ܗܘ, *is Satan—is a devil*—διάβολός ἐστιν—ܣܛܢܐ, (ch. xiii. 27, &c.) noun masc. def. *An adversary, accuser,—the Enemy, Satan.*

Heb. שָׂטָן, *An adversary*, Numb. xxii. 22:—with def. art. *Satan*, Job i. 6.—R. שָׂטַן, *Opposed himself*, Ps. xxxviii. 21, &c. Whence also שִׂטְנָה, n. f. *An accusation*, Ezr. iv. 6.

71. ܐܡܪ ܗܘܐ, *He had spoken, He spake*—Gr. ἔλεγε.

CHAPTER VII.

2. ܕܡܛܠܠܐ, *of Tabernacles*—Gr. ἡ σκηνοπηγία—Pl. def. of ܡܛܠܠܐ, noun masc. def. *A shady place, arbour, booth.*—Pl. ܡܛܠܠܢ, S. Matt. xvii. 4, &c. Form of Pael part. of ܛܠܠ, Pa. ܛܠܠ, *Overshadowed.*

3. ܫܢܐ ܠܟ, *depart*—μετάβηθι—See note, ch. v. 24.

4. ܒܛܘܫܝܐ, *in secret*—ἐν κρυπτῷ—ܛܘܫܝܐ, n. f. *A secret, secrecy.* Used only (in the N. T.) with pref. ܒ, adverbially. R. ܛܫܐ, *Lay hid.*

— ܕܒܓܠܝܐ ܢܗܘܐ, *that he should be in public—to be (known) openly*—Gr. ἐν παῤῥησίᾳ εἶναι—ܓܠܝܐ, a participial noun masc. def. *Manifestation, revelation*—Form of part. Peil of ܓܠܐ, *Revealed;*—as ܟܣܝܐ, *secrecy*, from ܟܣܐ, *hid.*

S. JOHN VII. 5—8.

Ver. 5. .... ܐܳܦ ܠܐ, Transl. *For not even His brethren believed in Jesus.*—ܒܗ pleonastic.

6. ܡܛܳܐ, *is come*—πάρεστιν—Verb Peal pret. *Came, approached, came to pass, arrived, fell to one's lot*, S. Luke i. 9.—Pret. 3. fem. ܡܛܳܬ݂, S. John xiii. 1:—and ܡܛܰܝ̈ (from ܡܛܳܝ) 1 Cor. x. 11.—Fut. ܢܡܛܶܐ.—Part. ܡܛܶܐ, used in the phrase ܡܛܶܐ ܒܐܝ̈ܕܝ ܡܪܗ, lit. *it comes into the hands of his Lord*, i. e. *his Lord hath power*, Rom. xiv. 4. Similarly 1 Cor. xvi. 2, with which compare Gen. xxxii. 14, מִן־דָּבָא בְיָדוֹ, *of what came into his hand*, i. e. *what he could.*—Part. fem. ܡܛܝܳܐ, S. Luke xv. 12:—used in phrase similar to the above, ܡܛܝܐ ܒܐܝ̈ܕܘܗܝ, *he is able*, 2 Tim. i. 12. Similarly, Hebr. xi. 19; Acts v. 39; xxv. 5.—Part. Peil fem. ܡܛܝܳܐ, similarly used, Acts xxiv. 13; 2 Cor. ix. 8; 2 Tim. ii. 2. Chald. מְטָא or מְטָה, Dan. iv. 8; vi. 25, &c.

— ܒܟܠܙܒܢ, *at every time, always*—πάντοτε—The words occur separately, S. Luke xviii. 1, 5.

— ܡܛܰܝܰܒ, *ready*—ἕτοιμος—Pael part. pass. of ܛܰܝܶܒ, *Was good.* Pa. ܛܰܝܶܒ, see note ch. xiv. 2, below.

7. ܠܡܣܢܳܝܟܘܢ, *to hate you*—μισεῖν ὑμᾶς—Inf. (following ܡܣܚܒ) of ܣܢܐ, see note, ch. iii. 20.—The final ܝ elided before the affix. All the Eds. read as above, except Schaaf, who reads ܠܡܣܢܝܘܬܟܘܢ.

8. ܣܩܘ, *go ye up*—ἀνάβητε—Imperat. pl. of ܢܣܩ, *Ascended.* Defective in the pret. which is supplied by the verb ܣܠܩ, see note, ch. i. 51. Fut. ܢܣܩ, S. Matt. xiii. 2, &c.—3. pl. ܢܣܩܘܢ, S. Matt. xiv. 22; S. Mark vi. 45.—Imperat. ܣܩ, Rev. iv. 1.—Inf. ܠܡܣܩ, Rev. xvii. 8.—Part. ܣܠܩ, Rev. xiv. 11. Heb. נָסַק, fut. 1. sing. אֶסַּק, Ps. cxxxix. 8.

— ܫܠܡ, *is fulfilled—full come*—πεπλήρωται—Verb Peal pret. *Completed, came to an end, filled up; agreed* or *consented*, S. Luke xxiii. 51. *Walked sincerely*, Rom. iv. 12.—Fut. ܢܫܠܡ, S. John xiii. 18, &c.:—Fem. ܬܫܠܡ (for ܬܫܠܡܝ), ch. xviii. 9, 32.—

Ver. 8. 3. pl. ܢܳܫܠܡܺܝܢ, S. Mark xiv. 49; S. Luke xxi. 24.—1. pl. ܢܳܫܠܰܡ, Gal. v. 25; Phil. iii. 16.—Part. ܡܫܰܠܰܡ, S. Luke xxiii. 51:—Fem. ܡܫܰܠܡܳܐ, S. Matt. xiii. 14; S. Luke v. 36.—Pl. masc. ܡܫܰܠܡܺܝܢ, Acts xxviii. 25, &c.—Pl. fem. ܡܫܰܠܡܳܢ, Acts xv. 15. From this verb are derived,

ܡܫܰܠܡܳܐ, adj. *Perfect, whole*—Pl. def. ܡܫܰܠܡܶܐ, *whole burnt-offerings*, ὁλοκαυτώματα—Hebr. x. 6, 8.

ܡܫܰܠܡܳܢܽܘܬܐ, noun fem. def. *Perfection: concord, peace*—2 Cor. vi. 15; xiii. 11.

Heb. שָׁלֵם, *Finished*, 1 Kings vii. 51.—Chald. שְׁלִים, part. Peil, Ezr. v. 16.

9. ܩܰܘܺܝ, *He abode*—ἔμεινεν—Verb Peal pret. 3. sing. ܩܰܘܺܝ ܗܘܳܐ, *Was still, remained*. Pronoun pleonastic, after a neuter verb.—Fut. ܢܩܰܘܶܐ.—Imperat. ܩܰܘܳܐ, S. Luke xxiv. 29.—Inf. ܠܰܡܩܰܘܳܝܽܘ, 1 Thess. iii. 1.—Part. ܡܩܰܘܶܐ, Phil. i. 25; Hebr. iv. 1.—Fem. ܡܩܰܘܝܳܐ, S. John xii. 24.

Transl. *These things He said, and remained in Galilee*.

10. ܐܰܝܟ ܕ, *as it were*—ὡς—*In order that*, S. Matt. ii. 13, 23.—*That*, Gr. ὅπως, S. Luke vii. 3.

11. ܐܰܝܟܰܘ, *where is?*—ποῦ ἐστιν;—Adverb compounded of ܗܽܘ + ܐܰܝܟܳܐ.

12. ܪܶܛܢܳܐ, *a murmuring*—γογγυσμός—Noun masc. def. R. ܪܛܰܢ, *Murmured*.

— ܥܠܰܘܗܝ, *concerning Him*—περὶ αὐτοῦ—See note, ch. i. 15.

— ܡܰܛܥܶܐ, *deceiving—He deceiveth*—Gr. πλανᾷ—Aphel part. of ܛܥܳܐ, *Wandered*.—Aph. ܐܰܛܥܺܝ (2 Cor. xi. 3), *Caused to wander, led into error*.—Pret. 3. fem. ܐܰܛܥܝܰܬ, with aff. Rom. vii. 11.—Fut. ܢܰܛܥܶܐ, 1 Cor. iii. 13:—with aff. S. Matt. xxiv. 4, &c.—3. pl. ܢܰܛܥܽܘܢ, S. Matt. xxiv. 5 (see note there), 11, &c.—2. pl. ܬܰܛܥܽܘܢ, S. James i. 22.—Inf. ܠܡܰܛܥܳܝܽܘ, Rev. xx. 8.—Part. fem. ܡܰܛܥܝܳܐ, Rev. ii. 20.—Pl. masc. ܡܰܛܥܶܝܢ, Rom. xvi. 18, &c.:—coalescing with ܠܰܢ, ܡܰܛܥܶܝܢܰܢ, 1 S. John i. 8.

S. JOHN VII. 12—15.

Ver. 12. Ethtaphal ܐܶܬ݂ܛܥܺܝ, *Was deceived.* Pret. 3. pl. ܐܶܬ݂ܛܥܺܝܘ, Rev. xviii. 23.

Heb. Hiph. הִטְעָה, *Led astray,* Ezek. xiii. 10.

13. ܓܰܠܝܳܐܺܝܬ݂, *openly*—Gr. παρρησίᾳ—Adverb.—R. ܓܠܳܐ, *Revealed.*

— ܕܶܚܠܬ݂ܳܐ, *fear*—τὸν φόβον—Def. of ܕܶܚܠܳܐ (S. Luke i. 74), noun fem. *Fear, terror,* also *Religion, reverence.*—Constr. ܕܶܚܠܰܬ݂, Acts ix. 31, &c.—Pl. def. ܕܶܚܠܳܬ݂ܳܐ, S. Luke xxi. 11.—R. ܕܚܶܠ, *Feared, reverenced.*

14. ܦܠܺܝܓ݂ܘ, *divided, were in the midst.* Transl. *But when the days of the Feast divided, i. e. were half over*—Gr. ἤδη δὲ τῆς ἑορτῆς μεσούσης—Pret. 3. pl. of ܦܠܰܓ݂ (Rom. xii. 3), *Divided, distributed, cut in two parts; set at variance.*—Fut. ܢܶܦܠܘܓ݂, with aff. S. Matt. xxiv. 51; S. Luke xii. 46.—1. sing. ܐܶܦܠܘܓ݂, S. Matt. x. 35.—Part. ܦܳܠܶܓ݂, S. Luke xii. 13 (where see note).—Pl. masc. ܦܳܠܓ݁ܺܝܢ, 1 Cor. ix. 13.—Part. Peil ܦܠܺܝܓ݂, Acts xiv. 4:—S. James i. 8.—Pl. masc. ܦܠܺܝܓ݂ܺܝܢ, S. Luke xii. 52.—Constr. ܦܠܺܝܓ݂ܰܝ̈ ܢܰܦܫܳܐ, Gr. δίψυχοι, S. James iv. 8.

Deriv. ܦܘܠܳܓ݂, noun masc. *Division, disputing; hesitation, diversity,* Phil. ii. 14.—Def. ܦܘܠܳܓ݂ܳܐ, Acts xi. 12.—Pl. def. ܦܘܠܳܓ݂ܶܐ, 1 Cor. xii. 4, &c.

Heb. (Kal not used) Niph. נִפְלַג, *Was divided,* Gen. x. 25.—Chald. פְּלַג, Part. Peil Dan. ii. 41.

15. ܣܶܦܪܳܐ, *literature, letters*—γράμματα—Def. of ܣܦܰܪ, noun masc. *A book, writing, literature, learning.* Pl. def. ܣܶܦܪ̈ܶܐ, *the Scriptures,* 2 Tim. iii. 15; Hebr. ix. 19.

Heb. סֵפֶר, Ps. xl. 8; lxix. 29, הַסְּפָרִים, *the Scriptures,* Dan. ix. 2.—Chald. סְפַר, pl. סִפְרִין, Ezr. iv. 15; Dan. vii. 10.—R. סָפַר, *Scratched, scraped, graved* on stone—whence, *Wrote*—Part. סֹפֵר, Ps. xlv. 2.—Syr. Pa. *Shaved,* Ethpa. *Was shaven,* Acts xviii. 18; 1 Cor. xi. 6.

Ver. 16. ܝܘܠܦܢܝ, *My doctrine*—ἡ ἐμὴ διδαχή—Noun with aff. ܝܘܠܦܢܐ (S. Matt. xvi. 12, &c.) noun masc. def. *Teaching, instruction.*—Pl. def. ܝܘܠܦܢ̈ܐ, S. Matt. xv. 9. R. ܝܠܦ, *Learned.*

17. ܡܣܬܟܠ, *knowing—he shall know*—γνώσεται—Ethpaal part. of ܣܟܠ, *Was foolish* (Peal not used).—Pael ܣܟܠ, *Made to understand, instructed.*—Part. pl. (with ܒܢܝ), Col. i. 28.—Ethpa. ܐܣܬܟܠ (S. Luke xx. 23), *Understood, considered.*—Pret. 3. pl. ܐܣܬܟܠܘ, S. Matt. xvi. 12, &c.—2. pl. ܐܣܬܟܠܬܘܢ, ch. xiii. 51, &c.—1. pl. ܐܣܬܟܠܢ, Acts xvi. 10.—Fut. ܢܣܬܟܠ, S. Matt. xxiv. 15; S. Mark xiii. 14.—1. sing. ܐܣܬܟܠ, Acts viii. 31.—3. pl. ܢܣܬܟܠܘܢ, S. John xii. 40, &c.—2. pl. ܬܣܬܟܠܘܢ, S. Matt. xiii. 14.—Imperat. ܐܣܬܟܠ, 2 Tim. ii. 7.—Pl. ܐܣܬܟܠܘ, S. Matt. xv. 10; S. Mark vii. 14.—Inf. ܠܡܣܬܟܠܘ, S. Luke xxiv. 45.—Part. with ܠܐ, *foolish*, Gr. ἀσύνετος, Rom. i. 21.—Pl. masc. ܡܣܬܟܠܝܢ, S. Matt. xiii. 13, &c. with ܒܢܝ, Hebr. xi. 3.

From this verb is derived the noun masc. ܣܘܟܠ, *Prudence, intelligence*, Eph. i. 8, &c. Def. ܣܘܟܠܐ, Rom. i. 20, &c.

Heb. (Kal not used) Pi. סִכֵּל, *Made foolish*, 2 Sam. xv. 31; Isa. xliv. 25.

18. ܡܢ ܓܒܘܬ ܪܥܝܢܗ, *of his own mind—of himself*—Gr. ἀφ' ἑαυτοῦ, rendered ܡܢ ܪܥܝܢ ܢܦܫܗ, ch. xvi. 13. For ܓܒܘܬ, see note, S. Matt. xviii. 19.

ܪܥܝܢ (Acts iv. 32), noun masc. *Mind, sense, opinion, understanding.* Constr. as above. Def. ܪܥܝܢܐ, S. Mark xii. 33, &c.—Pl. def. ܪ̈ܥܝܢܐ, 1 Cor. xv. 33.—R. ܪܥܐ, in the signification *Desired.*

Heb. רַעְיוֹן, *Desire*—Eccles. ii. 22.—Chald. the same—*Thought*, Dan. ii. 29, 30; iv. 16, &c.

— ܥܘܠܐ, *unrighteousness*—ἀδικία—noun masc. def. Pl. def. ܥܘ̈ܠܐ, *iniquities*, Rev. xviii. 5. Root, Arab. *Turned aside from right.*—Compare Heb. Pi. עִוֵּל, *Did wrong.*

Ver. 18. ܚܒܗ, *in his heart*, i.e. *in him*—Gr. ἐν αὐτῷ—ܠܒܐ (S. Matt. xii. 34, &c.) noun masc. *The heart.* Pl. of masc. form, with aff. ܠܒܘܬܗ, once, S. James iii. 14.—More usually of fem. def. form ܠܒܘܬܐ, S. Luke ii. 35; with aff. ch. xvi. 6, below.

Heb. לֵב, לֵבָב, Ps. xii. 3.—Chald. לֵב, Dan. vii. 28:—לְבַב, ch. ii. 30; iv. 13, &c.

20. ܕܝܘܐ, *a devil*—δαιμόνιον—noun masc. def.—Pl. def. ܕܝܘܐ, S. Matt. ix. 34, &c.

22. ܓܙܘܪܬܐ, *circumcision*—τὴν περιτομήν—Noun fem. def.—R. ܓܙܪ, *Cut off.*

— ܡܢܗ ܗܘ (pron. *menē-i*), *from him it is*, sc. from Moses—ܡܢܗ is pleonastic.

— ܓܙܪܝܬܘܢ ܐܢܬܘܢ (pron. *goz'ritun*) *ye circumcise*—περιτέμνετε—Part. pl. (forming present tense 2. pl.) of ܓܙܪ, *Cut, cut off;* always in the N. T. in the sense of *circumcised.* Pret. 3. sing. with aff. Acts vii. 8; xvi. 3.—Fut. ܢܓܙܘܪ, 1 Cor. vii. 18; Gal. ii. 3.—Inf. ܠܡܓܙܪ, Acts xv. 5;—with aff. pleon. S. Luke i. 59.—Part. ܓܙܪ.—Pl. masc. (passively) Acts xv. 1; Gal. vi. 13.—Part. Peil ܓܙܝܪ, 1 Cor. vii. 18.—Def. ܓܙܝܪܐ, Phil. iii. 5.—Pl. masc. ܓܙܝܪܝܢ, Acts vii. 51; xv. 24.—Def. ܓܙܝܪܐ, ch. x. 45.—From this verb is derived

ܓܙܪܬܐ, noun fem. def. *An island*, as being *cut off* from the mainland, Acts xiii. 6, &c.—Pl. def. ܓܙܪܬܐ, Rev. vi. 14.

Heb. גָּזַר, *Cut, divided*, Ps. cxxxvi. 13: also, *Decided, decreed*, Job xxii. 28.—Chald. גְּזַר, part. pl. גָּזְרִין, *the deciders of fate, astrologers*, Dan. ii. 27, &c.

23. ܡܬܓܙܪ, *being circumcised*—*be circumcised*—*receive circumcision*—Gr. περιτομὴν λαμβάνει—Ethpeel part. from the foregoing.—Ethpe. ܐܬܓܙܪ, *Was circumcised.*—Pret. 2. pl. ܐܬܓܙܪܬܘܢ, Col. ii. 11.— Fut. ܢܬܓܙܪ, S. Luke ii. 21.—2. pl. ܬܬܓܙܪܘܢ, Gal. v. 2, &c.

S. JOHN VII. 23—33.

Ver. 23. Chald. Ithpe. אֶתְגְּזַר, *Was cut off*, Dan. ii. 45;—and in the Heb. form, ver. 34.

N.B. Some editions read ܡܶܫܬ̇ܪܶܐ, Ethpaal.

— ܢܶܫܬ̇ܪܶܐ, *should be broken*—λυθῇ—Ethpeel fut. 3. sing. of ܫܪܳܐ, *Loosed*.—Ethpe. ܐܶܫܬ̇ܪܺܝ, (S. Mark vii. 35), *Was loosened, dismissed, broken to pieces, settled*.—Pret. 3. sing. fem. ܐܶܫܬ̇ܪܝܰܬ, Acts xiii. 43.—3. pl. ܐܶܫܬ̇ܪܺܝܘ, ch. iv. 23, &c.—Fut. 3. sing. fem. ܬܶܫܬ̇ܪܶܐ, S. Luke xiii. 16.—1. sing. ܐܶܫܬ̇ܪܶܐ, 2 Tim. iv. 6.—3. pl. ܢܶܫܬ̇ܪܽܘܢ, 2 S. Pet. iii. 10, 12.—2. pl. ܬܶܫܬ̇ܪܽܘܢ, S. Luke vi. 37.—Part. ܡܶܫܬ̇ܪܶܐ, Acts xix. 39.—Pl. masc. ܡܶܫܬ̇ܪܶܝܢ, ch. v. 38.—Pl. fem. ܡܶܫܬ̇ܪܝܳܢ, 2 S. Pet. iii. 11.

24. ܒܡܰܣܰܒ ܐܰܦ̈ܶܐ, Lit. *With acceptation of the person*, i.e. *with partiality*—Gr. κατ' ὄψιν, E. V. *according to the appearance*—The phrase answers to the Gr. ὑπόκρισις, S. Matt. xxiii. 28; S. Luke xii. 1;—προσωποληψία, Rom. ii. 11.

ܡܰܣܰܒ, noun masc. of form Aph. part. pass. of ܢܣܰܒ, *Took;* —see note, ch. i. 16.—Def. ܡܰܣܒܳܐ, *A receiving*, Phil. iv. 15.

ܐܰܦ̈ܶܐ, *The faces, persons*. See note, ch. xi. 44, below. The pref. ܒ is pleonastic.

For a similar phrase in Heb., see Ps. lxxxii. 2; 2 Chron. xix. 7.

26. ܐܰܪ̈ܟܽܘܢܶܐ, *the rulers*—οἱ ἄρχοντες—Pl. of ܐܰܪܟܽܘܢ, def. ܐܰܪܟܽܘܢܳܐ (S. Luke xv. 25.) *An elder, ruler, Bishop*, Gr. ἐπίσκοπος, 1 Tim. iii. 2, πρεσβύτερος, ch. v. 1.—Fem. form constr. ܐܰܪܟܽܘܢܰܬ, see note, S. Luke ii. 36.—Pl. def. ܐܰܪ̈ܟܽܘܢܶܐ, S. Matt. xv. 2, &c.—R. ܩܫܶܫ, *Was old*.

29. ܡܶܢ ܠܘܳܬܶܗ, *from Him*—παρ' αὐτοῦ—Compound preposition, with affixed pronoun.

32. ܗܶܢܽܘܢ, *they*, i.e. the Pharisees—Gr. οἱ Φαρισαῖοι.

— ܕܰܚܫ̈ܶܐ, *the officers*—ὑπηρέτας—noun masc. pl. def.

33. ܩܰܠܺܝܠ, *a little (while)*—μικρὸν (χρόνον)—Adj. *Short, small, light,* whence, *swift*. Often used as an adverb, see note ch. ii. 12.—

Ver. 33. ܩܠܝܠ ܩܠܝܠ, distributively, *a little for every one*, ch. vi. 7.— Also in the following adverbial expressions :—

ܒܩܠܝܠ ܩܪܝܒ, *almost*—Gr. ἐν ὀλίγῳ, Acts xxvi. 28.

ܒܡܠܐ ܩܠܝܠ, *almost, within a little*, lit. *in the fulness of a little*—Gr. ὄντως, *really, quite*, E. V. *clean*, 2 S. Pet. ii. 18. But the Alex. Vat. and some other MSS. read ὀλίγως.

ܡܢ ܐܬܪ ܩܠܝܠ, *in part*, lit. *from a little place*, Gr. ἀπὸ μέρους, Rom. xi. 25.

ܒܨܝܪ ܩܠܝܠ, *in part*, Gr. ἀπὸ μέρους, 2 Cor. ii. 5.

ܩܠܝܠ ܡܢ ܦܢܝܢ, *somewhat, in part*, Gr. ἀπὸ μέρους, Rom. xv. 24; 2 Cor. i. 14;—ἐκ μέρους, 1 Cor. xiii. 9, 12. Fem. ܩܠܝܠܬܐ, *light* burden, S. Matt. xi. 30.—Pl. fem. ܩܠܝܠܢ, *swift* feet, Rom. iii. 15. R. ܩܠ ܩܠܠ, *Was light, swift*,—occurring in the N. T. only in Aph. ܐܩܠ, *Lightened*;—pret. 3. pl. ܐܩܠܘ (followed by ܡܢ) *they lightened* the ship, Acts xxvii. 38.—Part. pl. ܡܩܠܝܢ, *making light of, insulting*, Gr. προκαλούμενοι, Gal. v. 26.

Heb. קַל, *Light, swift*, Isa. xix. 1.—As an adverb, ch. v. 26.

— ܬܘܒ, *yet*—Gr. ἔτι.

35. ܟܝ, a particle used in interrogations or exclamations, but always following another word, as ܠܡܐ, ܡܢܘ, ܡܢܐ, ܟܠܗ.—Gr. μή;—Lat. *numne? num forte?*—Compare also the *nam* in *quisnam;* and the Germ. denn, wohl.

— ܠܐܬܪܘܬܐ ܕܥܡܡܐ, *to the places of the nations*—Gr. εἰς τὴν διασπορὰν τῶν Ἑλλήνων.—For ܐܬܪ, *a region*, see note, ch. xi. 54.

— ܚܢܦܐ, *the heathen, Gentiles*—τοὺς Ἕλληνας—Pl. def. of ܚܢܦ, def. ܚܢܦܐ (S. Matt. xviii. 17.) *One who is polluted, profane.*—Fem. def. ܚܢܦܬܐ, S. Mark vii. 26.

Heb. חָנֵף, Job viii. 13, &c.—R. חָנֵף, *Was defiled*, Ps. cvi. 38.

38. ܢܗܪܘܬܐ, *rivers*—ποταμοί—Pl. def. of ܢܗܪ, def. ܢܗܪܐ (S. Matt. iii. 6, &c.) noun masc. *A river, stream.* Pl. abs. of masc. form in the

S. JOHN VII. 38, 39.

Ver. 38. expression ܒܝܬ ܢܗܪ̈ܝܢ, *between the rivers*, i.e. Mesopotamia, Acts ii. 9; vii. 2. But it takes the fem. form in pl. def. as above. Heb. נָהָר, Gen. ii. 10.—Chald. נְהַר, *A stream*, Dan. vii. 10.—Def. נַהֲרָא, נַהֲרָה, *the river*, i.e. the Euphrates, Ezr. iv. 10, 16, 17, 20.

— ܢܪܕܘܢ, *shall flow*—ῥεύσουσιν—Fut. 3. pl. of ܢܪܕ (Acts xviii. 18, 22), *Went forward, progressed, advanced; journeyed by land* (S. Mark x. 17), or *by sea* (S. Matt. xiv. 34).—From the notion of *progression*, it comes to signify, intransitively, *Exercised, gave one's attention, labour* to anything;—whence, transitively, *Caused others to be exercised; instructed, taught* (Col. iii. 16), as Gr. παιδεύειν—whence, again, *Admonished, chastised* (S. Luke xxiii. 16, 22). Pret. 3. pl. ܢܪܕܘ, S. Matt. xiv. 34.—1. pl. ܢܪܕܢ, Acts xx. 6, 13, &c.—Fut. ܢܪܕܘܢ, Acts xxvii. 9.—1. sing. ܐܪܕܐ, with aff. S. Luke xxiii. 16, 22.—1. pl. ܢܪܕܐ, S. Luke ii. 15.—Imperat. pl. ܪܕܘ, 1 Thess. v. 14.—Part. ܪܕܐ, S. Matt. ix. 20, &c.—Fem. ܪܕܝܐ, Acts ix. 31.—Pl. masc. ܪܕܝܢ, S. Mark vi. 48, &c.:—coalescing with ܒܢܝ, ܕܪܕܝܢ ܒܢܝ, 1 S. John i. 6.—Part. Peil ܪܕܐ, S. James iii. 13.—Pl. masc. ܪܕܝܢ (actively), Col. iii. 16: so Vienna Ed. and others, while some read ܪܕܝܢ.

Ethpeel ܐܬܪܕܝ, *Was informed, learned; was chastised*, Acts vii. 22.—Pret. 1. sing. ܐܬܪܕܝܬ, ch. xxii. 3.—Part. ܡܬܪܕܝܢ, Hebr. xii. 8.—Pl. with ܒܢܝ, and inf. ܡܬܪܕܝܘ, 1 Cor. xi. 32.

Deriv. ܪܕܘܝܐ, noun masc. def. *An instructor*, Rom. ii. 20.

ܡܪܕܘ, noun fem. *Instruction, learning;*—ܕܠܐ ܡܪܕܘ, *Unlearned*, 2 Tim. ii. 23.—Def. ܡܪܕܘܬܐ, 1 Cor. x. 11; Eph. vi. 4:—*Chastisement*, Hebr. xii. 7, 8, 11.

Cogn. Heb. רָדָה, *Laid low, had dominion over*, Ps. xlix. 15,—and יָרַד, *Descended, flowed down*, Ps. cvii. 23; Deut. ix. 21.

39. ܐܫܬܒܚ, *was glorified*—ἐδοξάσθη—Ethpaal pret. 3. sing. of ܫܒܚ (not used) Pa. ܫܒܚ, *Praised*. Ethpa. *Was praised, honoured.* —Pret. 3. sing. fem. ܐܫܬܒܚܬ, 2 Cor. iii. 10.—Fut. ܢܫܬܒܚ,

Ver. 39. S. John xi. 4, &c.—3. pl. ܢܫܬܒܚܘܢ, S. Matt. vi. 2.—1. pl. ܢܫܬܒܚ, Rom. viii. 17.—Part. ܡܫܬܒܚ, S. John xv. 8; S. Luke iv. 15:—Fem. ܡܫܬܒܚܐ, 2 Thess. iii. 1.—Pl. masc. ܡܫܬܒܚܝܢ, 1 Cor. iv. 10; xii. 26.

40. ܡ̈ܠܘܗܝ, *His words*—Gr. τὸν λόγον.

42. ܡܢ ܙܪܥܗ, *from his seed—the seed*—(aff. pleon.)—ἐκ τοῦ σπέρματος—ܙܪܥ, def. ܙܪܥܐ (S. Matt. xiii. 18, &c.), noun masc. *Seed*—Pl. def. ܙܪ̈ܥܐ, *seeds, sown fields*, S. Matt. xii. 1.—R. ܙܪܥ, *Sowed.*

Heb. זֶרַע, Gen. i. 11.—Chald. זְרַע, Dan. ii. 43.

— .... ܘܡܢ, Transl. *And (that) from Bethlehem, the town of David himself, comes the Messiah.*

43. ܦܠܓܘܬܐ, *a division*—σχίσμα—Def. of ܦܠܓܘܬ, noun fem. *Separation, part, portion.*—Pl. def. ܦܠ̈ܓܘܬܐ, Rom. xvi. 17, &c.—R. ܦܠܓ, *Divided.*

Compare Heb. פְּלֻגָּה, *A division*, of the priests, 2 Chron. xxxv. 5:—and Chald. the same, Ezr. vi. 18.

44. .... ܘܐܝܬ ܗܘܘ, Transl. *And there were men* (i.e. *some*) *of them who wished to take Him.*

46. .... ܠܐ ܡܡܠܠ ܗܘܐ, Transl. *Never thus spake man (son of man) as speaks this man.*—The Sin. MS. reads ...ὡς οὗτος λαλεῖ ὁ ἄνθρωπος.

47. ܛܥܝܬܘܢ (for ܛܥܝܢ ܐܢܬܘܢ), *are ye deceived?*—πεπλάνησθε;—Part. (forming pres. 2. pl.) of ܛܥܐ (S. Matt. xviii. 12), *Erred, strayed, was deceived; lay hid, escaped notice.*—Pret. 3. sing. fem. ܛܥܬ, 1 Tim. ii. 14:—with aff. S. Luke viii. 47.—3. pl. ܛܥܘ, S. Matt. xv. 24; xvi. 5, &c.—Fut. ܢܛܥܐ, S. Matt. xviii. 12;—Fem. ܬܛܥܐ, with aff. 2 S. Pet. iii. 8.—2. pl. ܬܛܥܘܢ, S. Luke xxi. 8.—Part. ܛܥܐ, Phil. iii. 13;—Fem. ܛܥܝܐ (for inf.), *let her fall off*, Gr. ἐκπεσεῖν, Acts xxvii. 32.—Pl. masc. ܛܥܝܢ, S. Matt. xxii. 29, &c.—Pl. fem. def. ܛܥܝܬܐ, 1 Tim. iv. 1.—Part. Peil ܛܥܐ, fem. ܛܥܝܐ, S. Luke xii. 6.—Pl. masc. ܛܥܝܢ, def. ܛܥܝܐ, Hebr. xi. 38.—Pl. fem. ܛܥܝܢ, Acts xxvi. 26.

Ver. 47. Ethpeel ܐܬܛܥܝ, *Was enticed*—Part. ܡܛܥܝܢ, S. James i. 25.
—From this verb is derived

ܛܘܥܝܐ, noun fem. def. *Ignorance, error, deceit*, Acts xvii. 30, Gr. ἄγνοια; Col. ii. 8, &c.

Heb. טָעָה (same as תָּעָה), once in Hiph. Ezek. xiii. 10.

49. אֶלָּא‎ ܐܢ, *unless, except*—Gr. ἀλλά.

— ܐܢܘܢ ܠܝܛܝܢ, *are cursed*—ἐπικατάρατοί εἰσι—Part. Peil pl. (forming pres. tense) of ܠܛ, *Cursed*—See note, S. Matt. v. 44.

N. B. ܐܢܘܢ and ܐܢܬ are nominatives when they represent the subst. verb.

Transl. *Unless this people, which know not the law, are cursed:*—Or, *Except this people which know not the law; accursed are they!*—or *accursed be they!*

51. ܡܚܝܒ, *condemning, judging—judgeth*—Gr. κρίνει—Pael part. (for present tense) of ܚܒ, *Was guilty.*—Pa. ܚܝܒ (Tit. iii. 11), *Judged guilty, condemned.*—Pret. 3. pl. ܚܝܒܘ, Acts xxvi. 10.—2. pl. ܚܝܒܬܘܢ, S. James v. 6.—Fut. ܢܚܝܒ, fem. ܬܚܝܒ, S. Luke xi. 31:—with aff. S. Matt. xii. 42.—3. pl. ܢܚܝܒܘܢ, with aff. ver. 41, &c.—2. pl. ܬܚܝܒܘܢ, S. Luke vi. 37. Inf. ܠܡܚܝܒܘ, with aff. Col. ii. 18.—Part. pl. masc. ܡܚܝܒܝܢ, S. Matt. xii. 7.—Part. pass. ܡܚܝܒ, S. Matt. v. 21, 22.—Pl. fem. ܡܚܝܒܢ, S. Jude ver. 7.

Heb. Pi. חִיֵּב, *Made liable to penalty*, Dan. i. 10.

53. ܟܠܢܫ, *every one, every man*—Gr. ἕκαστος—The words are separate, ܟܠ ܢܫ, Acts xvii. 27.

CHAPTER VIII.

It will be sufficient here to remind the student that the first eleven verses of this chapter, and the last verse of ch. vii. are not found in the Vienna, nor in any Edition prior to that of Elias Hutter (Norberg, 1600); who himself translated this and other missing portions of the N. T. into Syriac. The passage, as it now stands, was supplied by Bp. Walton in the Lond. Polyglott, from a MS. in the library of Abp. Ussher.

S. JOHN VIII. 1—5.

Ver. 1. ܕ݁ܙܰܝܬ݂ܶܐ, *of Olives*—τῶν Ἐλαιῶν—Pl. def. of ܙܰܝܬ݂ܳܐ (Rom. xi. 17), noun masc. def. *An olive, olive-tree.*
Heb. זַיִת, Ps. lii. 10.

2. ܒ݁ܨܰܦ݂ܪܳܐ, *in the morning*—Gr. ὄρθρου—Def. of ܨܰܦ݂ܪܳܐ, noun masc. *The morning.*

3. ܣܳܦ݂ܪܶܐ, *the Scribes*—οἱ Γραμματεῖς—Pl. def. of ܣܳܦ݂ܪܳܐ, def. ܣܳܦ݂ܪܶܐ (S. Matt. xiii. 52, &c.), noun masc. *One skilled in written Law.*—Form of part. act. of ܣܦ݂ܰܪ, Heb. סָפַר, *Graved, inscribed:*—whence
Heb. סֹפֵר, *A writer, scribe,* Ps. xlv. 2. Chald. סָפַר, Ezr. iv. 8, &c.; vii. 12, 21.

— ܕ݁ܶܐܬ݂ܬ݁ܰܚܕ݁ܰܬ݂, *who was taken*—Gr. κατειλημμένην—Ethpeel pret. 3. sing. fem. of ܐܰܚܰܕ݂, *Seized, held.*—Ethpe. ܐܶܬ݁ܬ݁ܰܚܕ݂ (S. Matt. xxv. 10), *Was seized, detained; was shut, closed:* for ܐܰܚܕ݂, see Cowper's Gr. § 111 (2).—Pret. 3. pl. ܐܶܬ݁ܬ݁ܰܚܕ݁ܘ, S. Luke iv. 25.—Fut. ܢܶܬ݁ܬ݁ܚܶܕ݂, Acts ii. 24.—3. pl. ܢܶܬ݁ܬ݁ܰܚܕ݂ܽܘܢ, Rev. xxi. 26.

— ܒ݁ܓ݂ܰܘܪܳܐ, *in adultery*—ἐν μοιχείᾳ—ܓ݁ܰܘܪܳܐ, noun masc. def. R. ܓ݁ܳܪ, *Committed adultery.*

— ܒ݁ܰܡܨܰܥܬ݂ܳܐ, *in the midst*—ἐν μέσῳ—Def. of ܡܨܰܥܬ݂ܳܐ, noun fem. *The middle.*—Constr. ܡܨܰܥܰܬ݂, S. Mark vi. 47, &c.—Whence is derived, ܡܨܰܥܳܝܳܐ, noun masc. def. *A mediator,* Gal. iii. 19, 20.

4. ܒ݁ܳܗ ܒ݁ܰܣܥܽܘܪܳܐ, *in the very act*—ἐπαυτοφώρῳ—Def. of ܣܥܽܘܪܳܐ, noun masc. *An act, deed; visitation,* S. Luke xix. 44.—Pl. def. ܣܥܽܘܪܶܐ, S. Luke i. 1.—R. ܣܥܰܪ, *Performed, visited, cared for.*
Transl. *This woman was taken openly in the very act of adultery.*

5. ܦ݁ܰܩܶܕ݂, *commanded*—ἐνετείλατο—Pael pret. 3. sing. of ܦ݁ܩܰܕ݂, *Visited, decreed.* Pa. *Gave commandment.*—Pret. 1. sing. ܦ݁ܰܩܕ݂ܶܬ݂, Acts xxiii. 30.—3. pl. ܦ݁ܰܩܶܕ݂ܘ, ch. iv. 15, 18.—1. pl. ܦ݁ܰܩܶܕ݂ܢ, ch. xv. 24.—Fut. ܢܦ݂ܰܩܶܕ݂, S. Matt. iv. 6; S. Luke iv. 10.—2. sing. ܬ݁ܦ݂ܰܩܶܕ݂, 1 Tim. i. 3.—1. sing. ܐܶܦ݂ܰܩܶܕ݂, with aff. 1 Cor. xi. 34.—2. pl. ܬ݁ܦ݂ܰܩܕ݂ܽܘܢ, Acts xv. 5.—Imperat. ܦ݁ܰܩܶܕ݂, 1 Tim. iv. 11.—Inf.

Ver. 5. ܦܩܰܕ݂, S. Matt. xi. 1.—Part. ܦܳܩܶܕ݂, S. John xv. 14, 17.— Pl. masc. ܦܳܩܕ݂ܺܝܢ, 2 Thess. iii. 10:—with ܒ, ver. 4, 12.

Ethpaal ܐܶܬ݂ܦܰܩܰܕ݂, *Was commanded.* Pret. 3. sing. fem. ܐܶܬ݂ܦܰܩܕ݂ܰܬ݂, Hebr. ix. 20.—3. pl. ܐܶܬ݂ܦܰܩܰܕ݂ܘ, Acts xxiii. 31.—2. pl. ܐܶܬ݂ܦܰܩܰܕ݂ܬ݁ܘܢ, Col. iv. 10.

Heb. Pi. פָּקַד, *Mustered,* Isa. xiii. 4.

— ܕ݁ܐܰܝܟ݂ ܗܳܠܶܝܢ, *that such as these*—Gr. τὰς τοιαύτας—compound of ܕ, *that,* ܠ of the object, the relative ܕ, and ܐܰܝܟ, *So.*

— ܢܶܪܓ݁ܘܡ, *we should stone*—Gr. λιθοβολεῖσθαι—Fut. 1. pl. of ܪܓܰܡ, *Stoned.*—Pret. 3. pl. ܪܓܰܡܘ, with aff. S. Matt. xxi. 35, &c.— Fut. ܢܶܪܓ݁ܘܡ, Acts v. 26.—3. pl. ܢܶܪܓ݁ܡܘܢ, ch. xiv. 5:—with aff. ver. 59, below.—Inf. ܠܡܶܪܓ݁ܰܡ, with aff. S. John x. 31; xi. 8.— Part. ܪܳܓܶܡ, S. Luke xx. 6.—Fem. constr. ܪܳܓܡܰܬ݂, S. Matt. xxiii. 37 (as ܩܳܛܠܰܬ݂, same verse).—Pl. masc. ܪܳܓܡܺܝܢ, S. John x. 32; with ܒ, ver. 33.

Ethpeel ܐܶܬ݂ܪܓ݂ܶܡ, *Was stoned.*—Pret. 3. pl. ܐܶܬ݂ܪܓ݂ܶܡܘ, Hebr. xi. 37.—Fut. 3. sing. fem. ܬ݁ܶܬ݂ܪܓ݂ܶܡ, ch. xii. 20. Pret. 1. sing. ܐܶܬ݂ܪܓ݂ܡܶܬ݂, 2 Cor. xi. 25, may be referred to Ethpe. or Ethpa.

Heb. Pi. רָגַם, Numb. xiv. 10; Josh. vii. 25.

Transl. *Now in the Law of Moses he commanded that we should stone such as these.*

6. .... ܐܺܝܬ݂, *so that there might be to them*—i.e. *that they might have*—Gr. ἵνα ἔχωσι.

— ܠܬܰܚܬ݁, *down*—κάτω—See note, ch. i. 48.

— ܐܶܬ݁ܓ݁ܗܶܢ, *He stooped*—Gr. κύψας—Ethpeel part. of ܓ݁ܗܶܢ, *Bent, stooped.* The Ethpe. conj. has here a reflexive force, *bent himself.* Fut. 1. sing. ܐܶܬ݁ܓ݁ܗܶܢ, S. Mark i. 7.

— ܡܟ݂ܰܬ݁ܶܒ݂ ܗ݈ܘܳܐ, *He was writing, kept writing*—*wrote*—ἔγραφεν—Pael part. (forming imperf. tense) of ܟ݁ܬ݂ܰܒ݂, *Wrote.*—Pa. ܟ݁ܰܬ݁ܶܒ݂.—The Par. and Lond. Polyglotts read ܡܰܟ݂ܬ݁ܶܒ݂, Aph. part.

Heb. Pi. כָּתַב, *Wrote down, decreed,* Isa. x. 1.

Ver. 7. ܟܰܬܰܪܘ, *they continued*—ἐπέμενον—Pael pret. 3. pl. of ܟܬܪ (not used) Pa. ܟܰܬܰܪ (ch. xi. 6), *Remained, lingered.* Pret. 2. pl. ܟܰܬܰܪܬܽܘܢ, S. Luke xxii. 28.—Fut. ܢܟܰܬܰܪ, Hebr. xiii. 1.—2. pl. ܬܟܰܬܪܽܘܢ, ver. 31, below.—Inf. ܠܡܟܰܬܳܪܽܘ, Rev. xvii. 10.—Part. ܡܟܰܬܰܪ, 2 S. Pet. iii. 4; 1 S. John ii. 10.—Pl. masc. ܡܟܰܬܪܺܝܢ, Acts xxvii. 31.—Pl. fem. ܡܟܰܬܪ̈ܳܢ, 1 Cor. xiii. 13.

Heb. Pi. כִּתֵּר, *Surrounded,* Ps. xxii. 13.—*Waited,* Job xxxvi. 2.

— ܐܶܬܦܫܶܛ, *He lifted up Himself*—Gr. ἀνακύψας—Ethpeel pret. 3. sing. of ܦܫܰܛ, *Extended.* Ethpe. with reflexive sense.—Pret. 3. sing. fem. ܐܶܬܦܫܶܛܰܬ, Gr. ἀνωρθώθη, S. Luke xiii. 13.—Fut. 3. sing. fem. ܬܶܬܦܫܶܛ, ver. 11.

— ܕܠܳܐ ܚܛܺܝܬܳܗ, Lit. *of no sin—without sin*—Gr. ἀναμάρτητος—ܚܛܺܝܬܳܗ, noun masc. *Sin.*—Def. ܚܛܺܝܬܳܐ, S. James iv. 17, &c.—Pl. ܚܛ̈ܗܶܝܢ, S. Matt. xii. 31.—Def. ܚܛ̈ܗܶܐ, S. John ix. 34, &c.—R. ܚܛܳܐ, *Sinned.*

Heb. חֵטְא, Ps. li. 7.—Chald. חֲטָי, Dan. iv. 24.

— ܢܶܫܕܶܐ, *he shall cast, let him cast*—βαλέτω—Fut. 3. sing. (for imperat.) of ܫܕܳܐ (ch. xxi. 7), *Threw, cast away, down, into.*—Pret. 3. sing. fem. ܫܶܕܝܰܬ, with aff. S. Mark i. 26.—3. pl. ܫܕܰܘ, Acts xxvii. 38.—1. pl. ܫܕܰܝܢ, ver. 18, 19.—Fut. 3. pl. ܢܶܫܕܽܘܢ, with aff. S. Luke iv. 29.—Imperat. ܫܕܺܝ, S. Matt. iv. 6.—Part. ܫܳܕܶܐ, 1 S. John iv. 18:—Fem. ܫܳܕܝܳܐ, Rev. vi. 13.—Pl. masc. ܫܳܕܶܝܢ. Constr. ܫܳܕ̈ܝܰܝ ܒܝܰܡܺܝܢܳܐ, *they that throw with the right hand, spearmen,* Gr. δεξιολάβους, Acts xxiii. 23.

9. ܟܰܕ ܫܰܪܺܝܘ, *when they had begun,* i.e. *beginning*—Gr. ἀρξάμενοι—Pael pret. 3. pl. of ܫܪܳܐ, *Loosed.* Pa. ܫܰܪܺܝ (S. Matt. iv. 17, &c.), *Loosened, began.* Pret. 3. sing. fem. ܫܰܪܝܰܬ, S. Mark xiv. 69.—1. sing. ܫܰܪܺܝܬ, ver. 25, below.—Fut. ܢܫܰܪܶܐ, S. Matt. xxiv. 49.—Imperat. ܫܰܪܳܐ, S. Matt. xx. 8.—Part. ܡܫܰܪܶܐ, Acts xiv. 11.—Pl. ܡܫܰܪܶܝܢ, with ܕܢܶܐ, 2 Cor. iii. 1.—Part. pass. ܡܫܰܪܰܝܢ, S. Matt.

Ver. 9. viii. 6.—Def. ܡܫܪܝܐ, ch. ix. 2, 6; S. Luke v. 24.—Pl. masc. def. ܡܫܪ̈ܝܐ, S. Matt. iv. 24.—Pl. fem. def. ܡܫܪ̈ܝܬܐ, Hebr. xii. 12.

Heb. Pi. שֵׁרָה, *Loosed*, Jer. xv. 11.—Chald. Pa. שָׁרֵא, *Dissolved* difficulties, Dan. v. 12;—*Begun*, Ezr. v. 2.

— ܐܫܬܒܩܬ, *she was left*.—Ethpeel pret. 3. sing. fem. of ܫܒܩ, *Left*. Ethpe. ܐܫܬܒܩ (S. Luke vii. 43), *Was left, was forgiven*, of sin. —Pret. 3. pl. ܐܫܬܒܩܘ, 1 S. John ii. 12.—Fut. ܢܫܬܒܩ, S. Matt. xii. 31, 32, &c.: Fem. ܬܫܬܒܩ (for ܬܫܬܒܩ) S. Matt. xxiv. 2, &c.—3. pl. ܢܫܬܒܩܘܢ, S. John xx. 23, &c. —Part. ܡܫܬܒܩ, S. Matt. xxiii. 38, &c.:—Fem. ܡܫܬܒܩܐ, S. Matt. xxiv. 41; S. Mark xiii. 2.—Pl. masc. ܡܫܬܒܩܝܢ, Hebr. vii. 23; S. James v. 15:—with ܢܢ, 2 Cor. iv. 9.—Those forms of Ethpeel, in which ܬ takes ܿ, are by some referred to Ethpaal.

Chald. Ithpe. אִשְׁתְּבִק, *Was left*, Dan. ii. 44.

— ܠܒܠܚܘܕܝܗ̇, *she alone*.—See note, ch. v. 18.

Transl. ver. 9, 10. *But they, when they heard, went out one by one, beginning from the elders; and the woman was left alone, being* (ܟܕ ܐܝܬܝܗ̇) *in the midst. But when Jesus lifted up Himself, He said unto the woman, Where are they? Hath no man condemned thee?*

11. .... ܐܙܠܝ, Transl. *Go, and from this time sin no more.*

14. ܐܦܢ, *though*—κἂν—Comp. of ܐܢ + ܐܦ—*Although*—also *Only, at least*, ch. xiv. 11, &c.—The words are written separately, 2 Cor. iv. 16; Gal. i. 8.

15. ܦܓܪܢܐܝܬ, *after the flesh*—Gr. κατὰ τὴν σάρκα—Adverb derived from ܦܓܪܢܐ, *Carnal*. Pl. def. 1 Cor. iii. 1, &c. ܦܓܪܢܝ̈ܐ, the same, pl. def. Hebr. vii. 16.

20. ܒܝܬ ܓܙܐ, *in the treasury*—ἐν τῷ γαζοφυλακίῳ—Lit. *house of treasure* —the prep. ܒ understood. ܓܙܐ, *Treasure;* with aff. fem. ܓܙܗ̇, Acts viii. 27.

Ver. 20. Compare Heb. בִּנְזֵי הַמֶּלֶךְ, *the king's treasuries*, Esth. iii. 9; iv. 7:—and Chald. גִּנְזַיָּא, *the treasures*, Ezr. vi. 1:—בֵּית גִּנְזַיָּא, *treasure house*, ch. v. 17. R. גְּנַז, Syr. ܓܢܰܙ, *Stored up*.

23. ܡܶܢ ܠܬܰܚܬ, *from beneath;* lit. *from those (who are) beneath*—ἐκ τῶν κάτω—See note, ch. i. 48.—Opposed to this is

— ܡܶܢ ܠܥܶܠ, *from (those that are) above*—ἐκ τῶν ἄνω—See note, ch. ii. 7.

24. ܐܶܡܪܶܬ ܠܟܽܘܢ, *I said unto you*—Gr. εἶπον οὖν ὑμῖν—οὖν is wanting in the Sin. MS.

25. ܫܰܪܺܝܬ ܕܶܐܡܰܠܶܠ, *I have begun to speak.* The verb ܫܰܪܺܝ, in the sense of *began*, is found in the following constructions:

    1. With ܕ prefixed to a verb in the future; as in this passage;
    2. With ܠ prefixed to the Infinitive; as ܫܰܪܺܝ ܠܡܰܫܳܓܽܘ, *He began to wash*, ch. xiii. 5;
    3. With a participle; as ܫܰܪܺܝܘ ܡܳܠܓܺܝܢ, *they began plucking, to pluck*, S. Matt. xii. 1.

Transl. *The Jews say, Who art thou? Jesus saith unto them, Although I have begun to speak with you, (26) I have (yet) much concerning you to say and to judge.*

26. .... ܒܥܳܠܡܳܐ, Transl. *And what things I have heard from Him, those speak I in the world*—Gr. εἰς τὸν κόσμον.—ܗܳܢܶܝܢ pleonastic—See Cowper's Gr. § 198 (1).

28. ܗܳܟܰܢܳܐ, *thus, similarly*—Adverb—same as ܐܳܟܰܢܳܐ, ch. v. 19.—ܗܳܢܶܝܢ following is pleonastic.

29. ܕܫܳܦܰܪ ܠܶܗ, *that pleaseth Him*—Gr. τὰ ἀρεστὰ αὐτῷ—Part. of ܫܦܰܪ (Rom. xv. 3), *Was beautiful, graceful, elegant; was pleasing, pleased*. Pret. 3. fem. ܫܶܦܪܰܬ, S. Matt. xiv. 6, &c.—Fut. ܢܶܫܦܰܪ, 1 Cor. vii. 32, 33;—Fem. ܬܶܫܦܰܪ, ver. 34.—1. sing. ܐܶܫܦܰܪ, Gal. i. 10.—2. pl. ܬܶܫܦܪܽܘܢ, Col. i. 10, &c.—1. pl. ܢܶܫܦܰܪ, Rom. xv. 1, &c.—Inf. ܠܡܶܫܦܰܪ, Rom. viii. 8.—Part. pl. masc. ܫܳܦܪܺܝܢ, 2 Cor. v. 9, &c.

www.ingramcontent.com/pod-product-compliance
Lightning Source LLC
Chambersburg PA
CBHW030339170426
43202CB00010B/1171